Justification and Application

Justification and Application

Remarks on Discourse Ethics

Jürgen Habermas

translated by Ciaran Cronin

The MIT Press, Cambridge, Massachusetts, and London, England

This edition © 1993 Massachusetts Institute of Technology. This English version includes three essays that were published in *Erläuterungen zur Diskursethik,* © 1991 Suhrkamp Verlag, Frankfurt am Main, Germany, and two additional pieces. The essay "To Seek to Salvage an Unconditional Meaning without God Is a Futile Undertaking: Reflections on a Remark of Max Horkheimer" was prepared for a festschrift in honor of Alfred Schmidt. The interview with Torben Hviid Nielsen was published in *Die nachholende Revolution,* volume 7 of Habermas's *Kleine Politische Schriften,* © 1990 Suhrkamp Verlag, Frankfurt am Main, Germany.

This book was set in Baskerville by DEKR Corporation and was printed and bound in the United States of America.

Library of Congress Cataloging-in-Publication Data

Habermas, Jürgen.
  Justification and application : remarks on discourse ethics /
Jürgen Habermas ; translated by Ciaran Cronin.
    p. cm. — (Studies in contemporary German social thought)
  "Includes three essays that were published in Erläuterungen zur
Diskursethik . . . and two additional pieces"—T.p. verso.
  Includes bibliographical references and index.
  Contents: On the pragmatic, the ethical, and the moral employments
of practical reason — Remarks on discourse ethics — Lawrence
Kohlberg and neo-Aristotelianism — To seek to salvage an
unconditional meaning without God is a futile undertaking —
Morality, society, and ethics : an interview with Torben Hviid
Nielsen.
  ISBN 0-262-08217-9
  1. Ethics. 2. Habermas, Jürgen—Interviews. 3. Habermas, Jürgen—
Ethics. I. Habermas, Jürgen. Erläuterungen zur Diskursethik.
II. Title. III. Title: Discourse ethics. IV. Series.
BJ1114.H264 1993
170—dc20   92-36599
                                              CIP

Contents

Preface

With this book I continue the investigations set forth in *Moral Consciousness and Communicative Action* (1990). The background to the discussion is formed primarily by objections against universalistic concepts of morality that can be traced back to Aristotle, Hegel, and contemporary [ethical] contextualism. Going beyond the sterile opposition between abstract universalism and a self-contradictory relativism, I endeavor to defend the primacy of the just (in the deontological sense) over the good. That does not mean, however, that ethical questions in the narrow sense have to be excluded from rational treatment.

It is my hope that these essays reflect a learning process. This holds at any rate for the explicit distinction between moral and ethical discourses. It is worked out for the first time in the Howison Lecture [which appears here under the title "On the Pragmatic, the Ethical, and the Moral Employments of Practical Reason"] delivered at Berkeley in 1988 and dedicated to my daughter Judith. Since then it would be more accurate to speak of a "discourse theory of morality," but I retain the term "discourse ethics," which has become established usage.

The "Remarks on Discourse Ethics" consutute the main text and derive from notes made during the years 1987 to 1990. They represent a confrontation with competing theoretical programs and are offered as a global critical evaluation of the relevant literature.

The discussions of the working group on legal theory that took place under the auspices of the Leibniz-Programm of the Deutsche Forschungsgemeinschaft contributed to clarifying my thoughts; I am indebted to the participants in the Thursday afternoon seminars.

Translator's Note

This book is a partial translation of Jürgen Habermas's book *Erläuterungen zur Diskursethik* (Frankfurt, 1991). Chapters 1, 2, and 3 correspond, respectively, to chapters 5, 6, and 4 of the German text.* Chapter 4 is a translation of "Einen unbedingten Sinn zu retten ohne Gott, ist eitel. Reflexionen über einen Satz von Max Horkheimer," which appeared in Matthias Lutz-Bachmann and Gunzelin Schmidt Noerr (eds.), *Kritischer Materialismus. Zur Diskussion eines Materialismus der Praxis* (Munich, 1991), pp. 125–142. Chapter 5 is a translation of "Interview mit T. Hviid Nielsen" from Habermas's *Die Nachholende Revolution. Kleine Politische Schriften VII* (Frankfurt, 1990), pp. 114–145. It consists of Habermas's written replies to questions posed by Nielsen. An anonymous translation previously appeared under the title "Jürgen Habermas: Morality, Society and Ethics: An Interview with Torben Hviid Nielsen," in *Acta Sociologica* 33 (1990), 2:92–114. Although it deviates significantly from the German version, I have benefited from it at a number of points and have adopted its title and critical apparatus.

*Of the remaining three chapters of the German text, chapter 1 has appeared in translation as "Morality and Ethical Life: Does Hegel's Critique of Kant Apply to Discourse Ethics?" in Jürgen Habermas, *Moral Consciousness and Comunicative Action*, trans. C. Lenhardt and S.W. Nicholsen (Cambridge, Mass., 1990), pp. 195–215, and chapter 3 as "Justice and Solidarity: On the Discussion Concerning 'Stage 6'" in Thomas Wren (ed.), *The Moral Domain: Essays in the Ongoing Discussion between Philosophy and the Social Sciences*, (Cambridge, Mass., 1990), pp. 224–251. To date chapter 2, "Was macht eine Lebensform rational?" has not appeared in English.

Translator's Introduction

Habermas's discourse theory of morality represents one of the most original and far-reaching attempts to defend a cognitivist, deontological ethical theory in contemporary moral philosophy.[1] His declared goal is to find a middle ground between the abstract universalism with which Kantian ethics is justly reproached and the relativistic implications of communitarian and contextualist positions in the tradition of Aristotle and Hegel. In pursuing this theoretical project Habermas is rowing against the prevailing tide of skepticism concerning the possibility of universally valid claims in ethics.[2] In the present work he undertakes a comprehensive defense of discourse ethics against its critics, especially those in the neo-Aristotelian camp, and in the process develops incisive criticisms of some of the major competing positions. Since the precise nature and strength of Habermas's ethical claims have so often been misunderstood, this introduction begins with a sketch of the argument on which discourse ethics rests. The second part addresses the main points of contention with several competing positions, with a view to situating Habermas's project in relation to important currents in contemporary Anglo-American moral thought. My goal is to show that he has philosophically robust responses to the (often serious) theoretical concerns underlying the criticisms commonly brought against discourse ethics.

I

While self-consciously Kantian in its cognitivism and its commitment to a universalistic interpretation of impartiality and autonomy, discourse ethics represents a sustained critique of the central role Kantian ethics has traditionally accorded individual reflection. Kant argued that reflection on what is implicit in everyday moral experience and judgment shows that the autonomous exercise of the will unconditioned by extraneous empirical motives—and hence the spontaneous activity of a noumenal self unencumbered by such motives—is a necessary precondition of genuinely moral action. For human agents who are affected by sensuous desires and inclinations, to act morally is to act for the sake of duty alone, which translates into the requirement that I reflect on whether I can consistently will that every other agent should act on my maxim of action as though it were a universal law. Understood as an elucidation of the grounds of validity of moral principles and judgments, the categorical imperative assumes that the meaning of moral validity can be adequately grasped from the perspective of an individual reflecting on his or her motives of action. Discourse ethics, however, is based on the conviction that, in the wake of the irreversible shift in philosophical concern from individual consciousness to language, monological reflection can no longer fulfill the foundational role accorded it by Kant. Once consciousness and thought are seen to be structured by language, and hence essentially social accomplishments, the deliberating subject must be relocated in the social space of communication where meanings—and hence individual identity which is structured by social meanings—are matters for communal determination through public processes of interpretation.[3]

For Habermas, however, this paradigm shift does not license a devaluation of the role of rational autonomy in ethical thought as urged by Aristotelians and Hegelians who subordinate the individual will to an encompassing communal ethical life, or *Sittlichkeit,* borne by the supraindividual forces of custom and tradition. For Habermas autonomy remains a central concept in ethical theory; it is defining for the social and political project of modernity to which his thought as a whole remains committed. With the historical transition from traditional to modern society—mirrored at the level of individual psychological development in the transition from conventional to postconventional moral consciousness[4]—religious and metaphysical worldviews lose their capacity to provide consensual justification of norms of social interaction and the autonomous individual becomes the center of the moral universe.[5] In light of this ineluctable historical transformation, the principal alternatives to rational autonomy as a source of moral validity seem to be (a) an arbitrary affirmation of one's own—or adopted—traditions and ways of life and the values underlying them as unconditionally valid, (b) a moral order based on a contractual agreement among self-interested utility calculators whose mutual solidarity would lack sufficient normative foundation to sustain communal goals, or (c) an unrestricted relativism of values and ways of life whose logical consequence would be complete practical disorientation. Given his commitment to a social theory that affords a normative standpoint for criticizing unjust social arrangements and their ideological justifications, none of these alternatives is viable for Habermas. Hence in his discourse ethics he undertakes to reconceptualize the notions of autonomy and practical reason with the goal of vindicating the cognitivist and universalist claims of Kant's moral theory within a dialogical framework.

This reappropriation of Kantian themes can be reconstructed in terms of three fundamental theoretical orientations: (i) a communicative theory of meaning, rationality, and validity that analyzes language in pragmatic terms; (ii) a "transcendental-pragmatic" elucidation of the validity-basis of moral judgment; and (iii) a procedural approach to moral justification.

(i) In contrast to a view that has wide currency in contemporary analytic philosophy of language, Habermas holds that meaning cannot be adequately understood in terms of semantic rules specifying truth conditions of proposition but must be viewed pragmatically in terms of acceptability conditions of utterances in which speakers raise different kinds of claims to validity.[6] The basic unit of meaning on this account is not the sentence, statement, or proposition but the speech act, whose primary function is to mediate ongoing communicative interaction. Speech acts structure social interactions through their illocutionary binding force.[7] This approach derives its power in part from the connections it establishes between meaning, rationality, and validity within a theoretical framework that ties them inextricably to human action. Habermas concurs with Wittgenstein and the pragmatists in viewing meaning as inseparable from the role of language in structuring practices and social interactions. His superordinate concept of validity allows for a more differentiated account of the interrelation between meaning and standards of validity than is possible on the dominant semantic views. Because they elucidate meaning in terms of truth conditions, semantic accounts accord preeminence to the assertoric use of language. But on Habermas's account truth is just one of a number of rationally criticizable validity claims raised in speech, and this permits a distinction crucial to his defense of ethical cognitivism.

Traditionally the issue of the objectivity of moral discourse has been understood to be whether moral judgments express claims that admit of truth and falsity. In Habermas's view this reflects a crucial misunderstanding of moral discourse that has led to fruitless investigations into the possibility of moral knowledge.[8] The claim raised in moral judgments, he argues, is not one to factual truth at all; the question of the cognitive status of moral discourse turns, rather, on identifying a *distinctive* validity claim raised in moral judgments, which, however, also admits of rational criticism on the basis of publicly intelligible reasons. This he characterizes as the claim to *normative rightness,* and the specific goal of his ethical theory is to show how it can be rationally redeemed, that is, adjudicated on publicly intelligible grounds in argumentative discourse. Neither the truth of factual statements nor the rightness of norms can be decided in a deductive fashion or by direct appeal to evidence or intuition. The only forum where such issues, once raised, can be decided without coercion and on a mutually acceptable basis is public discourse in which arguments and counterarguments are competitively marshaled and critically evaluated. Logically speaking, we can make sense of the notion of objectivity only in terms of the kinds of reasons that can be offered in argumentation for or against a validity claim, and in this respect claims to rightness are on a par with truth claims.[9]

Within the framework of his general theory, Habermas distinguishes between communicative action and discourse proper. For the most part communicatively mediated interaction proceeds on a consensual basis of accepted facts and shared norms. Indeed, communication is conceivable only against the background of broad agreement concerning the basic features of the natural and social worlds within which human life unfolds, since it is impossible to problematize all factual or normative claims simultaneously.[10] But where disagreements arise concerning the truth of assertions or the rightness of norms, consensual interaction is disrupted and can be resumed only when agreement on the contentious issues has been restored.[11] In such cases, restoring a disrupted consensus calls for a transition to a higher level of discourse where factual and normative claims are subjected to critical scrutiny in a process of argumentation freed from the imperatives of action.[12] Hence, on Habermas's account, truth and normative rightness are *essentially* discursive matters.

Elucidating truth and rightness in terms of the conditions of rational acceptability in critical discourse demands that rigorous idealizing conditions be set on such discourse. Truth and normative rightness cannot be identified without further ado with the rational consensus reached in any factual process of argumentation, since factual agreements are fallible in principle. Regardless of our assurance that a particular consensus is rational, it can always transpire that it involved ignoring or suppressing some relevant opinion or point of view, that it was influenced by asymmetries of power, that the language in which the issues were formulated was inappropriate, or simply that some evidence was unavailable to the participants.[13]
These considerations lead Habermas—taking his orientation from Peirce's notion of truth as the opinion fated to survive critical examination in an unlimited community of researchers—to elucidate validity in terms of the conditions of an "ideal speech situation," that is, the conditions that would ideally have to be satisfied by a form of communication free of the kinds of distortions that impede the argumentative search for truth or rightness. Clearly these ideal conditions of discourse—such as the absence of all forms of coercion and ideology and the unrestricted right of all competent subjects to participate—can never be realized fully in any real argumentation. Yet the notion of consensus under ideal conditions of discourse is not an empty ideal without relation to real discursive practices. Habermas maintains that the ideal has concrete practical implications because, insofar as participants in real discourses understand themselves to be engaging in a cooperative search for truth or rightness solely on the basis of good reasons, they must, as a condition of the intelligibility of the activity they are engaged in, assume that the conditions of the ideal speech situation are satisfied to a sufficient degree. And it is this normative presupposition that Habermas exploits in developing his "quasi-transcendental" grounding of a basic moral principle.

(ii) For Habermas, as for Kant, the goal of moral theory is to establish a basic principle of moral deliberation and judgment in terms of which the validity of moral norms can be decided. But the dialogical orientation of discourse ethics imposes distinctive requirements on such a basic principle: unlike the categorical imperative, it cannot take the form of a principle of private moral deliberation. Rather, it functions as a bridging principle in practical argumentation permitting participants to reach consensus on the validity of normative arrangements, with a view to their implications for the satisfaction of the needs and interests of all those potentially affected by them. Specifically, the moral principle takes the form of a procedural principle of universalization, 'U', which states that valid moral norms must satisfy the condition that "*All* affected can accept the consequences and the side effects its *general* observance can be anticipated to have for the satisfaction of *everyone's* interests (and these consequences are preferred to those of known alternative possibilities for regulation)."[14] A central question for discourse ethics is how the universal validity of such a principle could be established without recourse to the metaphysical assumptions Kant relied on in elucidating the categorical imperative. Habermas's justification strategy takes the form of a number of interlocking "transcendental-pragmatic" arguments.

Broadly speaking, transcendental arguments take some features of experience or practice accepted as indubitable or indisputable and argue to what must be the case if the features in question are to be possible.[15] Habermas, taking his lead from Karl-Otto Apel, employs such an argument to defend *normative* conclusions, specifically, the claim that argumentation necessarily involves pragmatic presuppositions from whose normative content a basic moral principle can be derived.[16] He presents his argument in the rhetorical form of a refutation of a moral skeptic who attempts to argue for the relativity of moral values. Already by engaging in argumentation, Habermas argues, the skeptic unavoidably makes certain presuppositions as a matter of the logic of the activity he or she is engaged in, presuppositions whose normative content contradicts the position he or she is explicitly defending, and thereby falls into a *performative* or *pragmatic contradiction*.[17] The success of this argumentative strategy depends on identifying appropriate features of a realm of experience or practice demonstrably unavoidable for us, in the sense that we cannot conceive of ourselves apart from it. Kant thought that the objective character of our experience and knowledge provided just such a ground from which to argue for conclusions concerning the necessary structure of human understanding; analogously, Habermas argues that practical argumentation constitutes a sphere of practice that is unavoidable for human agents. Communicative action, by its very structure, is oriented to discourse as the mechanism for repairing disruptions in the consensual basis of communicative interaction.[18] Hence, as social beings who are dependent on practical interactions for the preservation and reproduction of our identities, we are already implicitly committed to the normative presuppositions of argumentative discourse.[19]

(iii) It is not possible here to go into the details of the justification of the principle of universalization, but it is important to clarify some points concerning its logical status.[20] 'U' is intended as a *procedural* principle of practical argumentation that shows how a determinate range of practical issues can be decided in a way mutually acceptable to all participants. Its procedural character may be seen as a reinterpretation of the formal character of the categorical imperative: while it does not directly entail any particular normative principles, it specifies the condition such principles must meet in order to be justified. In doing so, it preserves the central role of autonomy by rejecting sources of moral authority external to the wills of rational agents, though autonomy is now construed in *intersubjective* terms as each participant's impartial concern with ends that can be willed *in common*. The structure imposed on practical argumentation by 'U' compels each participant to adopt the perspectives of all others in examining the validity of proposed norms, for it is their consequences for the needs and interests of those affected that constitute the relevant reasons in terms of which the issue of normative validity must be decided.[21] Now, clearly, not all practical questions admit of resolution in this manner since they do not necessarily involve potentially common interests. But practical discourse regulated by 'U' is not envisaged as a decision procedure for dealing with all kinds of practical questions and hence it is not coextensive with practical reason as such. Habermas differentiates between three distinct kinds of practical questions—pragmatic, ethical, and moral—which are correlated with different employments of practical reason.[22] Pragmatic questions address the technical issue of appropriate strategies and techniques for satisfying our contingent desires, ethical questions the prudential issue of developing plans of life in light of culturally conditioned self-interpretations and ideals of the good; neither can be answered in universally valid terms, and the scope of the correlative notions of practical rationality—respectively, the strategic and the prudential—is correspondingly limited. Only questions of the just regulation of social interaction—in other words, issues of the right—admit of universally valid consensual regulation, whereas ethical questions concern who I am (or we are) and who I (or we) want to be, and this cannot be abstracted from culturally specific notions of identity and the good life. Habermas treats the sphere of the moral as coextensive with questions of justice and hence excludes from its purview much of what has traditionally been included under the rubric of the ethical.

One final point is important for understanding Habermas's model of practical argumentation: while it involves strong counterfactual idealizations, it should not be understood in the manner of social contract constructions as a hypothetical model from which conclusions concerning valid principles of justice can be drawn in private reflection. Rawls's contractualist theory of justice provides a suitable contrast. In his more recent writings he has characterized the theoretical status of the original position variously as a "model-conception" and a "device of representation"[23] in terms of which we, as members of a modern liberal democracy, can clarify our intuitions concerning the right and justify basic principles of justice. On Habermas's approach to the theory of justice, by contrast, we cannot anticipate the outcome of *real* discourses concerning proposed principles of justice among those potentially affected by their observance. Participants alone are ultimately competent to adjudicate claims concerning their needs and interests, and only a consensus achieved in argumentation that sufficiently approximates to the conditions of the ideal speech situation can legitimately claim to be based on rational considerations, and hence to be valid. Thus the discourse theory of ethics demands that we go beyond theoretical speculations concerning justice and enter into real processes of argumentation under sufficiently propitious conditions.[24]

II

In order to situate Habermas's approach within the context of contemporary English-language debates in moral philosophy, I note
some fundamental points of conflict between discourse ethics and
neo-Aristotelian ethics and indicate briefly the burden of proof borne
by either side.[25] Perhaps the strongest thread uniting thinkers of a
neo-Aristotelian bent is a deep suspicion of what might be called the
project of modernity in ethical theory. Their suspicions are nourished
by the conviction that the modern ethics of autonomy cleave to an
individualistic understanding of the self at odds with a substantive
notion of community. In contrast to Aristotle, who saw the community, in the shape of the *polis,* as the bearer of the values and practices
that alone enable an agent to orient his deliberation and action to
practical goals and ideals of character, in the modern period the
individual comes to be viewed as an independent source of value
bound only by the dictates of his or her rational will. With this
individualistic turn, practical reason undergoes a profound transformation: it can no longer rely completely on a sustaining background
of values embodied in communal traditions and ways of life; indeed,
the practical interest in autonomy precludes any final appeal to such
substantive values as something extraneous to the rational will and
hence, in Kantian terms, heteronomous. Practical reason thereby
finds itself burdened with the task of generating decontextualized,
and hence unconditional, moral demands in a purely *immanent* fashion from formal requirements on practical deliberation, such as those
Kant expressed in the various formulations of the categorical
imperative.

Viewed through the lens of Aristotelian ethical concerns, these
theoretical orientations seem fundamentally misguided and lead inevitably to empty formalism at the level of moral principles, sterile
rigorism or impotence at the level of individual deliberation and
action, and incoherence and practical disorientation at the communal
level. The latter point encapsulates a communitarian critique of modernity that sees the tendencies toward fragmentation, alienation, an-
omie, and nihilism in modern societies as symptoms of the loss of a
coherent sense of community. Thus Alasdair MacIntyre paints a bleak
picture of the incoherent state of our moral culture: the currency of

contemporary moral debate, he suggests, is nothing but the debased remnants of conceptual schemes that have long since been severed from the totalities of theory and practice from which they originally derived their point; under such conditions moral disputes are vitiated by conceptual incommensurability and are fated to continue interminably, the participants lacking shared criteria in terms of which they could mediate their emphatic claims and counterclaims.[26] But while the pathologies of contemporary life may lend a certain plausibility to MacIntyre's critical posture, a critique of our moral language that depicts us as systematically deluded concerning the import of our own moral judgments would have to show that the modern ideal of autonomy is empty and that the philosophical project of grounding morality in requirements of practical reason is intrinsically untenable. MacIntyre's historical narrative of decline, which draws parallels between alleged inconsistencies in that project and incoherences in modern ethical culture, apart from exaggerating the importance of moral philosophy, is scarcely adequate to the task. It is open to a defender of modernity like Habermas to counter this story of the decay of a grand tradition in ethics extending from Aristotle through the Middle Ages with one in which Kant's moral theory marks the uncovering of an autonomous dimension of practical reason that remained implicit in the thought of his predecessors. Indeed, Habermas is here on relatively strong ground: against neo-Aristotelian critiques of the normative incoherence of modern life he can bring to bear the full weight of a sophisticated analysis of processes of social and cultural rationalization (grounded in his theory of communicative action) to argue that the modern period marks the culmination of an irreversible historical process of increased differentiation of spheres of validity and discourse.[27] As we have seen, Habermas maintains that communicative action—action oriented to reaching understanding on the basis of criticizable validity claims—is essential to social order and that claims to normative rightness constitute one of the dimensions of validity that structure communication. This enables him to paint a compelling picture of modernity as involving the emergence of forms of social organization explicitly structured by such claims. Moreover, he can counter that under conditions of irreducible pluralism, consensus concerning basic values and notions of the good life has permanently receded beyond the horizon of possibility, and hence that neo-Aristotelian appeals to tradition and community as a basis for coordinating social action simply fly in the face of historical reality. Under such circumstances we are left with no alternative except to locate the normative basis for social interaction in the rational structure of communication itself.

But ultimately the construction of competing interpretations of history cannot be decisive since they necessarily presuppose a guiding normative standpoint, as both Habermas and MacIntyre acknowledge. Viewed in this light, the issue between discourse ethics and neo-Aristotelianism comes down to the philosophical question of the internal coherence of their respective accounts of practical reason. Here neo-Aristotelians draw on a long tradition of powerful critiques of the apparent abstractness of the modern autonomous subject and the inevitable emptiness of formal principles grounded solely in the constraints of an unsituated reason. These and related criticisms can be traced back to one form or another of Aristotle's distinction between the realm of *theoria,* the unchanging realities of which we can have universal knowledge, and that of *praxis,* the changing social situations in which our actions unfold. The fact that the agent must always take account of the shifting features of practical situations in deliberating on how to act—or, in Aristotle's terms, the fact that action is necessarily rooted in the particular—means that theoretical cognition of universal truths, or *episteme,* has strictly limited relevance for practical reflection. Since theoretical knowledge can at best take account of the universal features of practical situations, action calls for a different form of cognition—prudential deliberation or *phronesis*—that cannot attain a high level of certainty or generality because it must remain sensitive to particulars.[28] Moreover, since maxims of prudence cannot be applied solely on the basis of intellectual insight, *phronesis* must be inculcated through training and practical experience and sustained through a stable personality structure comprising fixed traits of character. Thus practical reason for Aristotle essentially presupposes a background of communal traditions embodying ideals of individual virtue, and it is only through induction into the associated practices and forms of communal life that the individual acquires the capacity for ethical agency.

Because this account of practical reason gives expression to enduring insights concerning human agency, it provides ammunition for potentially damaging attacks on moral theories in the Kantian tradition. Viewed in Aristotelian terms, the primacy Kant accords the justification of universal principles of action, for example, must lead either to formalism and practical impotence, since unconditionally universal principles cannot presume to capture all of the practically relevant features of action situations, or to a sterile rigorism where principles are applied in a rigid fashion without regard to relevant contextual features. Correlative problems arise regarding the subject of deliberation and action and the sources of moral motivation. On Kant's account our grounds for acting morally must be immanent to practical reason as such, understood as independent of socially or naturally conditioned desires or prudential considerations of the individual good. Human nature or social context cannot provide points of application for the moral will, which must be viewed as generating moral value from within itself. This seems to presuppose a radically unsituated moral subject who can formulate coherent practical intentions in isolation from natural desires and a socially conditioned identity. But even aside from the intractable problem of how the yawning gap between such a faculty of reason and concrete intentions and actions could possibly be bridged (the problem of application), this position seems to render the sources of moral motivation inscrutable by divorcing questions of morally right action from considerations of the individual good. And once Kant's own seemingly boundless faith in reason is shaken, it is a short step to the voluntarist idea that moral values are grounded in free decisions of individual wills.

Whatever the merits of these criticisms of Kantian ethics in general, they cannot be applied to discourse ethics without significant qualifications that tend to neutralize their destructive potential. This becomes evident once we consider its treatment of the practical subject. One of the cornerstones of discourse ethics is its emphatic rejection of the unsituated notion of the subject criticized by neo-Aristotelians: it regards the capacity for agency as the result of socialization into forms of life structured by communicative action; hence autonomy and freedom are for Habermas *essentially* social matters. Even more significantly, discourse ethics goes beyond both Kant and the Aristotelian tradition in understanding practical reason from the perspective of the interaction of a plurality of subjects rather than that of the individual deliberating subject. On this account, thinkers such as Bernard Williams simply fail to comprehend the point of the modern notion of morality by accepting the ancient understanding of the issue of how one should live as essentially an *individual* problem.[29] In modern societies, where agents can no longer coordinate their actions solely by appeal to a background of shared values, the question of how one should live inevitably raises the question of *how we should regulate our interactions*. But the meaning of this question is such that it cannot in principle be elucidated from the perspective of the Aristotelian deliberating subject. It demands that individuals look beyond their own needs and interests and take account of the needs and interests of others—that is, that they go beyond the egocentric perspective of prudence. In addition, it requires that each adopt a perspective whose basic feature is captured in the universalization test of the categorical imperative, that is, the impartial perspective of principles of action that all could will. Impartiality in matters of the regulation of social interaction, Habermas claims, can only be achieved through a process of practical deliberation and reasoned agreement among all those potentially affected by a proposed norm of justice. In thus reinterpreting moral-practical reason as essentially communicative, and hence intersubjective, discourse ethics can legitimately claim to put the Kantian project on a new footing.[30]

It might nevertheless be objected that discourse ethics remains vulnerable to modified, though no less damaging, forms of the criticisms of emptiness and formalism. On Habermas's model, practical argumentation is a procedure for deliberating upon the validity claims of proposed principles of justice at a remove from the exigencies and constraints of action. Must not the same yawning gap between valid principles and real contexts of action that threatens to engulf Kant's construction again open up here? Moreover, Habermas's analysis of the normative presuppositions of practical argumentation only yields a procedural principle governing discourse but no substantive principles of justice as such. What practical guidance could agents hope to derive from such an abstract principle, and how can it claim validity beyond the sphere of discourse it regulates?

Habermas responds to the first concern by insisting on a clear distinction between discourses of justification and discourses of application.[31] An irreducible duality attaches to the notion of a valid norm: on the one hand, it should be capable of commanding the rational assent of all potentially affected by its observance and, on the other, its observance should be appropriate in all situations in which it is applicable. But these two requirements cannot be satisfied simultaneously because participants in a practical argumentation designed to test the validity of a proposed norm cannot take account of the relevant features of all possible situations in which the norm in question might be applicable. Thus if it is to be possible for finite subjects to reach any justified normative conclusions—the alternative being complete practical paralysis—the principle of universalization can demand at most that they take account of the consequences that the general observation of a norm can be *anticipated* to have on the basis of their present knowledge.[32] But this means that all conclusions concerning the validity of norms are open to reinterpretation in the light of unforeseen situations of application and that questions of their appropriateness to particular situations must be answered separately from the question of justification. In other words, application calls for a new discursive procedure, governed by a principle of *appropriateness,* which addresses the question of whether a norm should be observed in a particular situation in light of all of the latter's relevant features. Only the principles of universalization and appropriateness *together* do complete justice to the notion of impartiality underlying discourse ethics.

To the modified objection of formalism—that the proposed procedural moral principle does not generate any substantive principles of justice and can give no concrete guidance to action—Habermas responds that the very meaning of the notion of autonomy, as reinterpreted in intersubjective, discursive terms, dictates that *philosophical* reflection on the moral cannot itself generate substantive moral principles. Such reflection itself stipulates that questions of validity can be answered only through *real* processes of argumentation among those involved. Because the meaning of impartiality is elucidated in terms of adopting the perspective of everyone affected, and because this notion is given an operational interpretation in terms of a discursive procedure in which each participant has the opportunity to express his or her needs and interests, it is only by actually engaging in discourse with others that one can attain a rational conviction concerning the validity of a normative proposal.[33] As to the question of how discourse ethics can provide concrete guidance for action, this has already been addressed in part by the analysis of the problem of application. Moreover, Habermas never suggests that practical discourse could generate concrete practical principles from out of itself in an a priori fashion. Practical discourses respond to disruptions in normative consensus and hence, notwithstanding their idealizing presuppositions, are always situated within the life-world horizon of some particular group of people from which they derive the contents to be tested.[34]

Insofar as it bears on the issue of motivation, however, this criticism raises another problem for Habermas. Thus Herbert Schnädelbach has objected that in its one-sided cognitivist orientation and its anxiety to exorcize the ghost of decisionism, discourse ethics underestimates the significance of volition and decision in moral life.[35] Habermas's response is that the issue of motivation cannot be addressed at the level of moral *theory*. Nor can adherence to valid norms itself be assured by the outcomes of practical discourse. Argumentation can generate rational conviction concerning the validity of norms of interaction, but it cannot ensure that they will in fact be acted upon. Moral motivation has its sources in the affective psychological development of individuals, which is contingent on socialization into forms of communal life that foster and reinforce sensitivity and openness to the claims of others. In Habermas's words, "any universalistic morality is dependent on a form of life that *meets it halfway*. There has to be a modicum of congruence between morality and the practices of socialization and education. The latter must promote the requisite internalization of superego controls and the abstractness of ego identities."[36]

A more global criticism, which speaks to a sense of unease inspired in some by Habermas's unabashed advocacy of a universalist notion of practical reason, is that Kantian moral theory involves an ideal of public reason that strives for unlimited transparency in human life by demanding that all evaluative commitments be understood as voluntary commitments that are publicly justifiable.[37] The role discourse ethics assigns public argumentation would seem to make it particularly vulnerable to such criticism. But Habermas's concern with openness and publicity is motivated neither by an aspiration to unlimited explicitness nor by the mistaken assumption that all valid evaluative commitments must be entered into voluntarily (in the sense that they should ideally be accepted only on the basis of rational convictions resulting from discursive examination). Rather, he limits the demand for consensual legitimation to one clearly circumscribed sphere of practical questions—those concerning just norms of social interaction—where such an ideal is not merely appropriate but historically unavoidable. When confronted with the question of which norms should govern our interactions (itself inescapable given the character of life in modern industrial societies), we have no choice but to look to public norms to which all mature agents could freely assent, since we can no longer count on a shared *ethos* to sustain our interactions. But it would be a dangerous illusion to think that we could completely transform the normative parameters of our existence in this manner and that the moral community might thereby become coextensive with human life as such. Though as social actors we are under a moral obligation to adopt an impartial perspective on the needs and interests of all affected, such a demand is clearly inappropriate when it comes to deciding the ethical questions of who I am and who I want to be—what career I wish to pursue, who I wish to associate with in the sphere of intimate relations, and so forth. The network of identity-sustaining loyalties and evaluative commitments into which we are born and socialized is something that remains substantially untouched by the outcomes of practical discourses, except in the negative sense that we must renounce or modify commitments and loyalties that conflict with our moral obligations toward others.[38]

Neo-Aristotelian contrasts between abstract rights and principles and substantive ethical life, and between rational autonomy and the situated practical subject—to the detriment of the former term in each case—must be reconsidered in light of the intersubjective turn imparted the Kantian project by discourse ethics. At times Habermas stresses the discontinuity between the moral point of view operationalized in practical argumentation and the internal perspective of concrete ethical life from which issues of the individual and collective good are thematized: under the impartial moral gaze factual norms and values take on a merely problematic status and are examined as to their abstract validity.[39] By opposing the moral to the evaluative in such a stark fashion, he seems to lend substance to the view that morality as construed by discourse ethics is ultimately alien to the identities and interests of particular individuals. But a closer examination of his position reveals this impression to be at very least one-sided. We have already noted several points of mediation between universal principles and concrete contexts of action in discourse ethics: the issues addressed in practical discourse have their origin in contexts of interaction structured by existing norms and values; discourses of justification have to be supplemented by discourses of application sensitive to relevant, though unforeseeable, features of situations of action; and moral principles are dependent for translation into action on complementary sources of motivation rooted in structures of identity that are the result of socialization into appropriate forms of social life. Thus moral discourse is tied back into the lifeworld of socialized subjects both at the outset and in its issue.

Moreover, Habermas goes some way toward accommodating the neo-Aristotelian concern with community in terms of a moral commitment to *solidarity*. Since personal identity can be achieved only through socialization, the moral concern with autonomy and equal respect is inextricably bound up with an interest in the preservation and promotion of intersubjective relationships of mutual recognition, and hence of forms of communal life in which they can be realized.[40] Thus *morality* must be supplemented by a political *ethics* whose goal is to mediate between abstract principles of justice and collective identities via positive law and public policy. Nor is morality merely an arbitrary imposition of alien normative standards onto a recalcitrant substratum of communal forms of life: the lifeworld we moderns inhabit is already pervaded through and through by the universal principles of justice and corresponding abstract personality structures outlined by discourse ethics: "Because the idea of coming to a rationally motivated mutual understanding is to be found in the very structure of language, it is no mere demand of practical reason but is built into the reproduction of social life. . . . To the extent that normative validity claims become dependent on confirmation through communicatively achieved consensus, principles of democratic will-formation and universalistic principles of law are established in the modern state."[41]

Notes

1. The most important systematic exposition of his approach is "Discourse Ethics: Notes on a Program of Philosophical Justification" (henceforth *"DE"*) in *Moral Consciousness and Communicative Action*, trans. C. Lenhardt and S. W. Nicholsen (Cambridge, Mass., 1990), pp. 43–115, to which the present work may be seen as a companion volume.

2. Indeed he confronts the issue head on by casting his exposition in the form of a demonstration of the self-defeating character of ethical skepticism. Cf. *DE*, pp. 76–77.

3. Habermas's repeated criticisms of the "monological" character of the reflective procedure enjoined by the categorical imperative—in contrast with the dialogical procedure of practical argumentation central to discourse ethics—reflect his conviction that the paradigm shift from the "philosophy of consciousness" or "philosophy of the subject" to the philosophy of language and action marks an undeniable advance in our understanding of the central problems of modern philosophy. Cf. *The Philosophical Discourse of Modernity*, trans. F. Lawrence (Cambridge, Mass., 1987), especially pp. 296 ff.

4. Habermas regards Kohlberg's stage theory of moral-psychological development as providing essential empirical confirmation of his discourse theory of ethics. For a comprehensive treatment see "Moral Consciousness and Communicative Action," in Habermas, *Moral Consciousness*, pp. 116–194, and the third essay in the present volume.

5. In J. B. Schneewind's words, the transition to the modern period in moral and political thought is marked by "a movement from the view that morality must be imposed on human beings towards the belief that morality could be understood as human self-governance or autonomy." "Modern Moral Philosophy," in P. Singer, ed., *A Companion to Ethics* (Oxford, 1991), p. 147.

6. Cf. below pp. 55–56, 145–146, 162–163.

7. Cf. Habermas "What is Universal Pragmatics?" in *Communication and the Evolution of Society*, trans. T. McCarthy (Boston, 1979), pp. 65–68. For an illuminating discussion of Habermas's formal pragmatics in relation to analytic theories of meaning, see Kenneth Baynes, *The Normative Grounds of Social Criticism: Kant, Rawls, and Habermas* (Albany, NY, 1992), pp. 88–108.

8. Cf. his criticisms of moral intuitionism and value ethics, *DE*, pp. 50–57 and *Moral Consciousness*, p. 196. Bernard Williams's discussion of the objectivity of ethical judgments in terms of the question of the possibility of ethical knowledge is also open to this criticism—cf. *Ethics and the Limits of Philosophy* (Cambridge, Mass., 1985), pp. 132 ff.

9. Hence Habermas's insistence that the validity claim raised in moral judgments, while not a claim to truth, is *analogous* to a truth claim—see *DE*, pp. 57–62. Discourse ethics rejects the opposition governing the recent metaethical debate in analytic ethics concerning realist and anti-realist interpretations of moral discourse by implying that the question of whether or not there exist moral 'facts' described in moral judgments presupposes a mistaken interpretation of the logic of moral discourse on the model of factual discourse. See, for example, Michael Smith, "Realism," in Singer, ed., *Companion*, pp. 399–410, and G. Sayre-McCord, ed., *Essays on Moral Realism* (Ithaca, 1988).

10. Habermas elaborates this fundamental insight in his theory of the lifeworld—cf. *The Theory of Communicative Action* Vol. 2, trans. T. McCarthy (Boston, 1987), pp. 113 ff. and *Philosophical Discourse*, pp. 298–299, 342ff.

11. There are, of course, other possibilities. Interaction may be broken off altogether— an option of limited scope given the practical imperatives of communal coexistence— or it may continue on a curtailed consensual basis, where disputed factual issues are bracketed or a compromise is negotiated concerning disputed normative issues. Alternatively, belief and compliance can be assured through various forms of deception or coercion (e.g., propaganda, psychological manipulation, or straightforward threats), but such pseudo-consensus, apart from being morally and politically objectionable, is inevitably an unstable basis for ongoing interaction.

12. While communicative action and discourse are very closely interrelated—Habermas describes discourse as a reflective form of communicative action—only in discourse is the issue of validity thematized in a universalistic manner that transcends the limits of a particular community. Cf. Habermas, *Moral Consciousness*, pp. 201–202 and "Justice and Solidarity: On the Discussion Concerning 'Stage 6'," in Michael Kelly, ed., *Hermeneutics and Critical Theory in Ethics and Politics* (Cambridge, Mass., 1990), p. 48.

13. An important feature of Habermas's account of validity claims often overlooked by critics is how it combines a nonrelativistic defense of the objectivity of truth and normative rightness with a thoroughgoing fallibilism concerning particular factual and normative claims, however well supported by real argumentation. This applies to his own theoretical claims as well: he explicitly ties the fate of discourse ethics to reconstructions of implicit knowledge and competences that he acknowledges are fallible, and hence contestable, in principle. Cf. Habermas, *Moral Consciousness*, p. 119 and "Justice and Solidarity," n. 16, p. 52.

14. *DE*, p. 65.

15. Cf. Charles Taylor, "The Validity of Transcendental Arguments" in *Proceedings of the Aristotelian Society* 79 (1978–1979), pp. 151–165.

16. On the logical status of this "transcendental-pragmatic" argument, see *DE*, pp. 83–86.

17. Cf. *DE*, pp. 77ff.

18. On the concept of communicative action, see Habermas, "Remarks on the Concept of Communicative Action," in Gottfried Seebass and Raimo Tuomela, eds., *Social Action* (Dordrecht, 1985), pp. 151–178 and *The Theory of Communicative Action* Vol. 1, trans. T. McCarthy (Boston, 1984), pp. 94–101.

19. Cf. Habermas, *Moral Consciousness*, p. 130, and this volume, pp. 31, 83–84.

20. On the justification of 'U', cf. *DE*, pp. 86ff., and William Rehg, "Discourse and the Moral Point of View: Deriving a Dialogical Principle of Universalization," in *Inquiry* 34 (1991), pp. 27–48.

21. This construction represents a synthesis of Mead's notion of ideal role-taking and Peirce's discursive notion of truth. On the notion of ideal role-taking, see Habermas, "Justice and Solidarity," pp. 38–40.

22. See the first essay of the present volume, "On the Pragmatic, the Ethical, and the Moral Employments of Practical Reason."

23. See, respectively, "Kantian Constructivism in Moral Theory," *Journal of Philosophy* 77 (1980), pp. 520–522, and "Justice as Fairness: Political not Metaphysical," *Philosophy and Public Affairs* 14 (1985), pp. 236–237.

24. For Habermas's views on Rawls, see chapter 2, pp. 25ff., 92ff. This emphasis on public discourse is a development of a theme already present in his early historical-sociological account of the bourgeois public sphere (now belatedly available in English), *The Structural Transformation of the Public Sphere*, trans. T. Burger and F. Lawrence (Cambridge, Mass., 1989). In it he analyzes the legitimating function of public discussion concerning matters of general interest in the bourgeois public sphere which developed in seventeenth-century England and eighteenth-century France and traces its internal contradictions and vicissitudes up to its occlusion with the emergence of the social-welfare state in the nineteenth and twentieth centuries.

25. For present purposes the term *neo-Aristotelian* is used to designate ethical positions structured by recognizable successors to the fundamental orientations of Aristotle's ethics: the central role accorded communally shaped ideals of character and the human good, the distinction between theory and practice, and the distinctions between *praxis* and *poiesis* and between *phronesis* and *techne*. On this use of the term, see Herbert Schnädelbach, "What is Neo-Aristotelianism?" *Praxis International* 7 (1987/88), pp. 225–237.

26. Cf. *After Virtue* (Notre Dame, Ind., 1984), especially chapter 2.

27. For a concise statement, see Habermas, *Philosophical Discourse*, pp. 342–349.

28. *Phronesis* involves a kind of situational appreciation which Aristotle assimilates to perception and which does not admit of codification in terms of general rules or criteria of judgment. On this dimension of Aristotle's account of practical reason, see David Wiggins, "Deliberation and Practical Reason," in *Needs, Values, Truth* (Oxford, 1991), pp. 215–237.

29. Cf. Williams, *Ethics*, pp. 52–53, 67–69. Such criticisms as Sandel's against Rawls that contemporary liberalism repeats the error of its classical predecessors in presupposing "unencumbered" selves do not apply to discourse ethics, which views individuation from the outset as a product of socialization; but far from prejudging the issue against an ethics and politics of autonomy, Habermas argues, the social embeddedness of the subject demands that individual autonomy be reconceptualized in intersubjective terms.

30. Habermas rejects MacIntyre's and Williams's criticisms of attempts to derive a moral principle from the structure of human action as such on the grounds that they are based on a version of the argument (i.e. Alan Gewirth's) that remains tied to an individualistic notion of agency and a correspondingly restricted conception of practical reason. Cf. MacIntyre, *After Virtue*, pp. 66ff. and Williams, *Ethics*, pp. 55ff.

31. See chapter 2, pp. 35ff. In clarifying this distinction he draws on Klaus Günther's study *Der Sinn für Angemessenheit* (Frankfurt, 1988). For a summary of the argument of that work, see Günther, "Impartial Application of Moral and Legal Norms: A Contribution to Discourse Ethics," in David Rasmussen, ed., *Universalism vs. Communitarianism: Contemporary Debates in Ethics* (Cambridge, Mass., 1990), pp. 199–206.

Translator's Introduction

32. Cf. Günther, "Impartial Application," p. 200.

33. Cf. *DE*, p. 67. Habermas also avoids the narcissistic connotations of the Kantian concern with purity of motive in moral judgment by incorporating into his basic principle the discursive examination of the consequences of proposed moral norms, thereby accommodating valid consequentialist intuitions within a deontological ethical theory.

34. Cf. *DE*, p. 103 and "Morality and Ethical Life: Does Hegel's Critique of Kant Apply to Discourse Ethics?" in Habermas, *Moral Consciousness*, p. 204.

35. On the criticism of ethical intellectualism, see Schnädelbach, "Was ist Neoaristotelismus?" in Wolfgang Kuhlmann, ed., *Moralität und Sittlichketi* (Frankfurt, 1986), pp. 57–59. (This discussion does not appear in the translation cited above, n. 25.)

36. Habermas, *Moral Consciousness*, p. 207.

37. Cf. Williams, *Ethics*, pp. 18, 37–38, 100–101, 174ff. Fredric Jameson expresses a related unease of postmodernists when he (somewhat tendentiously) attributes to Habermas a "vision of a 'noisefree,' transparent, fully communicational society," in his introduction to Jean-François Lyotard, *The Postmodern Condition* (Minneapolis, 1984), p. vii.

38. Cf. *DE*, p. 104 and chapter 1 of this volume.

39. See especially *DE*, pp. 107–109.

40. Cf. Habermas, "Justice and Solidarity," pp. 47ff. As he says in another place, "the free actualization of the personality of one individual depends on the actualization of freedom for all," *Moral Consciousness*, p. 207.

41. Habermas, *Theory of Communicative Action* Vol. 2, p. 96; cf. also *Philosophical Discourse*, pp. 344–345.

1
On the Pragmatic, the Ethical, and the Moral Employments of Practical Reason

For Judith

Contemporary discussions in practical philosophy draw, now as before, on three main sources: Aristotelian ethics, utilitarianism, and Kantian moral theory. Two of the parties to these interesting debates also appeal to Hegel who tried to achieve a synthesis of the classical communal and modern individualistic conceptions of freedom with his theory of objective spirit and his "sublation" (*Aufhebung*) of morality into ethical life. Whereas the communitarians appropriate the Hegelian legacy in the form of an Aristotelian ethics of the good and abandon the universalism of rational natural law, discourse ethics takes its orientation for an intersubjective interpretation of the categorical imperative from Hegel's theory of recognition but without incurring the cost of a historical *dissolution* of morality in ethical life. Like Hegel it insists, though in a Kantian spirit, on the internal relation between justice and solidarity. It attempts to show that the meaning of the basic principle of morality can be explicated in terms of the content of the unavoidable presuppositions of an argumentative practice that can be pursued only in common with others. The moral point of view from which we can judge practical questions impartially is indeed open to different interpretations. But because it is grounded in the communicative structure of rational discourse as such, we cannot simply dispose of it at will. It forces itself intuitively on anyone who is at all open to this reflective form of communicative action. With this fundamental assumption, discourse ethics situates itself squarely in the Kantian tradition yet without leaving itself vulnerable to the objections with which the abstract ethics of conviction has met from its inception. Admittedly, it adopts a narrowly circumscribed conception of morality that focuses on questions of justice. But it neither has to neglect the calculation of the consequences of actions rightly emphasized by utilitarianism nor exclude from the sphere of discursive problematization the questions of the good life accorded prominence by classical ethics, abandoning them to irrational emotional dispositions or decisions. The term *discourse ethics* may have occasioned a misunderstanding in this connection. The theory of discourse relates in different ways to moral, ethical, and pragmatic questions. It is this differentiation that I propose to clarify here.

Classical ethics, like modern theories, proceeds from the question that inevitably forces itself upon an individual in need of orientation faced with a perplexing practical task in a particular situation: how should I proceed, what should I do?[1] The meaning of this "should" remains indeterminate as long as the relevant problem and the aspect under which it is to be addressed have not been more clearly specified. I will begin by taking the distinction between pragmatic, ethical, and moral questions as a guide to differentiating the various uses of practical reason. Different tasks are required of practical reason under the aspects of the purposive, the good, and the just. Correspondingly, the constellation of reason and volition changes as we move between pragmatic, ethical, and moral discourses. Finally, once moral theory breaks out of the investigative horizon of the first-person singular, it encounters the reality of an alien will, which generates problems of a different order.

I

Practical problems beset us in a variety of situations. They "have to be" mastered; otherwise we suffer consequences that are at very least annoying. We *must* decide what to do when the bicycle we use every day is broken, when we are afflicted with illness, or when we lack the money necessary to realize certain desires. In such cases we look for reasons for a rational choice between different available courses of action in the light of a task that we *must* accomplish if we *want* to achieve a certain goal. The goals themselves can also become problematic, as, for example, when holiday plans fall through or when we must make a career decision. Whether one travels to Scandinavia or to Elba or stays at home or whether one goes directly to college or first does an apprenticeship, becomes a physician or a salesperson—such things depend in the first instance on our preferences and on the options open to us in such situations. Once again we seek reasons for a rational choice but in this case for a choice between the goals themselves.

In both cases the rational thing to do is determined in part by what one wants: it is a matter of making a rational choice of means in the light of fixed purposes or of the rational assessment of goals in the light of existing preferences. Our will is already fixed as a matter of fact by our wishes and values; it is open to further determination only in respect of alternative possible choices of means or specifications of ends. Here we are exclusively concerned with appropriate techniques—whether for repairing bicycles or treating disease—with strategies for acquiring money or with programs for planning vacations and choosing occupations. In complex cases decision-making strategies themselves must be developed; then reason seeks reassurance concerning its own procedure by becoming reflective—for example, in the form of a theory of rational choice. As long as the question "What should I do?" has such pragmatic tasks in view, observations, investigations, comparisons, and assessments undertaken on the basis of empirical data with a view to efficiency or with the aid of other decision rules are appropriate. Practical reflection here proceeds within the horizon of purposive rationality, its goal being to discover appropriate techniques, strategies, or programs.[2] It leads to recommendations that, in the most straightforward cases, are expressed in the semantic form of conditional imperatives. Kant speaks in this connection of rules of skill and of counsels of prudence and, correspondingly, of technical and pragmatic imperatives. These relate causes to effects in accordance with value preferences and prior goal determinations. The imperative meaning they express can be glossed as that of a *relative ought,* the corresponding directions for action specifying what one "ought" or "must" do when faced with a particular problem if one wants to realize certain values or goals. Of course, once the values themselves become problematic, the question "What should I do?" points beyond the horizon of purposive rationality.

In the case of complex decisions—for example, choosing a career—it may transpire that the question is not a pragmatic one at all. Someone who wants to become a manager of a publishing house might deliberate as to whether it is more expedient to do an apprenticeship first or go straight to college; but someone who is not clear about what he wants to do is in a completely different situation. In the latter case, the choice of a career or a direction of study is bound up with one's "inclinations" or interests, what occupation one would find fulfilling, and so forth. The more radically this question is posed, the more it becomes a matter of what life one would like to lead, and that means what kind of person one is and would like to be. When faced with crucial existential choices, someone who does not know what he wants to be will ultimately be led to pose the question, "Who am I, and who would I like to be?" Decisions based on weak or trivial preferences do not require justification; no one need give an account of his preferences in automobiles or sweaters, whether to himself or anyone else. In the contrasting case, I shall follow Charles Taylor in using the term *strong preferences* to designate preferences that concern not merely contingent dispositions and inclinations but the self-understanding of a person, his character and way of life; they are inextricably interwoven with each individual's identity.[3] This circumstance not only lends existential decisions their peculiar weight but also furnishes them with a context in which they both admit and stand in need of justification. Since Aristotle, important *value decisions* have been regarded as clinical questions of the good life. A decision based on illusions—attaching oneself to the wrong partner or choosing the wrong career—can lead to a failed life. The exercise of practical reason directed in this sense to the good and not merely to the possible and expedient belongs, following classical usage, to the sphere of ethics.

Strong evaluations are embedded in the context of a particular self-understanding. How one understands oneself depends not only on how one describes oneself but also on the ideals toward which one strives. One's identity is determined simultaneously by how one sees oneself and how one would like to see oneself, by what one finds oneself to be and the ideals with reference to which one fashions oneself and one's life. This existential self-understanding is evaluative in its core and, like all evaluations, is Janus faced. Two components are interwoven in it: the descriptive component of the ontogenesis of the ego and the normative component of the ego-ideal. Hence, the clarification of one's self-understanding or the clinical reassurance of one's identity calls for an *appropriative* form of understanding— the appropriation of one's own life history and the traditions and circumstances of life that have shaped one's process of development.[4] If illusions are playing a role, this hermeneutic self-understanding can be raised to the level of a form of reflection that dissolves self-deceptions. Bringing one's life history and its normative context to awareness in a critical manner does not lead to a value-neutral self-understanding; rather, the hermeneutically generated self-description is logically contingent upon a critical relation to self. A more profound self-understanding alters the attitudes that sustain, or at least imply, a life project with normative substance. In this way, strong evaluations can be justified through hermeneutic self-clarification.

One will be able to choose between pursuing a career in management and training to become a theologian on better grounds after one has become clear about who one is and who one would like to be. Ethical questions are generally answered by unconditional imperatives such as the following: "You must embark on a career that affords you the assurance that you are helping other people." The meaning of this imperative can be understood as an "ought" that is not dependent on subjective purposes and preferences and yet is not absolute. What you "should" or "must" do has here the sense that it is "good" for you to act in this way in the long run, all things considered. Aristotle speaks in this connection of paths to the good and happy life. Strong evaluations take their orientation from a goal posited absolutely for me, that is, from the highest good of a self-sufficient form of life that has its value in itself.

The meaning of the question "What should I do?" undergoes a further transformation as soon as my actions affect the interests of others and lead to conflicts that should be regulated in an impartial manner, that is, from the moral point of view. A contrasting comparison will be instructive concerning the new discursive modality that thereby comes into play. Pragmatic tasks are informed by the perspective of an agent who takes his preferences and goals as his point of departure. Moral problems cannot even be conceived from this point of view because other persons are accorded merely the status of means or limiting conditions for the realization of one's own individual plan of action. In strategic action, the participants assume that each decides egocentrically in accordance with his own interests. Given these premises, there exists from the beginning at least a latent conflict between adversaries. This can be played out or curbed and brought under control; it can also be resolved in the mutual interest of all concerned. But without a radical shift in perspective and attitude, an interpersonal conflict cannot be perceived by those involved *as* a moral problem. If I can secure a loan only by concealing pertinent information, then from a pragmatic point of view all that counts is the probability of my deception's succeeding. Someone who raises the issue of its permissibility is posing a *different* kind of question—the moral question of whether we all could will that anyone in my situation should act in accordance with the same maxim.

Ethical questions by no means call for a complete break with the egocentric perspective; in each instance they take their orientation from the telos of one's own life. From this point of view, other persons, other life histories, and structures of interests acquire importance only to the extent that they are interrelated or interwoven with my identity, my life history, and my interests within the framework of an intersubjectively shared form of life. My development unfolds against a background of traditions that I share with other persons; moreover, my identity is shaped by collective identities, and my life history is embedded in encompassing historical forms of life. To that extent the life that is good for me also concerns the forms of life that are common to us.[5] Thus, Aristotle viewed the *ethos* of the individual as embedded in the *polis* comprising the citizen body. But ethical questions point in a different direction from moral questions: the regulation of interpersonal conflicts of action resulting from opposed interests is not yet an issue. Whether I would like to be someone who in a case of acute need would be willing to defraud an anonymous insurance company just this one time is not a moral question, for it concerns my self-respect and possibly the respect that others show me, but not equal respect for all, and hence not the symmetrical respect that everyone should accord the integrity of all other persons.

We approach the moral outlook once we begin to examine our maxims as to their compatibility with the maxims of others. By maxims Kant meant the more or less trivial, situational rules of action by which an individual customarily regulates his actions. They relieve the agent of the burden of everyday decision making and fit together to constitute a more or less consistent life practice in which the agent's character and way of life are mirrored. What Kant had in mind were primarily the maxims of an occupationally stratified, early capitalist society. Maxims constitute in general the smallest units in a network of operative customs in which the identity and life projects of an individual (or group) are concretized; they regulate the course of daily life, modes of interaction, the ways in which problems are addressed and conflicts resolved, and so forth. Maxims are the plane in which ethics and morality intersect because they can be judged alternately from ethical and moral points of view. The maxim to allow myself just one trivial deception may not be *good* for me—for example, if it does not cohere with the picture of the person who I would like to be and would like others to acknowledge me to be. The same maxim may also be *unjust* if its general observance is not equally good for all. A mode of examining maxims or a heuristic for generating maxims guided by the question of how I want to live involves a *different* exercise of practical reason from reflection on whether from my perspective a generally observed maxim is suitable to regulate our communal existence. In the first case, what is being asked is whether a maxim is good for me and is appropriate in the given situation, and in the second, whether I can will that a maxim should be followed by everyone as a general law.

The former is a matter for ethical deliberation, the latter for moral deliberation, though still in a restricted sense, for the outcome of this deliberation remains bound to the personal perspective of a particular individual. My perspective is structured by my self-understanding, and a casual attitude toward deception may be compatible with my preferred way of life if others behave similarly in comparable situations and occasionally make me the victim of their manipulations. Even Hobbes recognizes a golden rule with reference to which such a maxim could be justified under appropriate circumstances. For him it is a "natural law" that each should accord everyone else the rights he demands for himself.[6] But an egocentrically conceived universalizability test does not yet imply that a maxim would be accepted by all as the moral yardstick of their actions. This would follow only if my perspective necessarily cohered with that of everyone else. Only if my identity and my life project reflected a universally valid form of life would what from my perspective is equally good for all in fact be equally in the interest of all.[7]

A categorical imperative that specifies that a maxim is just only if *all* could will that it should be adhered to by everyone in comparable situations first signals a break with the egocentric character of the golden rule ("Do not do unto others what you would not have them do unto you"). *Everyone* must be able to will that the maxims of our action should become a universal law.[8] Only a maxim that can be generalized from the perspective of all affected counts as a norm that can command general assent and to that extent is worthy of recognition or, in other words, is morally binding. The question "What should I do?" is answered morally with reference to what *one* ought to do. Moral commands are categorical or unconditional imperatives that express valid norms or make implicit reference to them. The imperative meaning of these commands alone can be understood as an "ought" that is dependent on neither subjective goals and preferences nor on what is for me the absolute goal of a good, successful, or not-failed life. Rather, what one "should" or "must" do has here the sense that to act thus is just and therefore a duty.

II

Thus, the question "What should I do?" takes on a pragmatic, an ethical, or a moral meaning depending on how the problem is conceived. In each case it is a matter of justifying choices among alternative available courses of action, but pragmatic tasks call for a different *kind of action,* and the corresponding question, a different *kind of answer,* from ethical or moral ones. Value-oriented assessments of ends and purposive assessments of available means facilitate rational decisions concerning how we must intervene in the objective world in order to bring about a desired state of affairs. This is essentially a matter of settling empirical questions and questions of rational choice, and the *terminus ad quem* of a corresponding pragmatic discourse is a recommendation concerning a suitable technology or a realizable program of action. The rational consideration of an important value decision that affects the whole course of one's life is quite a different matter. This latter involves hermeneutical clarification of an individual's self-understanding and clinical questions of a happy or not-failed life. The *terminus ad quem* of a corresponding ethical-existential discourse is advice concerning the correct conduct of life and the realization of a personal life project. Moral judgment of actions and maxims is again something different. It serves to clarify legitimate behavioral expectations in response to interpersonal conflicts resulting from the disruption of our orderly coexistence by conflicts of interests. Here we are concerned with the justification and application of norms that stipulate reciprocal rights and duties, and the *terminus ad quem* of a corresponding moral-practical discourse is an agreement concerning the just resolution of a conflict in the realm of norm-regulated action.

Thus, the pragmatic, ethical, and moral employments of practical reason have as their respective goals technical and strategic directions for action, clinical advice, and moral judgments. Practical reason is the ability to justify corresponding imperatives, where not just the illocutionary meaning of "must" or "ought" changes with the practical relation and the kind of decision impending but also the *concept of the will* that is supposed to be open to determination by rationally grounded imperatives in each instance. The "ought" of pragmatic recommendations relativized to subjective ends and values is tailored to the *arbitrary choice* (*Willkür*) of a subject who makes intelligent decisions on the basis of contingent attitudes and preferences that form his point of departure; the faculty of rational choice does not extend to the interests and value orientations themselves but presupposes them as given. The "ought" of clinical advice relativized to the telos of the good life is addressed to the striving for self-realization and thus to the *resoluteness* (*Entschlußkraft*) of an individual who has committed himself to an authentic life; the capacity for existential decisions or radical choice of self always operates within the horizon of a life history, in whose traces the individual can discern who he is and who he would like to become. The categorical "ought" of moral injunctions, finally, is directed to the *free will* (*freien Willen*), emphatically construed, of a person who acts in accordance with self-given laws; this will alone is autonomous in the sense that it is completely open to determination by moral insights. In the sphere of validity of the moral law, neither contingent dispositions nor life histories and personal identities set limits to the determination of the will by practical reason. Only a will that is guided by moral insight, and hence is completely rational, can be called autonomous. All heteronomous elements of mere choice or of commitment to an idiosyncratic way of life, however authentic it may be, have been expunged from such a will. Kant confused the autonomous will with an omnipotent will and had to transpose it into the intelligible realm in order to conceive of it as absolutely determinative. But in the world as we experience it, the autonomous will is efficacious only to the extent that it can ensure that the motivational force of good reasons outweighs the power of other motives. Thus, in the plain language of everyday life, we call a correctly informed but weak will a "good will."

To summarize, practical reason, according to whether it takes its orientation from the purposive, the good, or the just, directs itself in turn to the choice of the purposively acting subject, to the resoluteness of the authentic, self-realizing subject, or to the free will of the subject capable of moral judgment. In each instance, the constellation of reason and volition and the concept of practical reason itself undergo alteration. Not only the addressee, the will of the agent who seeks an answer, changes its status with the meaning of the question "What should I do?" but also the addresser, the capacity of practical deliberation itself. According to the aspect chosen, there result three different though complementary interpretations of practical reason. But in each of the three major philosophical traditions, just one of these interpretations has been thematized. For Kant practical reason is coextensive with morality; only in autonomy do reason (*Vernunft*) and the will attain unity. Empiricism assimilates practical reason to its pragmatic use; in Kantian terminology, it is reduced to the purposive exercise of the understanding (*Verstand*). And in the Aristotelian tradition, practical reason assumes the role of a faculty of judgment (*Urteilskraft*) that illuminates the life historical horizon of a customary *ethos*. In each case a *different* exercise is attributed to practical reason, as will become apparent when we consider the respective discourses in which they operate.

III

Pragmatic discourses in which we justify technical and strategic recommendations have a certain affinity with empirical discourses. They serve to relate empirical knowledge to hypothetical goal determinations and preferences and to assess the consequences of (imperfectly informed) choices in the light of underlying maxims. Technical or strategic recommendations ultimately derive their validity from the empirical knowledge on which they rest. Their validity does not depend on whether an addressee decides to adopt their directives. Pragmatic discourses take their orientation from *possible contexts* of application. They are related to the actual volitions of agents only though subjective goal determinations and preferences. There is no *internal* relation between reason and the will. In ethical-existential discourses, this constellation is altered in such a way that justifications become rational motives for changes of attitude.

The roles of agent and participant in discourse overlap in such processes of self-clarification. Someone who wishes to attain clarity about his life as a whole—to justify important value decisions and to gain assurance concerning his identity—cannot allow himself to be represented by someone else in ethical-existential discourse, whether in his capacity as the one involved or as the one who must weigh competing claims. Nevertheless, there is room here for discourse because here too the steps in argumentation should not be idiosyncratic but must be comprehensible in intersubjective terms. The individual attains reflective distance from his own life history only within the horizon of forms of life that he shares with others and that themselves constitute the context for different individual life projects. Those who belong to a shared lifeworld are potential participants who can assume the catalyzing role of impartial critics in processes of self-clarification. This role can be refined into the therapeutic role of an analyst once generalizable clinical knowledge comes into play. Clinical knowledge of this sort is first generated in such discourses.[9]

Self-clarification draws on the context of a specific life history and leads to evaluative statements about what is good for a particular person. Such evaluations, which rest on the reconstruction of a consciously appropriated life history, have a peculiar semantic status, for "reconstruction" here signifies not just the descriptive delineation of a developmental process through which one has become the individual one finds oneself to be; it signifies at the same time a critical sifting and rearrangement of the elements integrated in such a way that one's own past can be accepted in the light of existing possibilities of action as the developmental history of the person one would like to be and continue to be in the future. The existential figure of the "thrown projection" (*geworfener Entwurf*) illuminates the Janus-faced character of the strong evaluations justified by way of a critical appropriation of one's own life history. Here genesis and validity can no longer be separated as they can in the case of technical and strategic recommendations. Insofar as I recognize what is good for me, I also already in a certain sense make the advice my own; that is what it means to make a conscious decision. To the extent that I have become convinced of the soundness of clinical advice, I have also already made up my mind to transform my life in the manner suggested. On the other hand, my identity is only responsive to—even at the mercy of—the reflexive pressure of an altered self-understanding when it observes the same standards of authenticity as ethical-existential discourse itself. Such a discourse already presupposes, on the part of the addressee, a striving to live an authentic life or the suffering of a patient who has become conscious of the "sickness unto death." In this respect, ethical-existential discourse remains contingent on the *prior* telos of a *consciously* pursued way of life.

IV

In ethical-existential discourses, reason and the will condition one another reciprocally, though the latter remains embedded in the life-historical context thematized. Participants in processes of self-clarification cannot distance themselves from the life histories and forms of life in which they actually find themselves. Moral-practical discourses, by contrast, require a break with all of the unquestioned truths of an established, concrete ethical life, in addition to distancing oneself from the contexts of life with which one's identity is inextricably interwoven. The higher-level intersubjectivity characterized by an intermeshing of the perspective of each with the perspectives of all is constituted only under the communicative presuppositions of a universal discourse in which all those possibly affected could take part and could adopt a hypothetical, argumentative stance toward the validity claims of norms and modes of action that have become problematic. This impartial standpoint overcomes the subjectivity of

the individual participant's perspective without becoming discon-
nected from the performative attitude of the participants. The objectivity of the so-called ideal observer would impede access to the
intuitive knowledge of the lifeworld. Moral-practical discourse represents the ideal extension of each individual communication community from within.[10] In this forum, only those norms proposed that
express a common interest of all affected can win justified assent. To
this extent, discursively justified norms bring to expression simultaneously both insight into what is equally in the interest of all and a
general will that has absorbed into itself, *without repression,* the will of
all. Understood in this way, the will determined by moral grounds
does not remain external to argumentative reason; the autonomous
will is completely internal to reason.

Hence, Kant believed that practical reason first completely comes
into its own and becomes coextensive with morality in its role as a
norm-testing court of appeal. Yet the discourse-ethical interpretation
of the categorical imperative we have offered reveals the one-sided-
ness of a theory that concentrates exclusively on questions of justification. Once moral justifications rest on a principle of universalization
constraining participants in discourse to examine whether disputed
norms could command the well-considered assent of all concerned,
detached from practical situations and without regard to current
motives or existing institutions, the problem of how norms, thus
grounded, could ever be *applied* becomes more acute.[11] Valid norms
owe their abstract universality to the fact that they withstand the
universalization test only in a decontextualized form. But in this
abstract formulation, they can be applied without qualification only
to standard situations whose salient features have been integrated
from the outset into the conditional components of the rule as conditions of application. Moreover, every justification of a norm is
necessarily subject to the normal limitations of a finite, historically
situated outlook that is provincial in regard to the future. Hence *a
forteriori* it cannot already explicitly allow for all of the salient features
that at some time in the future will characterize the constellations of
unforeseen individual cases. For this reason, the *application* of norms
calls for argumentative clarification in its own right. In this case, the
impartiality of judgment cannot again be secured through a principle
of universalization; rather, in addressing questions of context-sensi-

tive application, practical reason must be informed by a principle of appropriateness (*Angemessenheit*). What must be determined here is which of the norms already accepted as valid is appropriate in a given case in the light of all the relevant features of the situation conceived as exhaustively as possible.

Of course, discourses of application, like justificatory discourses, are a purely cognitive undertaking and as such cannot compensate for the uncoupling of moral judgment from the concrete motives that inform actions. Moral commands are valid regardless of whether the addressee can also summon the resolve to do what is judged to be right. The autonomy of his will is a function of whether he is capable of acting from moral insight, but moral insights do not of themselves lead to autonomous actions. The validity claim we associate with normative propositions certainly has obligatory force, and duty, to borrow Kant's terminology, is the affection of the will by the validity claim of moral commands. That the reasons underlying such validity claims are not completely ineffectual is shown by the pangs of conscience that plague us when we act against our better judgment. Guilt feelings are a palpable indicator of transgressions of duty, but then they express only the recognition that we lack good reasons to act *otherwise*. Thus, feelings of guilt reflect a split within the will itself.

V

The empirical will that has split off from the autonomous will plays an important role in the dynamics of our moral learning processes.[12] The division of the will is a symptom of weakness of will only when the moral demands against which it transgresses are in fact legitimate and it is *reasonable* (*zumutbar*) to expect adherence to them under the given circumstances. In the revolt of a dissident will, there all too often also come to expression, as we know, the voice of the other who is excluded by rigid moral principles, the violated integrity of human dignity, recognition refused, interests neglected, and differences denied.

Because the principles of a will that has attained autonomy embody a claim analogous to that associated with knowledge, validity and genesis once again diverge here as they do in pragmatic discourse. Thus, behind the facade of categorical validity may lurk a hidden, entrenched interest that is susceptible only of being pushed through. This facade can be erected all the more easily because the rightness of moral commands, unlike the truth of technical or strategic recommendations, does not stand in a contingent relation to the will of the addressee but is intended to bind the will rationally from within. Liberating ourselves from the merely presumptive generality of selectively employed universalistic principles applied in a context-insensitive manner has always required, and today still requires, social movements and political struggles; we have to learn from the painful experiences and the irreparable suffering of those who have been humiliated, insulted, injured, and brutalized that nobody may be excluded in the name of moral universalism—neither underprivileged classes nor exploited nations, neither domesticated women nor marginalized minorities. Someone who in the name of universalism excludes another who has the right to *remain* alien or other betrays his own guiding idea. The universalism of equal respect for all and of solidarity with everything that bears the mark of humanity is first put to the test by radical freedom in the choice of individual life histories and particular forms of life.

This reflection already oversteps the boundaries of individual will formation. Thus far we have examined the pragmatic, ethical, and moral employments of practical reason, taking as a guide the traditional question, "What should *I* do?" But with the shift in horizon of our questions from the first-person singular to the first-person plural, more changes than just the forum of reflection. Individual will formation by its very nature is already guided by public argumentation, which it simply reproduces *in foro interno*. Thus, where moral life runs up against the boundaries of morality, it is not a matter of a shift in perspective from internal monological thought to public discourse but of a transformation in the problem at issue; what changes is the role in which other subjects are encountered.

Moral-practical discourse detaches itself from the orientation to personal success and one's own life to which both pragmatic and ethical reflection remain tied. But norm-testing reason still encounters the other as an opponent in an *imaginary*—because counterfactually extended and virtually enacted—process of argumentation. Once the other appears as a *real* individual with his own unsubstitutable will, new problems arise. *This* reality of the alien will belongs to the primary conditions of collective will formation.

The fact of the plurality of agents and the twofold contingency under which the reality of one will confronts that of another generate the additional problem of the communal pursuit of collective goals, and the problem of the regulation of communal existence under the pressure of social complexity also takes on a new form. Pragmatic discourses point to the necessity of compromise as soon as one's own interests have to be brought into harmony with those of others. Ethical-political discourses have as their goal the clarification of a collective identity that must leave room for the pursuit of diverse individual life projects. The problem of the conditions under which moral commands are reasonable motivates the transition from morality to law. And, finally, the implementation of goals and programs gives rise to questions of the transfer and neutral exercise of power.

Modern rational natural law responded to this constellation of problems, but it failed to do justice to the intersubjective nature of collective will formation, which cannot be correctly construed as individual will formation writ large. Hence, we must renounce the premises of the philosophy of the subject on which rational natural law is based. From the perspective of a theory of discourse, the problem of agreement among parties whose wills and interests clash is shifted to the plane of institutionalized procedures and communicative presuppositions of processes of argumentation and negotiation that must be actually carried out.[13]

It is only at the level of a discourse theory of law and politics that we can also expect an answer to the question invited by our analyses: Can we still speak of practical reason in the singular after it has dissolved into three different forms of argumentation under the aspects of the purposive, the good, and the right? All of these forms of argument are indeed related to the wills of possible agents, but as we have seen, concepts of the will change with the type of question and answer entertained. The unity of practical reason can no longer be grounded in the unity of moral argumentation in accordance with the Kantian model of the unity of transcendental consciousness, for there is no metadiscourse on which we could fall back to justify the choice between different forms of argumentation.[14] Is the issue of whether we wish to address a given problem under the standpoint of the purposive, the good, or the just not then left to the arbitrary choice, or at best the prediscursive judgment, of the individual? Recourse to a faculty of judgment that "grasps" whether a problem is aesthetic rather than economic, theoretical rather than practical, ethical rather than moral, political rather than legal, must remain suspect for anyone who agrees that Kant had good grounds for abandoning the Aristotelian concept of judgment. In any case, it is not the faculty of reflective judgment, which subsumes particular cases under general rules, that is relevant here but an aptitude for discriminating problems into different kinds.

As Peirce and the pragmatists correctly emphasize, real problems are always rooted in something objective. The problems we confront thrust themselves upon us; they have a situation-defining power and engage our minds with their own logics. Nevertheless, if each problem followed a unique logic of its own that had nothing to do with the logic of the next problem, our minds would be led in a new direction by every new kind of problem. A practical reason that saw its unity only in the blind spot of such a reactive faculty of judgment would remain an opaque construction comprehensible only in phenomenological terms.

Moral theory must bequeath this question unanswered to the philosophy of law; the unity of practical reason can be realized in an unequivocal manner only within a network of public forms of communication and practices in which the conditions of rational collective will formation have taken on concrete institutional form.

2

Remarks on Discourse Ethics

Discourse ethics has met with objections directed, on the one hand, against deontological theories generally and, on the other, against the particular project of offering an explication of the moral point of view in terms of universal communicative presuppositions of argumentation. Here I here take up some of these objections and discuss them in a metacritical fashion by way of explicating once again, though in an unsystematic fashion, the theoretical program I share, in its essentials, with Karl-Otto Apel.

In the following sections I shall refer to theses of Bernard Williams, John Rawls, Albrecht Wellmer, Klaus Günther, Ernst Tugendhat, Stephen Lukes, Charles Fried, Charles Taylor, Apel, Thomas McCarthy, Alasdair MacIntyre, and Günther Patzig, discussing in succession the following topics:

1. The relation between theoretical and practical reason.

2. Similarities and differences between the mode of validity of truth claims and that of norms.

3. Some interrelations between rationality and morality.

4. The relation between the justification and the application of norms.

5. The relation between the validity of norms, sanctions, and self-respect.

6. The discourse-ethical interpretation of the moral point of view.

7. The role of idealizations in this explication of the moral point of view.

8. The distinction between negative and positive rights and duties.

9. The attempt to develop a postmetaphysical ethics of the good.

10. The meaning of "ultimate justifications" in moral theory.

11. The primacy of the right over the good.

12. The relation between tradition and modernity constitutive for the concept of "postconventional moral consciousness."

13. The challenge posed by an ecological ethics for an anthropocentric conception.

1. The cognitivism of Kantian ethics has repeatedly met with the incomprehension of those who judge practical reason by the standards of what Kant called the understanding. Thus, empiricism disputes whether moral questions can even be decided in a rational manner. Normal language use—so runs a *prima facie* plausible objection—should already make the cognitivist wary: when we act immorally, we are not necessarily behaving irrationally. This is indeed indisputable if we understand "rational" in terms of intelligent, pragmatically astute, and, hence, purposively rational action. But then, of course, our way of using language can no longer serve as an unbiased witness, since it is already informed by an outlook that limits the rational to the sphere of purposive action. Certainly we cannot simply assimilate moral insight to epistemic knowledge without further ado, for the former tells us what we ought to do, whereas we only know something, strictly speaking, when we know how things stand in the world. Practical questions do not seem to admit of theoretical treatment. In fact, our everyday moral intuitions neither depend on an ethical theory nor can they in the normal course of events derive much benefit from one. But it does not follow that intuitively mastered everyday knowledge is not knowledge at all. On the contrary, our practices of criticizing immoral actions and of disputing moral questions by appealing to reasons suggest rather that we associate a cognitive claim with moral judgments. Kant too shows no small regard for the "moral knowledge of common human reason" and is

cognizant of the fact "that neither science nor philosophy is needed in order to know what one has to do."[1]

It must be asked, therefore, whether, in the light of the "moral knowledge of common human reason," moral theory is not itself subject to narrow constraints. Moral judgments give authors like Bernard Williams occasion to reflect on the "limits of philosophy."[2] They acknowledge that moral reflection is indeed cognitive in character but only in the weak sense of a reflective confirmation of the familiar conditions under which we live or would like to live. This corresponds to an Aristotelian approach that views practical reason as limited essentially to ethical self-understanding and consequently to the sphere of the good. Aristotle advocated the thesis that expressions such as "moral judgment" and "moral justification" have a specific, nonempirical meaning and held that ethics is not a matter of knowledge in the strict sense but of practical deliberation.

Aristotle defined this faculty of *phronesis* (*prudentia,* "prudence") in a negative fashion in contrast to the strong claims of *episteme*—the faculty of knowledge concerned with the universal, necessary, and supratemporal dimension of existence and, ultimately, of the cosmos—but without completely denying its cognitive status. However, *modern* Aristotelians can no longer uncritically appeal to such a faculty of metaphysical knowledge as a point of contrast. The fallible conception of knowledge that informs the sciences involves the renunciation of all metaphysical aspirations, and it is not clear that significant modifications could still be made to this weak, postmetaphysical conception of knowledge without jeopardizing its fundamental cognitive status. On the other hand, the theoretical knowledge secured by the modern empirical sciences can no longer be employed in genuinely practical contexts; at best, it permits calculations of means and ends (technical and strategic recommendations) that are indifferent to moral concerns. On these premises it becomes questionable whether our everyday ethical knowledge can be viewed as genuine knowledge.

Modern Aristotelians can circumvent this difficulty by appealing to the distinction between naive, contextual, everyday knowledge, on the one hand, and generalized, theoretical, reflective knowledge, on the other. Williams expounds the thesis that we can speak of ethical as well as scientific *knowledge,* because the former enables us to orient ourselves in the social world, just as the latter enables us to orient ourselves in the objective world of things and events. Ethical knowledge retains its capacity to provide orientation, however, only within the horizon of the established everyday practice of individuals socialized into a specific culture, whereas empirical knowledge becomes prey to illusions precisely in everyday contexts and can be shown to be universally valid factual knowledge only from the detached perspective of scientific reflection. The empirical sciences adopt a critical attitude toward the kind of everyday intuitions on which we immediately rely in our moral judgments. On the other hand, we would destroy our ethical knowledge by submitting it to scientific examination, because theoretical objectification would dislodge it from its proper place in our life.

Williams recognizes that Aristotelian reflections such as these lead us up a blind alley. Modern life is characterized by a plurality of forms of life and rival value convictions. For this reason—and not on account of the empty misgivings of moral theorists—the traditional, established knowledge of concrete ethical life is drawn into a dynamic of problematization that no one today can elude. This awareness of contingency also pervades ethical knowledge and compels it to reflect upon itself: "the urge to reflective understanding of society and our activities goes deeper and is more widely spread in modern society than it has ever been before. . . . There is no route back from reflectiveness."[3] In view of this situation, the attempt to shield traditional powers and institutions from the pressure of reflection, in the manner of an Arnold Gehlen, is hopelessly reactionary. Equally implausible, on the other hand, is the decisionistic attempt to evade the growing contingency besetting value convictions by making certainty a function of pure decision. Like other noncognitivist proposals, decisionism is counterintuitive, for a moment of passivity always attaches to convictions, which *take shape* gradually and are not produced by us like decisions. And, finally, if we do not cynically reject the phenomena as they force themselves upon us from the participant perspective in favor of a relativism informed by the observer perspective, and if we refuse to follow Nietzsche and the historicists in simply repudiating the clear language of our moral feelings, then we are faced with an acute dilemma: How can we appropriate naive, everyday ethical knowledge in a critical fashion without at the same time destroying it through theoretical objectification? How can ethical knowledge become reflective from the perspective of the participants themselves?

The answer Williams offers points in the direction of ethical self-reflection. Just as an individual can reflect on himself and his life as a whole with the goal of clarifying who he is and who he would like to be, so too the members of a collectivity can engage in public deliberation in a spirit of mutual trust, with the goal of coming to an understanding concerning their shared form of life and their identity solely through the unforced force of the better argument. In such ethical-political discourses, as I propose to call them, participants can clarify who they are and who they want to be, whether as members of a family, as inhabitants of a region, or as citizens of a state. The strong evaluations that shape the self-understanding of the person or of the community as a whole are here up for discussion. An individual life history or an intersubjectively shared form of life is the horizon within which participants can critically appropriate their past with a view to existing possibilities of action. Such processes of self-understanding lead to conscious decisions that are judged according to the standard of an authentic way of life. Insofar as any kind of theoretical knowledge can be of any help in these processes, it is generalized therapeutic knowledge rather than philosophical knowledge: "How truthfulness to an existing self or society is to be combined with reflection, self-understanding, and criticism is a question that philosophy itself cannot answer. It is the kind of question that has to be answered through reflective living. The answer has to be discovered, or established, as a result of a process, personal or social, which essentially cannot formulate the answer in advance, except in an unspecific way. Philosophy can play a part in the process, as it plays a part in identifying the question, but it cannot be a substitute for it."[4] Philosophy can at best clarify the most general features of ethical self-reflection and the form of communication appropriate to it.[5]

But if this is the task that Williams assigns to philosophy, then philosophy must also be in a position to differentiate specifically moral questions from ethical ones and to give them their proper due. Williams does accord moral questions in a narrower sense—those dealing with rights and duties—a special status and even a certain urgency, but his differentiations are not sufficiently incisive. He does not make clear that morality is not oriented to the *telos* of a successful life with a view to answering the question, "Who am I, (or who we are) and who would I (or we) like to be?" Rather, it is concerned with the categorially different question of the norms according to which we want to live together and of how practical conflicts can be settled in the common interest of all. The peculiarly moral problematic detaches itself from the egocentric (or ethnocentric) perspective of each individual's (or our) way of life and demands that interpersonal conflicts be judged from the standpoint of what *all* could will in common. A moral theory can accomplish no less with this question than in Williams's view it is supposed to accomplish in the ethical case: clarification of the conditions under which the participants could find a rational answer for themselves. In the Kantian tradition, this is called the explication of the moral point of view, that is, a point of view that permits the impartial treatment of questions of justice. In moral argumentation, as in the case of ethical discourse, it must be left to the participants themselves to find concrete answers in particular cases; it cannot be known in advance. Moral questions, like ethical questions, must be addressed from the perspective of the participants if the questions and answers are not to be robbed of their normative substance and their binding force. For both discourses, the proposition holds equally: "If the agreement were to be uncoerced, it would have to grow from inside human life."[6]

The moral point of view, however, requires that maxims and contested interests be generalized, which compels the participants to *transcend* the social and historical context of their particular form of life and particular community and adopt the perspective of *all* those possibly affected. This exercise of abstraction explodes the culture-specific lifeworld horizon within which processes of ethical self-understanding take place. Furthermore, it places the neo-Aristotelian demarcation of theoretical from everyday practical knowledge in question for a second time. It was already recognized that ethical knowledge had cast off the naiveté of everyday knowledge and attained reflective status. But moral knowledge that raises a claim to universal validity must in addition detach itself from the contexts in which ethical knowledge remains embedded (though with the qualifications to which all discursive knowledge is subject).

This step is incompatible with Williams's paradoxical attempt to accord practical knowledge a status that divorces it from strict knowledge on an analogy with the way in which *phronesis* was once divorced from *episteme*. Today *all* discursive knowledge is taken to be fallible and more or less context dependent, more or less general, more or less rigorous; correlatively, it is not *just* the nomological knowledge of the objectifying empirical sciences that raises a claim to universal validity. Logic, mathematics, and grammar are also sciences that reconstruct the intuitive knowledge of competent judging and speaking subjects. In an analogous fashion, moral theory engages in a task of rational reconstruction when it elicits from everyday moral intuitions the standpoint of the impartial judgment of interpersonal practical conflicts. In this reflection, of course, it cannot abandon the performative attitude of participants in interaction; only in this way can it maintain contact with the intuitive knowledge acquired through socialization that makes moral judgments possible. To this extent, the connection to the pretheoretical knowledge of everyday life remains intact. Williams does not allow for this possibility because he remains committed to an empirically truncated concept of theoretical knowledge: "I do not believe, then, that we can understand reflection as a process that substitutes knowledge for beliefs attained in unreflective practice. We must reject the objectivist view of ethical life as in that way a pursuit of ethical truth."[7] Williams fails to recognize that theory does not necessarily take the form of objectifying knowledge that explains everyday knowledge in terms of prior dispositions instead of reconstructing it in terms of the underlying generative knowledge of the participants.

2. With his method of "reflective equilibrium," John Rawls has developed just such a reconstructive theory of morality and justice that takes its orientation from everyday situations.[8] He also addresses the question of the relation between theoretical and practical reason. He wants to justify principles of justice, though he understands his justification in constructivist rather than strictly empirical terms. He develops a contract theory of the validity of moral commands because in this way he can bracket the question of "moral truth" and avoid committing himself to either realism or subjectivism concerning values. In his view, these are the only alternatives because he regards

truth exclusively as a property of assertoric propositions. Propositional truth concerns the existence of states of affairs; assertoric propositions say what is the case. But if the meaning of the assertoric mode were the only model in terms of which we could interpret the meaning of normative propositions, and thus the validity of "moral truths," a cognitivist interpretation of morality would present us with a choice between two equally counterintuitive interpretations. Either we would have to accept something like moral facts and understand "moral truth" in the sense of a correspondence theory of truth, as the conformity of propositions with an antecedent realm of value objects that is ultimately independent of the self-understanding and the needs of agents, or we would have to deny that normative propositions can be true or false at all and hold that behind the apparent validity claim to moral truth there is concealed something purely subjective—feelings, attitudes, or decisions that we attribute to ourselves. The former contradicts the grammatical intuition that we can express neither the existence of things nor their actual configurations by means of normative propositions. The latter alternative contradicts another grammatical intuition: that we do not merely express what we feel, wish, intend, or prefer by means of normative propositions. Rawls rightly regards this alternative as unacceptable because, while moral commands, unlike constative utterances, do not relate to anything in the objective world, yet like them they have something objective in view. What ought to be is neither an entity nor a mere experience.

In an attempt to escape this alternative Rawls brings, in addition to the objective and subjective worlds, the concept of a *social world* into play—a world produced by the actors themselves but in accordance with standards that are not at their disposition and that, in a similar though less rigid manner to the existence of states of affairs, are independent of them: "What justifies a conception of justice is not its being true to an order antecedent to and given to us, but its congruence with our deeper understanding of ourselves and our aspirations, and our realization that, given our history and the traditions embedded in our public life, it is the most reasonable doctrine for us. We can find no better basic charter for our social world. Kantian constructivism holds that moral objectivity is to be understood in terms of a suitably constructed social point of view that all can accept. Apart from the procedure of constructing the principles of justice, there are no moral facts."[9] Both moments—the moment of passivity inscribed in reason and the moment of activity attributable to the will—must be such that they can be related to one another in the concept of a procedural morality. We do not determine the procedure through which norms can be judged and accepted as valid—it imposes itself upon us; at the same time, the procedural practice performs the function of *generation* or construction no less than that of *discovery*, that is, of moral cognition of the principles of a correctly regulated communal life. This procedure admits of different characterizations and takes on a different meaning as we highlight one or the other moment of the procedural practice. If the procedure is interpreted on the model of an agreement between private contracting subjects, the moment of voluntary construction comes to the fore, whereas the model of argumentation oriented to justification suggests an overhasty assimilation of moral cognition to forms of knowledge.

Rawls opts for the model of the social contract and develops a constructivist account of the rational production of principles of justice: "It recasts ideas from the tradition of the social contract to achieve a practicable conception of objectivity and justification founded on public agreement in judgment on due reflection. The aim is free agreement, reconciliation through public reason."[10] Like many earlier formulations familiar from *A Theory of Justice*, this statement is in an interesting way ambiguous. Rawls shares this ambiguity with the tradition of rational natural law in which the justification of principles of natural law took on a different meaning according to the manner in which the autonomy of the contracting parties was understood. Parties such as those envisaged by Hobbes who are equipped only with freedom of choice can justify their contractual agreements exclusively on purposive grounds, with the result that their reasons remain tied to the contingent interests and preferences of participants. The agreement that they reach is, in accordance with the model of civil law, essentially an act of will of subjects who possess power. Parties such as those of Kant, by contrast, who are equipped with freedom of will must justify their contractual agreements from the moral point of view—and thus by recourse to the moral law—with the result that their reasons become independent from the egocentric perspectives of participants and are bound up with the discovery of norms that admit of general assent and the shared interests that underlie them. The agreement in this case rests on the insight of morally judging subjects into what they could all will in common.

In *A Theory of Justice* Rawls still mistakenly took the two readings to be compatible but later explicitly adopted the Kantian reading.[11] In fact, he had already integrated the determinations of practical reason into the procedure of will formation under the guise of the specific limitations to which the parties in the original position are subject.

Nevertheless, Rawls fails to distance himself from the voluntaristic implications of a pure contractualist model for the justification of principles of justice. Since the latter are constructed rather than discovered, the corresponding procedure cannot be understood epistemologically as a procedure for discovering truth. Rawls does not merely differentiate the procedure of rational will formation from theoretical cognition but goes so far as to dissociate it from processes of belief formation oriented to truth in a way similar to that in which neo-Aristotelians dissociate prudence or practical deliberation from knowledge as such. What still sets him apart from the neo-Aristotelians is a stronger Kantian concept of practical reason; but on his present conception, this should no longer be introduced as a procedure of rational will formation. The proposed procedure no longer owes its rationality directly to the idealized conditions of a communicative practice that makes agreement in the sense of rationally motivated assent possible, as was still the case in the *A Theory of Justice*. Rather, this procedure is now supposed to derive its rationality from the rational capacities of the participants. As a consequence, the concept of a *person* now bears the full explanatory weight in demonstrating the normative content of practical reason. Everyday moral intuitions presuppose the existence of persons who are so constituted that they possess a sense of justice, form conceptions of the good, regard themselves as sources of legitimate claims, and accept the conditions of fair cooperation. In short, the theoretical problem of justification is shifted from characteristics of procedures to qualities of persons. But since a substantive normative concept of the person cannot be justified straightforwardly in anthropological terms, Rawls in his more recent publications is of two minds as to whether he should give up the claim to moral-theoretical justification in favor of a political ethics. He is now widely interpreted as attempting to found his postmetaphysical, political concept of justice on the self-understanding of a particular political tradition: the two-hundred-year-old American tradition of the constitutional state.[12]

Regardless of where one stands on this question, a neo-Aristotelian retreat from the strong claims to justification of a Kantian theory of justice would be consistent with Rawls's fear of an epistemological assimilation of practical to theoretical reason. But his apprehension becomes groundless once we dissociate the idea of a rationally grounded consensus from a mistaken concept of truth.[13] Here I cannot go into the difficulties of the correspondence theory of truth that have been repeatedly raised since Peirce. But if we understand propositional truth as a claim raised in constative speech acts that can be redeemed discursively only under the exacting communicative presuppositions of argumentation, the claim to rightness raised in regulative speech acts, which is analogous to the claim to truth, can be freed from assumptions concerning correspondence. The concept of a *validity claim* is of a higher level of generality and leaves open the possibility of specifying a number of different validity claims. A validity claim says that the conditions of validity of an utterance—be it an assertion or a moral command—are satisfied, something that cannot be shown by direct appeal to decisive evidence but only through discursive redemption of the claim to propositional truth or normative rightness. The conditions of validity that are not directly accessible are interpreted in terms of reasons that can be advanced in discourse, and the kinds of reasons relevant to discursive redemption of a validity claim cast light on the specific meaning of the validity claim raised in a given instance. Just as the assertoric mode of utterance can be explicated in terms of the existence of the states of affairs asserted, so too the deontological mode can be explicated in terms of the actions enjoined being equally in the interest of all possibly affected.

Moreover, this interpretation of the notion of validity in terms of the logic of argumentation finds support in epistemological considerations. The epistemological view with which the proposed theory of validity claims accords best is undoubtedly a constructivist one, but *this* constructivism applies equally to practical and to theoretical reason. The objectifying knowledge of the empirical sciences is also contingent on the constitutive and meaning-disclosing accomplishments of the expert community of researchers; such accomplishments are by no means the prerogative of the public communication community of citizens. Pragmatism, genetic structuralism, and epistemological anthropology have highlighted in their respective ways the phenomenon described in an ontological fashion by Heidegger as "being-ahead-of-oneself" in a "thrown projection." The anticipatory character of understanding is universal; the moments of projection and discovery complement each other in *all* cognitive activities. In this connection, Peirce, Piaget, and Merleau-Ponty can appeal to Kant, Marx, and Nietzsche. The constellations of elements do indeed vary; at one time, the passive moment of experience through which the world acts upon us predominates, and at another the active moment of an anticipation of possible effects upon us; but both moments, those of discovery and construction, intermesh, and the relative proportions vary already within the sphere of theoretical reason. From physics to morality, from mathematics to art criticism, our cognitive accomplishments form a continuum within the common, though shifting, terrain of argumentation in which validity claims are thematized.

3. Empiricist objections to cognitivist approaches in moral theory can be explained in part as a reflection of restricted concepts of knowledge, rationality, and truth that are oriented to the modern empirical sciences and eliminate practical reason in the Kantian sense. From this perspective, moral judgments are assimilated to either feelings, attitudes, or decisions or to strong evaluations resulting from processes of self-clarification.[14] A different kind of objection is directed against the *specific* justification strategy of discourse ethics: grounding the moral principle in the normative content of our practice of argumentation. Albrecht Wellmer maintains that moral obligations cannot be derived from such implicitly presupposed conditions of rationality: "Obligations to rationality are concerned with arguments regardless of who voices them, whereas moral obligations are concerned with people regardless of their arguments."[15] Although this formulation is striking, it can count as an objection only if one at-

tributes a mistaken premise and a false conclusion to discourse ethics.[16]

Anyone who seriously engages in argumentation must presuppose that the context of discussion guarantees in principle freedom of access, equal rights to participate, truthfulness on the part of participants, absence of coercion in adopting positions, and so on. If the participants genuinely want to convince one another, they must make the pragmatic assumption that they allow their "yes" and "no" responses to be influenced solely by the force of the better argument. This must be distinguished from the institutional arrangements that obligate specific groups of people to engage in argumentation, and consequently to accept the rationality assumptions alluded to, in addressing certain topics and on certain occasions—for example, in university seminars, in court, or in parliamentary hearings. One could concur with Wellmer in holding that such institutions impose "obligations to rationality," since norms alone—here the norms through which discourses are *institutionalized*—can ground obligations to behave in a more or less rational fashion. But Wellmer blurs an important distinction. The general pragmatic presuppositions that must always be made by participants when they enter into argumentation, whether institutionalized or not, do not have the character of practical obligations at all but that of transcendental constraints. Even prior to institutionalization, argumentation leaves participants without a choice; just in virtue of undertaking to engage in such a practice as such, they must accept certain idealizations in the form of presuppositions of communication.

The latter have "normative" content *in a broad sense* that cannot be equated with the obligatory force of norms of interaction. Presuppositions of communication do not have regulative force even when they point beyond actually existing conditions in an idealizing fashion. Rather, as *anticipatory* suppositions they are constitutive of a practice that without them could not function and would degenerate at the very least into a surreptitious form of strategic action. Presuppositions of rationality do not impose *obligations* to act rationally; they *make possible* the practice that participants understand as argumentation.

The program of justification pursued by discourse ethics sets itself the task of deriving from suppositions of rationality of this kind a rule of argumentation for discourses in which moral norms can be justified. It attempts to show that moral questions can be decided rationally as a general rule. Among the premises of such a "derivation," moreover, belong not only the suppositions of rational argumentation as such (expressed in the form of rules) but also a more detailed specification of what we intuitively appeal to when we wish to *justify* a moral action or an underlying norm. Knowing what "justification" signifies in this context is not of itself to prejudge the further question of whether moral justifications and justificatory discourses are indeed possible. This further issue can be resolved only by specifying a rule of argumentation that can perform a role in practical discourse similar to, for example, that played by the principle of induction in empirical-theoretical discourses.

The controversies concerning assertions have made clear what justifications consist in and are generally supposed to accomplish. They resolve disputes about facts—disputes, that is, concerning the truth of corresponding assertoric propositions—through arguments and thereby lead to argumentatively achieved consensus. Furthermore, everyday life teaches us what disputes concerning the rightness of normative sentences involve. We have an intuitive mastery of the language game of norm-guided action in which agents adhere to or deviate from rules while possessing rights and duties that can clash with one other and lead to practical conflicts understood in normative terms. Thus, we are also aware that moral justifications resolve disputes concerning rights and duties, that is, concerning the rightness of the corresponding normative statements. If this is the (weak) sense of normative justification[17] and if anyone who engages in a corresponding argumentative praxis must make idealizing presuppositions of the sort indicated, then it follows from the normative content of these suppositions of rationality (openness, equal rights, truthfulness and absence of coercion) that, insofar as one's sole aim is to justify norms, one must accept procedural conditions that implicitly amount to the recognition of a rule of argumentation, (U): "Every valid norm must satisfy the condition that the consequences and side effects its *general* observance can be anticipated to have for the satisfaction of the interests of *each* could be freely accepted by *all* affected (and be preferred to those of known alternative possibilities for regulation)."[18]

This moral principle yields a precise specification of the validity claim that attaches to obligatory norms of interaction. The obligatory character of justified norms involves the notion that they regulate problems of communal life in the common interest and thus are "equally good" for all affected. For this reason, moral obligations relate, on the one hand, to "persons regardless of their arguments," if by this one understands "without taking into account egocentric convictions that may be bound up with generally valid arguments from the perspective of individual persons." On the other hand, the moral principle owes its rigorously universalistic character precisely to the assumption that arguments deserve equal consideration regardless of their origin and, hence, also "regardless of who voices them."

Furthermore, the opposition between rationality and morality Wellmer presents gains superficial plausibility from the erroneous assumption that cognitivist ethical positions assert or are committed to asserting that moral insight is already a sufficient motive for moral action. But it is part of the cognitivist understanding of morality that justified moral commands and corresponding moral insights only have the weak motivating force of good reasons. No *direct* action-regulating force outside the context of argumentation may (or need) be ascribed to the "normative" content of presuppositions of argumentation that cannot be denied without falling into a performative contradiction or to the moral principle based upon them. The moral principle performs the role of a rule of argumentation only for justifying moral judgments and as such can neither obligate one to engage in moral argumentation nor motivate one to act on moral insights. A valid moral judgment does indeed *signify* in addition an obligation to act accordingly, and to this extent every normative validity claim has rationally motivating force grounded in reasons. Hence, for Kant too, only a will determined by moral insight counts as autonomous. But insight is compatible with weakness of will. Without the support of complementary processes of socialization and structures of identity, without a background of complementary institutions and normative contexts, a moral judgment that is accepted as valid can establish only one thing: that the insightful addressee then knows he has no good reason to act *otherwise*. The weak motivating force of moral insights is manifested empirically in the fact that someone who acts against his better judgment must not only face the moral rebukes of others but is also prey to self-criticism, and thus to "bad conscience." Hence Wellmer is simply asserting a consequence of the cognitivist understanding of morality, and not making an objection against discourse ethics, when he asserts "that the effectiveness of moral arguments remains dependent on preconditions which are not only cognitive, but also affective in nature. . . . A rational equivalent to a moral agreement supported by sacred or religious authority is only possible in so far as a successful adaptation to conditions of mutual recognition between persons—in both cognitive *and* affective terms—has taken place."[19]

The uncoupling of moral judgment from moral action may initially appear counterintuitive because judgments of obligations, like assertoric judgments, are associated with an unconditional validity claim. We say that moral commands are "right" or "wrong" and understand this in a sense analogous to truth. It is no coincidence that we speak of "moral truths" to express the categorical character of normative validity, but with this validity claim, reason affects a will whose contingency consists in its ability to choose to act differently. A will that lets itself be *bound* by moral insight, though it could choose otherwise, is autonomous. Kant mistakenly identified this quality with the act of liberating the will from all empirical motives. This residuum of Platonism disappears once we abandon the idealistic conception of the catharsis of a will purging itself of all earthly impurities. Then the autonomous will is not *eo ipso* a repressive will that suppresses inclinations in favor of duties.

Since Schiller, the rigidity of the Kantian ethics of duty has been repeatedly and rightly criticized. But autonomy can be reasonably expected (*zumutbar*) only in social contexts that are already themselves rational in the sense that they ensure that action motivated by good reasons will not of necessity conflict with one's own interests. The validity of moral commands is subject to the condition that they are *universally* adhered to as the basis for a general practice. Only when this condition is satisfied do they express what all could will. Only then are moral commands in the common interest and—precisely because they are equally good for all—do not impose supererogatory demands. To this extent rational morality puts its seal on the abolition of the victim. At the same time, someone who obeys the Christian commandment to love one's neighbor, for example, and makes sacrifices that could not reasonably be morally required of him, is deserving of our moral admiration. Supererogatory acts can be understood as attempts to counteract the effects of unjust suffering in cases of tragic complication or under barbarous living conditions that inspire our moral indignation.

4. Wellmer touches on another aspect of the relation between rationality and morality in his objection regarding the alleged inapplicability of the principle of universalization in the form proposed by discourse ethics. Universalism seems to overtax the limited capacities of our rational faculty and to necessitate the operations of a divine intellect. If we understand the fundamental moral question "What ought I (or we) to do?" immediately as a concrete question that arises for me (or for us) in a context-dependent manner in a determinate situation, it is indeed unclear how the application of the rule of argumentation (U) could lead to an unambiguous solution. Wellmer assumes that we wish to determine "what is the right way of acting under the *given circumstances*" by directly addressing the particular case and that we propose to answer this question by appeal to a corresponding singular command by means of a discursively generated operation of generalization. Then it must be acknowledged that "this increases enormously the difficulty of the task of determining the consequences and side-effects of a *universal* observance of norms for *each* individual and, beyond that, of finding out whether *all* would be able to accept without coercion these consequences and side effects, as they would arise for each individual."[20]

This characterization, however, misrepresents the role of the principle of universalization in the logic of argumentation, which is solely that of justifying generalized behavioral expectations or modes of action, that is, of justifying the norms that underlie a general practice. (U) belongs properly to *justificatory discourses* in which we test the validity of universal precepts (or their simple or double negations—prohibitions and permissions). Since Kant neglects the problem of *application,* his formulations may suggest another view, or at least a misunderstanding of his view. Discourse ethics has learned from this and makes a careful distinction between the validity—or justice—of norms and the correctness of singular judgments that prescribe some particular action on the basis of a valid norm. Analytically, "the right thing to do in the given circumstances" cannot be decided by a *single* act of justification—or within the boundaries of a single kind of argumentation—but calls for a two-stage process of argument consisting of justification followed by application of norms.

Klaus Günther has drawn on this conclusion to rebut Wellmer's objection convincingly.[21] Moral rules claim validity for an abstract state of affairs, for a way of regulating some practical matter. But the meaning of the validity claim in question can be differentiated in *two ways*: in terms of the rationally motivated assent of all potentially affected that a valid norm earns and in terms of the totality of possible situations to which the norm capable of commanding assent in this manner can be applied: "Does not recognizing a norm as valid for each participant in discourse mean that he regards its observance in all situations in which the norm is applicable as appropriate?"[22] Hence the idea of impartiality, which is expressed in the moral point of view and gives determinate meaning to the validity claim of moral judgments, demands that we take into account a norm's rational acceptance among all those possibly affected with reference to all situations of application *appropriate* to it. Günther formulates this duality in the following manner: "A norm is valid and appropriate whenever the consequences and side effects of its general observance for the interests of each individual in every particular situation can be accepted by all."[23] Of course, participants in argumentation could apply this formula properly only if they had unlimited time at their disposal or were privy to complete knowledge that enabled them to predict reliably all situations that could possibly arise. But the principle of universalization, as a rule of argumentation, must retain a rational, and thus operational, meaning for finite subjects who make judgments in particular contexts. Hence it can demand at most that in justifying norms, those consequences and side effects be taken into account that general adherence to a norm can be *anticipated* to have for the interests of each on the basis of the information and reasons available to them at a particular time.

Clearly, only situations actually used by participants, on the basis of their state of knowledge, for purposes of paradigmatically explicating a matter in need of regulation can be taken into account in the conditional components of a valid norm. The principle of universalization must be formulated in such a way that it does not impose impossible demands; it must relieve participants in argumentation of the burden of taking into account the multitude of completely unforeseeable future situations in justifying norms. Hence, Günther proposes the formula: "A norm is valid if the consequences and side effects of its general observance for the interests of each individual *under unaltered circumstances* can be accepted by all."[24] The *rebus sic stantibus* clause here expresses the qualification that the validity claim of a norm that has withstood the universalization test bears a "time and knowledge index." This reservation ensures that justificatory discourses cannot completely exhaust the notion of impartiality but can only specify its meaning in relation to universal and reciprocal worthiness of recognition. Prima facie valid norms remain open to further interpretation in the light of particular constellations of unforeseeable situations of application. The question of whether norms determined to be valid with reference to anticipated typical situations cited as exemplars are also *appropriate* for similar situations actually occurring in the future in the light of the relevant features of *these* situations is left unanswered by justificatory discourses. This question can be answered only in a further discursive step, specifically, from the *changed* perspective of a discourse of application.

In discourses of application, the principle of appropriateness takes on the role played by the principle of universalization in justificatory discourses. Only the two principles taken together exhaust the idea of impartiality: "In justification only the norm itself, independently of its application in a particular situation, is relevant. The issue is whether it is in the interest of all that everyone should follow the rule. . . . In application, by contrast, the particular situation is relevant, regardless of whether general observance is also in the interest of all (as determined by the prior discursive examination). The issue here is whether and how the rule should be followed in a given situation in light of all of the particular circumstances. . . . What must be decided is not the validity of the norm for each individual and his interests but its appropriateness in relation to all of the features of a particular situation."[25] Discourses of application bring to bear the hermeneutic insight that the appropriate norm gains concrete significance in the light of the salient features of the situation, and the situation is described in turn in the light of the conditions specified in the norm.

Here I do not need to go into the principle of appropriateness and the logic of discourses of application, since these matters have been investigated in detail by Günther.[26] The problem to which both respond becomes apparent in the case of conflict between norms, for in such cases it must be determined which of the prima facie valid norms that are candidates for application proves to be the one most appropriate to a situation, described as exhaustively as possible in all of its relevant features. The norms that are eclipsed by the norm actually applied in a given case do not thereby lose their validity but form a *coherent normative order* together with all other valid rules. From the standpoint of coherence, the relations within this order shift with each new case that leads to the selection of the "single appropriate norm." Thus, it is the system of rules as a whole that ideally permits just one correct solution for every situation of application. Conversely, it is the particular situation whose appropriate interpretation first confers the determinate shape of a coherent order on the unordered mass of valid norms.

Moreover, this result enables us to account for an unsettling asymmetry between the treatment of moral-practical questions, on the one hand, and of empirical-theoretical questions, on the other. In justifying factual claims, we find no analogue of the peculiar division of the impartial judgment of moral conflicts of action into the steps of justification and application. Although the discursive redemption of assertoric validity claims is subject to the fallibilistic qualification that we cannot know definitively whether the assertion taken to be true will withstand all future objections, in this case a justification does not stand in need of supplementation in the same way as in the case of the prima facie validity of a norm; valid empirical knowledge is not *logically* contingent on the resolution of questions of application.

Practical knowledge, by contrast, is of its very nature related to action. This fact provides an explanation of the asymmetry only if it is understood in a particular way. Given its relation to action, moral knowledge of how things should go in the social world is influenced differently by history from empirical knowledge of how things do go in the objective world. The fallibilism that characterizes *all* knowledge, and hence also the fruits of moral discourses of justification and application, amounts to the acknowledgment of the critical potential of superior future knowledge, that is, of history in the shape of our own unforeseeable learning processes. The *specific* reservation that expresses itself in the fact that we take well-grounded norms of action to be prima facie valid only in a provisional sense can indeed be explained in terms of the limitedness of our knowledge but not in terms of its fallibility. The more far-reaching reservation concerning incompleteness cannot be explained in terms of cognitive provinciality in view of potentially better future knowledge; it is rather a function of existential provinciality resulting from historical transformations in the objects themselves, and thus in the contexts in which future actions will be determined by rules accepted at present.

The social world toward which we are oriented in the normative attitude is *historical* in a different sense from the laws and regularities that constitute the realm of describable events and states of affairs in the objective world. The incompleteness of what can be accomplished by discourses of moral justification can be ultimately explained by the fact that the social world, as the totality of legitimately ordered interpersonal relations, has a different ontological constitution from the objective world. Whereas in the objectifying attitude we presuppose the objective world as the totality of existing states of affairs, the social world as such has a historical character. Günther's normative concept of coherence seeks to do justice to this "intrinsic" historicality: "If every valid norm is dependent on coherent supplementation by all others in situations in which norms are applicable, then their meaning changes in every situation. In this way we are dependent on history, since it first produces the unforeseeable situations that compel us in each instance to produce a new interpretation of all valid norms."[27] Deontological ethical conceptions assume in the final analysis only that the moral point of view remains identical; but neither our understanding of this fundamental intuition, nor the interpretations we give morally valid rules in applying them to unforeseeable cases, remain invariant.

5. Only cognitivist basic assumptions can do justice to the phenomena and the experiences of a posttraditional morality that has detached itself from the religious and metaphysical contexts from which it arose. Kantian ethics derives its plausibility not from the justification

of the categorical imperative in particular, or from the construction of a Kingdom of Ends, and definitely not from the architectonic of the two-worlds theory as a whole but from moral intuitions to which a cognitivist interpretation can appeal. Moral experiences are a response to the violation of what Kant called duty, respect, and free will; they crystallize around the harm inflicted on a person by immoral action—the humiliation and abasement of a person whose integrity has been violated, and the reproaches that the injurious action as well as the wrongdoer bring upon themselves. With this, the peculiar mode of validity of moral injunctions becomes the focus of interest as a phenomenon in need of explanation. Hence, the interpretation of the mode of validity of normative statements on an analogy with the truth of assertoric statements is opposed (a) to the empiricist notion that the illocutionary force of moral commands rests on mere feelings of obligation originating in the internalization of threatened sanctions and (b) to the noncognitivist notion that the reciprocal interest in the observance of norms can ultimately be traced back to an interest in self-respect.

(a) "Ought" sentences expressing obligations are the primary linguistic form in which morality finds expression. Duties prescribe actions or omissions. Prohibitions are the negations of permissions, permissions the negations of prohibitions. Obligations have their experiential basis not in perceptions but, as Strawson has shown, in moral feelings. The latter point as a general rule to violations of duties, transgressions against norms from which duties and rights (i.e., legitimate expectations concerning actions in accordance with duties) can be derived. Feelings of offense and resentment are second-person reactions to violations of our rights by others; feelings of shame and guilt are reactions to our own transgressions; and outrage and contempt are reactions of one present but not directly involved to the violation of a recognized norm by a third person. Thus, these affective states correspond to the perspectives and roles of the participants in interaction—ego and alter—and of a neutral party who is not presently involved but whose perspective should not be confused with that of a mere observer, his view being that of a representative of universality. They all belong to a community in which interpersonal relations and actions are regulated by norms of interaction and can be judged in the light of these norms to be justified or unjustified.

These *affective responses* to violations that find expression in turn in reproaches, confessions, condemnations, and so forth and can lead to accusations, justifications, or excuses constitute the *experiential basis* of obligations, though they do not exhaust their semantic meaning. The normative sentences in which these obligations are expressed point to a background of normatively generalized behavioral expectations. Norms regulate contexts of interaction by imposing practical obligations in a justifiable manner on actors who belong to a shared community. Conventions are norms of interaction that define reciprocal behavioral expectations in such a way that their content does not need to be justified. "Mere" conventions bind, so to speak, in a groundless fashion by custom alone; we do not associate a moral claim with them. Duties, by contrast, derive their binding force from the validity of norms of interaction that claim to rest on good reasons. We feel obligated only by norms of which we believe that, if called upon to do so, we could explain why they both deserve and admit of recognition on the part of their addressees (and of those affected).

The internal connection between norms and justifying grounds constitutes the *rational foundation of normative validity*. This can be confirmed at the phenomenological level by the corresponding sense of obligation. Duties *bind* (*binden*) the will but do not *bend* (*beugen*) it. They point the will in a certain direction and give it orientation but do not compel it as impulses do; they motivate through reasons and lack the impulsive force of purely empirical motives. Hence the empiricist notion that norms obligate only to the extent that they are backed up by well-founded expectations of sanctions neglects the fundamental intuition that the noncoercive binding force is transferred from the validity of a valid norm to the duty and the act of feeling obligated. Only the affective reactions to the violation and the perpetrator—resentment, outrage, and contempt—are expressed in the sanctions that result from transgressions of norms.

But the violation of legitimate expectations, to which these feelings are reactions, already presupposes the validity of the underlying norms. Sanctions (however much they are internalized) are not constitutive of normative validity; they are *symptoms* of an already felt, and thus antecedent, violation of a normatively regulated context of life. Hence Kant correctly presupposes the primacy of the "ought" over sanctions—as indeed does Durkheim—in explaining the original phenomenon of insight into, and the moral feeling of, being obligated to do something in terms of the interrelation between autonomy of the will and practical reason.[28]

We do not adhere to recognized norms from a sense of duty because they are *imposed* upon us by the threat of sanctions but because we *give* them to ourselves. Of course, this preliminary reflection does not provide an adequate basis for developing a notion of self-legislation. Norms we give to ourselves may express our own orders, and thus mere choices (*Willkür*), in which case they lack the very quality that would make them binding norms. It is not because recognized norms are *certified* by custom and tradition that we observe them from a sense of duty but because we take them to be *justified*. But even these reflections viewed in themselves are not a sufficient basis for developing the concept of a norm-testing reason. For example, we might want to justify norms as we do facts, thereby overlooking precisely what makes reason practical. Only by combining both reflections do the concepts of "autonomous will" and "practical reason" emerge as coeval with one another.

Only a will that is open to determination by what all could will in common, and thus by moral insight, is autonomous; and that reason is practical which conceives of everything that is justified in accordance with its impartial judgment as the product of a legislating will. *Voluntas* and *ratio* are interwoven in a remarkable fashion in these two concepts without the one being reduced to the other. These moments no longer confront each other abstractly as, respectively, an active faculty that intervenes in the world and a passive faculty that mirrors facts. An autonomous will *gives itself* only rationally grounded laws, and practical reason *discovers* only laws that it simultaneously formulates and prescribes. A cognitive moment inheres as much in self-determination as a constructive moment does in norm-testing reason. Even Kant could not ultimately give a satisfactory explanation of this perplexing interrelation; it becomes intelligible only when we cease to regard freedom and reason as merely subjective faculties.

From the standpoint of the theory of intersubjectivity, autonomy does not signify the discretionary power of a subject who disposes of himself as his own property but the independence of a person made possible by relations of reciprocal recognition that can exist only in conjunction with the correlative independence of the other. The intersubjective character of freedom and practical reason becomes manifest when we analyze the role an expression such as "respect" assumes in the language game of morality.

(b) In the various stages of its development, Ernst Tugendhat's moral theory exhibits a tendency to combine the empiricist conception of normative validity just discussed with an intersubjective conception of morality through the mediation of the concept of self-respect.[29] Tugendhat understands morality as a "system of norms that exist in a society as a product of social pressure."[30] This description is intended to hold not only from the observer's perspective but also from that of the participant. Hence, he believes that the phenomenon of normative validity can be elucidated by a suitable description of the social sanctions consequent on the transgression of moral norms. This approach yields a noncognitivist conception of morality, since immoral actions cannot be viewed as irrational: "What happens when one violates a moral order is rather that one experiences a social sanction."[31] For this reason Tugendhat thinks that we must give up the attempt to justify morality "in the strict sense." Rationality in the practical sphere he takes to be synonymous with purposive rationality. At the same time Tugendhat takes issue with theories that appeal to these empiricist assumptions as a basis for reducing morality to purposive considerations, with the goal of demonstrating that everyone has good reasons grounded in premoral or natural interests to accept a certain system of externally imposed constraints of reciprocal concern. Mackie, for example, with his appeal to enlightened self-interest and prudent accommodation to external promises of rewards and threats of punishment, completely ignores the obligating sense of norms that is clearly expressed in moral feelings. Tugendhat outlines the intuition he wishes to oppose to this reductionism as follows: "In the one case we have a community constituted by norms that subserve reciprocal utility, in the other a community constituted by (substantially the same) norms, but their meaning now consists in the fact that in them reciprocal respect comes to expression."[32]

The phenomenon of *reciprocal respect* must here be understood in terms of the empiricist premises that Tugendhat shares. The key to this is provided by inner sanctions, that is, the feelings of guilt and shame that result from the internalization of outer sanctions. Tugendhat understands moral shame and guilt as reactions to the loss of one's sense of self-worth; thus, it is ultimately my self-respect that is endangered when I act immorally. One who violates moral norms not only exposes himself to the contempt of others but also feels contempt for himself because he has internalized this sanction. A norm counts as "justified," therefore, only insofar as it is in the interest of each, viewed from his own perspective, that everyone should engage in a practice regulated by the exchange of signs of respect.

If we follow Tugendhat in assuming that everyone has an interest in self-respect and being respected as a person by others, we can explain why moral norms are good for me only when they are good for all, for self-respect requires *reciprocal* respect, since I can affirm myself only if I am valued by those who behave in such a way that they, in turn, are worthy of respect and can also be valued by me.[33] The outcome of Tugendhat's reflections is a morality of mutual respect that seems to boil down to the familiar universalistic principle of equal respect for all. But the premises of this position come into conflict with precisely this intuition. If my esteem for other persons and their respect for me are ultimately rooted in the fact that each individual can respect *himself* only if he is respected by others whom he does not hold in contempt, then there is something purely instrumental about the mutuality of recognition: respect for others is mediated by the concern with self-respect. But my respect for others cannot be made conditional on the satisfaction of my interest in self-respect if relations of mutual respect are to generate the *perfectly symmetrical* structures of recognition commensurate with our intuitive understanding of noninstrumental relations between autonomously acting persons. The egocentric character of the underlying need to be respected by others postulated as primary is transmitted to the structures of recognition based upon it and undermines the complete reciprocity of relations of recognition.[34]

Reciprocal respect represents a necessary pragmatic precondition of participants in interaction ascribing themselves rights and duties only when understood in the sense of *complete* reciprocity. Tugendhat has since adopted a new approach in an effort to free his project—elucidating the phenomenon of reciprocal recognition from the perspective of each individual's sense of self-respect—from the lingering suspicion of egocentricity. In his most recent work, he links the central capacity to experience moral shame and guilt *from the outset* with the status of membership in a community. My understanding of myself as a person is interwoven with my social identity in such a way that I can value myself only if the community of which I view myself as a part and whose authority is binding for me confirms me in my status as a member. What I have internalized as a sanction is the fear of expulsion from a community with which I have identified. Tugendhat introduces this foundation of self-respect in *antecedent* social relations of recognition through an account of what it means to respect someone as a person.

Respect in the sense of esteem is not always a moral matter. We hold someone in esteem as an athlete or as a scientist because of his outstanding achievements. We value someone as a colleague or a friend for his competence or reliability—in short, on account of some outstanding personal qualities he possesses. The example of a friend need be altered only slightly for us to recognize that we can also value someone for his moral qualities—as someone, for example, who refrains from acting improperly, or even opportunistically, in difficult situations and who is willing to make a sacrifice or, in extreme cases, even to sacrifice himself. In all such cases respect can be transformed into admiration, since respect here is a function of greater or lesser estimation of actions and qualities of character. By contrast, respect for a person *as* a person admits of no gradations; we respect a person as such not on account of some outstanding characteristic or other. We respect a person as such on account of his capacity to act autonomously, that is, to orient his actions to normative validity claims; we respect him solely on account of the accomplishment or quality that makes him a person. One cannot possess this constitutive capacity to a greater or lesser degree; it is definitive of what it means to be a person as such. We do not respect someone as a person because he impresses us or because he is worthy of esteem in some way or other—or even because he is a good person or lives a good life—but because he is, and by his conduct shows himself to be, fundamentally capable of being a "member of a community," that is, capable of observing norms of communal life *as such*.

With this the concept of *social membership* assumes the privileged status previously enjoyed by the concept of self-respect. Self-respect cannot be an original phenomenon for the simple reason that it is unclear what the respectworthiness of the isolated subject is supposed to consist in prior to all socialization. Tugendhat initially thought that the intrinsic worth that qualified the subject by his very nature, so to speak, to claim the respect of others could be understood as the value that this subject ascribes to his life as a whole.[35] But clearly the dignity of a person cannot be reduced to the value he confers on his life, since on occasion we may risk our life in order to preserve our self-respect. In fact, the self of self-respect is tied to an extremely vulnerable personality structure; but the latter first emerges in the context of relations of reciprocal recognition. The unconditional relations of mutual respect in which individuals confront one another as responsible acting persons are *coeval* with the phenomenon of self-respect, and thus with the consciousness of being worthy of the respect of others. Hence, Tugendhat adopts a conception of the social constitution of the self from which it follows that nobody adequately understands his own identity who does not derive his sense of self-respect from his status as a member of a community, a status that is recognized by all other members.[36]

On this account, the phenomenon of reciprocal recognition is no longer explained in terms of an original interest in *self*-respect or of an initial fear of the inner sanction of loss of one's sense of *self*-worth. The self is no longer the primary phenomenon but is viewed as the product of a process of socialization that itself already presupposes the structure of relations of reciprocal recognition. What is fundamental is the idea of a community "in which each member derives his sense of self-worth from the observance of the norms that make a community possible and demands the same of others. Thus reciprocity does not here consist in exchange relations but in reciprocally understanding one another in a certain way and in reciprocally demanding such understanding of one another."[37] But in that case it may be asked whether the meaning of the moral "ought" grounded in the reciprocal demand for mutual recognition is still to be sought "in the inner sanction," as Tugendhat would have it, or whether the central feelings of shame and guilt, which are coeval with outrage and contempt, are not secondary phenomena to the extent that they are *reactions* to the violation of legitimate expectations grounded ultimately in the reciprocity of the structures of recognition underlying communities in general. In short, Tugendhat confuses genesis and validity. He is misled by the observation that in the process of socialization, conscience is formed through the internalization of external sanctions to suppose that, even *from the participant perspective* of the conscientious individual who has been socialized in this manner, behind the moral "ought" there is concealed a sanction, the inner sanction of loss of self-respect, instead of the unforced force of the good reasons in terms of which moral insights impress themselves on consciousness as convictions.

The understanding of postconventional morality that Tugendhat proposes itself reveals the cognitive meaning of the mode of validity of moral norms, which cannot be analyzed in terms of inner sanctions. In traditional societies, moral norms are indeed so closely bound up with religious worldviews and shared forms of life that individuals learn what it means to enjoy the status of membership in a community thus founded through identification with the contents of this established concrete ethical life. But in modern societies, moral norms must detach themselves from the concrete contents of the plurality of attitudes toward life that now manifest themselves; they are grounded solely in an abstract social identity that is henceforth circumscribed only by the status of membership in *some* society, not in this or that particular society. This explains the two salient features of a secularized morality that has *transcended* the context of an overarching social ethos. A morality that rests only on the normative content of universal conditions of coexistence in a society (founded on mutual respect for persons) *in general* must be universalistic and egalitarian in respect of the validity and sphere of application of its norms; at the same time, it is formal and empty in the content of its norms. But from its formal and empty character there follows a consequence that is incompatible with a noncognitivist understanding of morality.

The generalized structure of the reciprocal recognition of subjects who confront each other simultaneously as nonreplaceable individuals and as members of a community henceforth amounts only to the viewpoint of the impartial judgment of practical questions that remain to be decided by argument among those affected. When Tugendhat also speaks ultimately of the "enlightened perspective" from which "only that which can be agreed upon is decisive" and comes to the conclusion that "the viable core of all morality reduces to the basic stock of natural or rational norms to which contractualism also appeals and without which there could not be anything like a community,"[38] then he abandons his empiricist premises and falls back on an intersubjectivist interpretation of Kant—on a construction such as that of Rawls, for example, who analyzes moral obligation, and thus the validity of moral principles and institutions, in terms of the idea that they can be rationally justified under conditions of impartial judgment. The general structure of the relations of recognition that make the understanding of self as a person and as a member of a community simultaneously possible is presupposed in communicative action and is preserved in the communicative presuppositions of moral argumentation. Just this structure compels each participant in argumentation to adopt the perspective of all others.

6. The fact of a form of life structured by communicative action can no more be circumvented in moral judgment than in moral action. This becomes manifest once we analyze the rule specifying how one can regard something "from the moral point of view." This is the name we give the standpoint from which moral questions can be judged impartially. Interestingly enough, all attempts to characterize this standpoint as that of a *neutral observer* have miscarried, whether the latter is represented as surveying the moral world as a whole from a transcendental vantage point (as in Kant) or as an empirical observer who occupies a position in the world but is equipped with ideal knowledge (as in utilitarian theories). The observer standpoint seems to guarantee an exceptional degree of objectivity of judgment because of its third-person perspective, but in fact it is unsuitable for judging the question of whether actions or norms are in the common interest or contribute to the common good. The ideal observer operates as an isolated subject, collecting and assessing his information in the light of his own individual understanding of the world and of himself. Impartiality of judgment, by contrast, is essentially dependent on whether the conflicting needs and interests of *all* participants

are given their due and can be taken into consideration from the viewpoint of the participants *themselves*. The privileged position, which initially appears to be advantageous because it promises to liberate the observer from the perspectival interpretations of the disputing parties, has the disadvantage that it isolates him in a monological fashion from the interpretive horizons of the participants and denies him hermeneutic access to an intersubjectively shared moral world that reveals itself only *from within*.

One who wishes to examine something from the moral point of view must not allow himself to be excluded from the intersubjective context of participants in communication who engage in interpersonal relations and who can understand themselves as addressees of binding norms only in this performative attitude. Controversial questions of normative validity can be thematized only from the first-person plural perspective, that is, in each instance "by us"; for normative validity claims are contingent on "our" recognition. We cannot attain an impartial standpoint by turning our back on the context of linguistically mediated interaction and by abandoning the participant perspective completely, but only by extending the individual participant perspective in a *universal* fashion.[39] Each of us must be able to place himself in the situation of all those who would be affected by the performance of a problematic action or the adoption of a questionable norm. What G. H. Mead recommends with his notion of ideal role taking cannot be performed privately by each individual but must be practiced by us *collectively* as participants in a public discourse.

Once it becomes clear that the goal of such an inclusive process of communication (uncoerced agreement) can be achieved only through the mediation of good reasons, the reflective character of what Mead calls "universal discourse" takes on sharper contours. It should not be conceived simply as a kind of net of communicative action that encompasses all potentially affected. On the contrary, as the reflective form of communicative action, it is a form of argumentation in the strict sense.

Viewed in this way, Mead's construction loses the quality of a mere projection, for in every real process of argumentation the participants unavoidably undertake such a "projection." They must make a pragmatic presupposition to the effect that all affected can in principle freely participate as equals in a cooperative search for the truth in which the force of the better argument alone can influence the outcome. On this fact of universal pragmatics is founded the fundamental principle of discourse ethics: only moral rules that could win the assent of all affected as participants in a practical discourse can claim validity. In virtue of the *idealizing* assumptions that everyone who seriously engages in argumentation must make *as a matter of fact,* rational discourse can play the role of a procedure that explicates the moral point of view. Practical discourse may be understood as a communicative process that induces all participants *simultaneously* to engage in ideal role taking in virtue of its form, that is, solely on the basis of unavoidable universal presuppositions of argumentation.

This explanation of the moral point of view privileges practical discourse as the form of communication that secures the impartiality of moral judgment together with universal interchangeability of participant perspectives. It also explains why there is a reasonable prospect of deriving the fundamental principle of universalistic morality from the necessary practical presuppositions of argumentation in general without committing a naturalistic fallacy. Discourses overlay communication oriented to reaching understanding as their reflective form; in the symmetry conditions and reciprocity expectations of everyday speech oriented to reaching understanding, there already exist *in nuce* the basic notions of equal treatment and general welfare on which all morality turns, even in premodern societies. The ideas of justice and solidarity are already *implicit* in the idealizing presuppositions of communicative action, above all in the reciprocal recognition of persons capable of orienting their actions to validity claims. Of course, the normative obligations that children assume in virtue of the mere form of socializing interaction do not *of themselves* point beyond the limits of a concrete lifeworld (of the family, the clan, the city, or the nation). These barriers must first be breached in rational discourse. Arguments by their very nature point beyond particular individual lifeworlds; in their pragmatic presuppositions, the normative content of presuppositions of communicative action is generalized, abstracted and enlarged, and extended to an ideal communication community encompassing all subjects capable of speech and action (as Apel claims following Peirce).

The standpoint of morality differs from that of concrete ethical life in its *idealizing extension* and reversal of interpretive perspectives that are tied to particular, established cultural lifeforms and are the result of individual processes of development. This transition to the idealizing presuppositions of a socially and spatiotemporally unlimited communication community in every actually carried out discourse is an anticipation of, and approximation to, a regulative idea. At the same time, actually engaging in discourse belongs to that very idea, since otherwise the solipsistic character of an examination of norms undertaken "in the privacy of individual reflection" would reassert itself. Even an advocatory discourse, or one pursued *in mente*, is still different from the essentially *monological* procedure of examining maxims in accordance with the categorical imperative in that it clarifies the meaning and burden of proof of the principle of universalization. Admittedly, Kant too makes a distinction between an ego-oriented mode of generalization in the weak sense of the Golden Rule and the rigorously universalistic operation of generalization commensurate with the pragmatic implications of forming a general will.[40] But as long as the isolated subject, in his role as custodian of the transcendental, arrogates to himself the authority to examine norms on behalf of all others, the difference between his supposition concerning a *general* will and an intersubjective agreement concerning a *common* will never comes to light. The perspective from which I test the generalizability of all concerned interests remains in each instance an unquestioned background assumption, for as long as each autonomous will can regard itself as one with all other intelligible beings in the Kingdom of Ends, the maxims that I (in the light of my own self-understanding and view of the world) can will to be rules governing a general practice are valid. But once we abandon the metaphysical doctrine of two separate spheres of reality, subjects encounter each other as individuals who can no longer rely on this antecedent transcendental agreement. They, and hence we, must confront the problem of reaching an adequate intersubjective understanding of the interests of each individual.

In such a situation the principle "Do unto others as you would have them do unto you" will be found wanting because it remains bound in an egocentric fashion to an unthematized individual understanding of self and world. Only an intersubjective process of argumentation in which all potentially affected could participate makes radical generalization at once possible and necessary—in other words, only a test of the generalizability of modes of action that excludes all surreptitious privileging of individual viewpoints and demands the coordination of all of the interpretive perspectives that tend toward individualism and pluralistic fragmentation, at least in modern societies. Given the communicative presuppositions of an inclusive and noncoercive discourse among free and equal partners, the principle of universalization requires each participant to project himself into the perspectives of all others; at the same time, it remains possible for each participant to test whether he can will a disputed norm as a general law from his own point of view on the basis of reciprocal criticism of the appropriateness of interpretive perspectives and need interpretations.

The notion that ideal role taking—that is, checking and reciprocally reversing interpretive perspectives under the general communicative presuppositions of the practice of argumentation—becomes both possible and necessary loses its strangeness when we reflect that the principle of universalization merely makes explicit what it means for a norm to be able to claim validity. Already in Kant the moral principle is designed to explicate the meaning of the validity of norms; it expresses, with specific reference to normative propositions, the *general* intuition that true or correct statements are not valid just for you or me alone. Valid statements must admit of justification by appeal to reasons that could convince anyone irrespective of time or place. In raising claims to validity, speakers and hearers transcend the provincial standards of a merely particular community of interpreters and their spatiotemporally localized communicative practice. The moral principle articulates a notion of transcendence or self-overcoming already contained in assertoric validity claims. Thus, Peirce, in explicating the *meaning of truth,* already engages in extensions or idealizations of the social and temporal dimensions of the practice of communication similar to those required by an intersubjective principle of universalization.[41]

The world as the totality of possible facts is always constituted by some community of interpreters whose members come to an understanding with one another, within an intersubjectively shared lifeworld, about something in the world. What is "real" can be expressed in true statements, where "true" can be explained in terms of the claim that an individual addresses to others when he makes a statement. With the assertoric meaning of his utterance, the speaker raises a criticizable claim to the validity of the asserted proposition; and since we have no direct access to uninterpreted conditions of validity, "validity" (*Gültigkeit*) must be understood epistemically as "validity (*Geltung*) that is established for us." Every justified truth claim advocated by someone must be capable of being defended with reasons against the objections of possible opponents and must ultimately be able to command the rationally motivated agreement of the community of interpreters as a whole. Here an appeal to some particular community of interpreters will not suffice. Hence, Peirce explicates truth by appealing to the counterfactual redemption of criticizable validity claims under the communicative conditions of a community of interpreters extended ideally in social space and historical time. The projection of an *unlimited* communication community serves to substitute for the infinite (or transtemporal) character of "unconditionality" the idea of an open but goal-directed process of interpretation that transcends the boundaries of social space and historical time from within, from the perspective of a finite existence situated within the world. In time, according to Peirce, the learning processes of the unlimited communication community should erect a bridge that spans all temporal distance; in the world, the conditions that must be assumed to be sufficiently satisfied as a precondition of the unconditional claim of transcending validity claims should be realizable. That degree of fulfillment counts as "sufficient" which qualifies our argumentative practice in a given instance as a spatiotemporally localized component of the universal discourse of an ideally extended community of interpreters that we necessarily presuppose. This projection has the effect of shifting the tension between facticity and validity into presuppositions of communication, which, despite the fact that their *ideal* content can only ever be approximately realized, must *as a matter of fact* be made by all participants every time they assert or dispute the truth of a statement and undertake to justify this validity claim in argumentation.

Peirce's discursive conception of truth shows how the concept of normative validity, understood on the model of truth, can be explicated in terms of a moral principle that links the requisite notion of ideal role taking to the communicative form of practical discourse. Correct normative propositions do not refer to existing states of affairs in the objective world as do true statements but to legitimately ordered interpersonal relations in the social world. But in addition to being constructed, just social orders are also discovered. The role of the idealizations to which an intersubjective explanation of the moral principle repeatedly appeals is, of course, in need of further explanation.

7. If normative rightness, like validity (*Gültigkeit*) in general, is construed as the three-place relation "validity (*Geltung*)-of-something-for-someone," then the counterfactual meaning of rational accep*tability* cannot be reduced to that of accep*tance* within a community of interpreters. On the other hand, the idea of an ideally extended communication community is paradoxical in that every known community is limited and distinguishes members from nonmembers through rules of inclusion. Precisely this difference would have to be effaced through reflective extension of social space and historical time. Even the image of an ideal audience (Chaim Perelman) is still too concrete. The model of a public sphere accessible to all participants, issues, and contributions comes closest to the notion envisaged, for these pictures merely serve to express in tangible form limiting concepts for specifying an ideal *structure* of communication. The idealizations relate to the possible *structure* of a communicative practice that operates in a self-reflexive and self-correcting manner and results in a progressive derelativizing of the conditions under which validity claims that are raised in a particular context, but are context transcending in their meaning can be redeemed.

We speak of "idealizations" in a variety of different contexts. The ideal generality of concepts and meanings generates at first sight few difficulties because it seems to establish itself in the rarefied medium of thought. But in fact the universality of meaning already depends on the linguistic idealizations that enable us to recognize the same sign type in individual sign tokens and the same grammatically structured sentence in different utterances. Geometrical figures that we, like Euclid, can realize only approximately in the sand or on the blackboard exhibit a different kind of ideal generality. With them we associate the idea of perfection or perfectibility—we can draw a circle only with a greater or lesser degree of exactitude. Physical measuring operations also rest on the counterfactual assumption that we can approximate ideal quantities to an arbitrary degree of exactitude; as a practical matter, we cannot produce a perfectly level plane. In a similar way experiments may be based on the assumption of an ideal gas, a perfect vacuum, or such like. Simulations have a different, though related, significance. We can remove in thought the operation of gravity and simulate on earth conditions of weightlessness actually encountered in outer space. Finally, with the concept of a regulative idea, the mathematical model of infinite approximation is transposed from the sphere of instrumental action to interactions. These few comparative illustrations must here suffice to lend plausibility to the notion that to *idealize forms of communication,* that is, to think of processes of communication as if they took place under idealized conditions, is not *per se* absurd.

The idealizations undertaken in the sphere of communicative praxis have an air of arbitrariness about them only when viewed from the perspective of a semantically abridged conception of language. Once we reflect on the use of linguistic expressions in the performative attitude of speakers and hearers, we experience idealizations as those simultaneously unavoidable and trivial accomplishments that sustain communicative action and argumentation. We attribute identical meanings to expressions, attach context-transcending significance to validity claims, and ascribe rationality or accountability to speakers. These and similar attributions remain for the most part implicit and have their proper locus in pragmatic presuppositions. In performing an act of communication, we can assume in a self-reflexive fashion that a pragmatic precondition of this communication is fulfilled even though this assumption may not be objectively correct; when our communication does not actually fulfill the assumed condition, we have acted under a *counterfactual presupposition.*

An idea whose comprehension is a major source of difficulties is the transcendental-pragmatic assumption that language use oriented to reaching understanding, whether in communicative action or in argumentation, *always* demands that participants make certain formal pragmatic presuppositions if the practice is to exist *at all*—and this independently of whether they turn out *post hoc* to be counterfactual. We know at least intuitively that certain of these presuppositions cannot be fulfilled under normal empirical restrictions, yet we must nevertheless assume that these idealizing presuppositions are *sufficiently* fulfilled. It is in this sense that in rational discourse, where the speaker seeks to convince his audience through the force of the better argument, we presuppose a dialogical situation that satisfies ideal conditions in a number of respects, including, as we have seen, freedom of access, equal rights to participate, truthfulness on the part of participants, absence of coercion in taking positions, and so forth. It must be shown for each of these conditions of a so-called ideal speech situation (through the demonstration of performative self-contradictions) that they belong to the *unavoidable* presuppositions of argumentation. Every speaker knows intuitively that an alleged argument is not a serious one if the appropriate conditions are violated—for example, if certain individuals are not allowed to participate, issues or contributions are suppressed, agreement or disagreement is manipulated by insinuations or by threat of sanctions, and the like.

The general presuppositions of argumentation cannot be easily fulfilled because of their rigorous idealizing content. Rational discourses have an improbable character, existing like islands in the sea of everyday practice. At the same time, they constitute an irreducible order and cannot be replaced by functional equivalents. In the contemporary world, discourses have specialized social functions—such as the production of knowledge, therapy, art criticism, the administration of justice, political will formation, and so forth—and have to be institutionalized. The rules in accordance with which discourses are institutionalized in modern societies are for the most part legal norms—in the first instance, organizational and procedural norms that specify qualifications for participation, areas of jurisdiction, subjects for discussion, deliberative procedures, decision processes, obligations to justify decisions, and so on. Rules regulating the order of business in deliberative bodies provide an example of how deliberations are regulated with the goal of ensuring the probability of adequate fulfillment of demanding communicative presuppositions under temporal, social, and practical limitations. The institutionalization of specific regions of discourse such as these relieves participants of the considerable motivational and cognitive burdens that every presupposition-laden cooperative quest for the truth imposes when it is pursued in an *ad hoc* fashion in the form of unregulated, spontaneous argumentation. From the perspective of the legislator who institutionalizes rules of discourse, the degenerate forms in which such quasi-natural, informal deliberative practices appear constitute the resistant substrate in which the "geometrical forms" of an ideal deliberative process must be realized in an approximate fashion.

The most serious misgivings do not concern the possibility of effectively institutionalizing rational discourse, which is a matter for a discourse theory of law and politics; skeptical objections are directed against the idealizations involved in the discourse model as such.[42]

(a) Thus Steven Lukes asks in what form actors could satisfy the preconditions for participating in a practical discourse that is supposed to offer the prospect of a rationally motivated agreement among all affected on the basis of ideal role taking. A consensus on generalizable interests can be expected, he claims, only if the theory postulates either homogeneous societies or abstract discourse participants such as Rawls's parties in the original position and thereby assumes that flesh-and-blood actors are surreptitiously transformed into intelligible beings under the communicative presuppositions of rational discourse. But participants in argumentation who must alter their identity to such an extent that they no longer bear any discernable relation to the agents involved in conflicts in need of regulation would become disengaged from their own interests and problems. A form of argumentation uncoupled from real life in this way would necessarily lose sight of its true object: "Even if it were so, the greater the change from the actual agents to the ideally rational agents, capable of reaching the requisite consensus, the less relevant would be the deliberations of the latter to the purpose at hand—which is to establish how the actual participants would think and feel, were alleged structures of domination to be overthrown."[43] In a similar context, Williams objects that the dream of an ideal communication community—by which he means Kant's Kingdom of Ends—is too far removed from social and historical reality to preserve any relevance for concrete issues.[44] But these objections rest on a mistaken conception of idealization.

Anyone who seriously engages in argumentation must indeed presuppose that the conditions of an "ideal speech situation" alluded to are sufficiently realized. But this idealization does not bear on the

objects treated in argumentation; it leaves the identity of the participants and sources of conflict originating in the lifeworld untouched.
The moral point of view calls for the extension and reversibility of
interpretive perspectives so that alternative viewpoints and interest
structures and differences in individual self-understandings and
worldviews are not effaced but are given full play in discourse. Klaus
Günther's operational interpretation of the idea of impartiality
underlines what is essential to the meaning of the validity of singular
moral judgments: just one of the norms that are equally in the interest
of all must be appropriate to a given situation when all of its relevant
features are taken into consideration. In justificatory discourses it is
necessary to abstract from the contingent contextual embeddedness
of a proposed norm only to ensure that the norm, assuming it with-
stands the generalization test, is sufficiently open to context-sensitive
application. It must not be so selective that it admits only of standard
interpretations and excludes the differentiations of a maximally exhaustive situation description that must be taken into account in
discourses of application.

(b) A further objection against procedural interpretations of the
moral principle is that practical discourse cannot stipulate a *sufficiently
determinate* procedure. The procedure of argumentation cannot ensure the choice of correct answers solely on the basis of presuppositions of communication. It would have to have access to independent
criteria for assessing reasons. The procedurally correct practice of an
intersubjective exchange of arguments could not be the decisive fac-
tor in this regard, for in the final analysis only the substantive grounds
that each participant can just as well ponder for himself are significant.[45] Objections of this kind rest on either a pragmatically truncated
concept of argumentation or a semantically truncated concept of
justification, or both.

I understand argumentation as a procedure for the exchange and
assessment of information, reasons, and terminologies (or of new
vocabularies that make a revision of descriptions possible). Of course,
the procedure cannot itself generate these elements; its task is to
ensure that the argumentative exchange can proceed on the basis of
all relevant information and reasons available at a particular point in
time and within the most fruitful and appropriate descriptive framework in each instance. I follow Peirce in holding that arguments are

essential components of reflective learning processes that for their part certainly cannot be explicated solely in terms of argumentation. But procedures and reasons are so closely interwoven with each other that there cannot be any evidence or criteria of assessment that are completely *prior* to argumentation that do not have to be justified in turn in argumentation and validated by rationally motivated agreement reached in discourse under the presuppositions of argumentation. Deductive arguments alone are not informative, and experiences or moral feelings do not constitute a foundation independent of interpretation. Because there cannot be "ultimate" evidence or "decisive" arguments in dealing with substantive questions, we must appeal to the pragmatics of the procedure of argumentation in order to explain why we can even think ourselves capable of raising and redeeming context-transcending validity claims.

(c) Finally, it is asked whether we can expect *exclusively correct* answers in argumentation and in particular in practical argumentation.[46] Because of the ideal content of the central presuppositions of argumentation in general, we can never be certain that the statements we take to be true or correct at this stage of discussion belong among the statements that will withstand all future criticism. But this fallibilism built into the theory of discourse is merely the converse side of the postulate that every sufficiently precise question admits of just one valid answer. Even if we find this convincing for assertoric propositions, things appear to be otherwise in the case of normative questions. Is there only one correct answer to the abortion question, for example? At this stage of the debate, both sides in this dispute appear to have good, perhaps even equally good, arguments. For the time being, therefore, the issue remains undecided. But insofar as what is at issue is in fact a moral matter in the strict sense, we must proceed from the assumption that in the long run it could be decided one way or the other on the basis of good reasons. However, *a forteriori* the possibility cannot be excluded that abortion is a problem that cannot be resolved from the moral point of view at all. From this point of view, what we seek is a way of regulating our communal life that is equally good for all. But it might transpire that descriptions of the problem of abortion are always inextricably interwoven with individual self-descriptions of persons and groups, and thus with their identities and life projects. Where an internal connection of this sort exists, the question must be formulated differently, specifically, in ethical terms. Then it would be answered differently depending on context, tradition, and ideals of life. It follows, therefore, that the moral question, properly speaking, would first arise at the more general level of the legitimate ordering of coexisting forms of life. Then the question would be how the integrity and the coexistence of ways of life and worldviews that generate different ethical conceptions of abortion can be secured under conditions of equal rights.

In other cases it is possible to deduce from the inconclusive outcome of practical discourses that the problems under consideration and the issues in need of regulation do not involve generalizable interests at all; then one should not look for moral solutions but instead for fair compromises. *ethical solution regulated by moral procedures*

8. The communication-theoretical interpretation of morality and the discourse-ethical version of the moral principle have the advantage of avoiding a confusion that creeps in under the premises of the philosophy of the subject. A narrow moral concept tailored to the private sphere of the individual and initially removed from the public sphere of socially organized communal life follows from the deontological distinction between normative questions of right action and evaluative questions of the good life only if one takes as one's underlying assumption a narrow, individualistic concept of the person. By contrast, once we take a concept of the individual as essentially socialized as our point of departure and regard the moral point of view as implicit in the structure of reciprocal recognition among communicatively acting subjects, there is no longer a distinction in principle between private morality and public justice but only in respect of the degree of organization and institutional mediation of interaction.[47] It then becomes clear that persons, understood as mutually respecting *individuals,* are morally obligated in precisely the same way as persons understood as *members* of a community engaged in the activity of realizing collective goals.

The narrow, individualistic conception of morality rests on a negative reading of the categorical imperative understood as being applied in a monological fashion. This is meant to serve the justification of moral injunctions by way of prohibiting nongeneralizable modes of action. Negative duties such as "You should not lie" or "You should not inflict harm on anyone" provide models for this form of justification. If I cannot will that the maxim that permits me to deceive and inflict harm on others in order to procure advantages for myself should become a general norm, then we have a duty not to act in this manner. If, on the other hand, I come to the conclusion that a maxim is fit to hold as a general law, it does not follow that we have a duty, but only that we are permitted, to act in accordance with this maxim.[48] This reading derives its plausibility from the fact that it gives precedence to negative over positive duties and the fact that negative duties seem to express the deontological meaning of moral injunctions with special force. Categorical prohibitions such as "You should not kill" or "You should not lie" are addressed in the second person to all subjects capable of action and demand that we *refrain* from specific actions regardless of the consequences. These norms owe their force (a) to the unconditional character of their validity, (b) the determinateness of their content, and (c) the lack of ambiguity concerning their addressees. Only when these three conditions are fulfilled can *each* individual know *unequivocally* what satisfies and what violates the norm.

From the perspective of a potential victim, to every duty there corresponds a right—for example, to the duty to refrain from killing corresponds the right to the inviolability of one's life and body. A moral principle that makes possible only the justification of general prohibitions gives precedence to the class of negative rights and duties as the essential core of morality. This coheres with liberal convictions, for the rights that correspond to the negative duties circumscribe the spheres of freedom in which, according to the formulation of the Kantian principle of right, the choice (*Willkür*) of each can coexist with the freedom of all in accordance with a general law. If this followed conclusively from the deontological approach itself, the discourse-ethical principle, whose application extends beyond the formation of a *negative* general will, would be too unspecific and in reality a basic principle not of moral but of political will formation. For this reason Albrecht Wellmer, for example, distinguishes a negatively understood and privately applicable moral principle from a public democratic principle of legitimacy that leads to the formation of a common positive will: "In *either* case the way of distinguishing between 'right' and 'wrong' involves an appeal to the idea of a common will formed in the absence of coercion. . . . But the nature of this appeal to a common will should be understood differently in each case. In the case of moral judgment we are concerned with finding a way of acting in concrete situations which we should be able, in B. Gert's terminology, to 'publicly advocate' as a generalizable one. . . . The question that arises in each specific instance is whether we—as rational beings—are able to will that a particular way of acting should become universal. And only the *negative* answer to this question constitutes a moral 'ought.'"[49] Against this view I will show that the precedence accorded negative rights does not follow from the deontological approach as such but only from it in conjunction with a narrow, individualistic concept of the person.

To the deontological distinction between the right and the good corresponds the distinction between normative judgments about what we ought to do and evaluative judgments about something in the world that is more or less good or bad for us. This distinction draws initial support from the fact that the grammar of commands is related internally to action, which is not the case with the grammar of evaluations. Normative judgments always relate to the choice between alternative possibilities of action; evaluations relate to objects or states of affairs independently of whether they are described as ends or goods from the perspective of a purposively acting subject. More important is the nonteleological significance of commands. Norm-guided actions do indeed have good or bad consequences for those directly involved and those affected. But a moral judgment about an action can claim general validity only because it is made with reference to an underlying valid norm of action and does not depend on an *ad hoc* evaluation of the consequences of action judged more or less desirable by the standards of someone directly involved or some collection of individuals affected. Evaluations express what in a given case is more or less good and useful or bad and harmful "for me" or "for us." Binary encoded commands prescribe which modes of action are right or wrong, without reference to specific addressees and without considering their contingent preferences or evaluative orientations. Murder and deceit are not wrong merely because they are not good for those whom they victimize. As norms of action they are wrong *in general* because they do not express a *generalizable* interest. Hence the unconditional or categorical character of normative validity would be compromised if the obligatoriness of impartially grounded actions and norms of action were not divorced from values and preferences that arise only from the evaluative perspective of particular persons or reference groups. In this respect, normative judgments are oriented to rules rather than ends.

Rules of action coordinate the plans of a variety of agents; ends are the intended results of the interventions of an individual or collective agent in the world. One who wishes to act morally decides between alternative available courses of action in the light of norms he believes to be right, and the correctness of these norms is determined by whether they are equally in the interest of all potentially affected. One who wishes to act purposively decides between alternative available courses of actions in the light of preferred goals and selects his goals in the light of values. From a deontological viewpoint, therefore, moral deliberations must be kept completely free from goal-directed reflections. Because general prohibitory norms undoubtedly satisfy this condition, they appear to be capable of grounding moral duties in an exemplary fashion. Against this I will show under the three above headings (a) through (c) that positive norms of action can also ground duties in the strict sense.

In regard to (a), prohibitions of the form "You should not kill" create the impression that such conduct is forbidden "unconditionally" in the sense of strict generality—that is, for everyone under all circumstances and for all time, in short, *categorically*. This, at least, is how Kant understood the validity of the maxims justified as general laws by the categorical imperative; the meaning of moral obligation, the meaning of the moral "ought," is expressed with special force in the notion of *unconditional* or absolute validity. On closer inspection, though, we find that negative rights and duties can no more claim "absolute" validity than can positive duties.

An untruthful statement that saves the life of another is no less morally commanded than killing in cases of self-defense or refraining from offering assistance to avoid a greater evil are morally permissible. Valid norms are valid only in a "prima facie" sense. Regardless of whether they rest on double negations, *all* rights and duties play the same role in discourses of application, namely, that of reasons. In cases of conflict between norms, it can be shown only on the basis of a maximally complete description of all relevant features of the given situation *which* of the competing norms is appropriate to a particular case.[50] Norms that are overruled by this "single appropriate" norm do not lose their validity because they are not "pertinent." They remain valid even if they do not apply to the given case. This already entails that the deontological force of normative validity cannot be interpreted simply as an *unconditional* or absolute ought, as it is by an *ethics of conviction.*

On the contrary, normative validity has the intersubjective sense that a behavioral expectation is equally good "for all," not that it has desirable consequences for a particular addressee: a connection with good and bad is not categorically excluded, but the norm is qualified through generalization as a regulation that is *equally good for all.* Because of these intersubjective relations inscribed in moral norms, no norm, regardless of whether it involves negative or positive rights and duties, can be justified or applied privately in the solitary monologue of the soul with itself. It is not a foregone conclusion that maxims generalizable from my point of view must also be acknowledged to be moral obligations from the perspective of others, let alone of all others. Kant could disregard this fact because, as I noted, he assumed that all subjects in the Kingdom of Ends share the *same* conception of themselves and of the world. With this abstract preunderstanding at the level of "consciousness as such" is correlated, at the level of the world of appearances, the assumption of an abstract equality of interest among individual persons who are conceived, on the model of possessive individualism, as standing in a relation of ownership to themselves.[51] Once we abandon these premises it becomes imperative to submit all norms—and not just general prohibitions—to a *public,* discursive, generalization test that necessitates reciprocal perspective taking.

In regard to (b), prohibitions of the form "You should not kill" have the merit of *determinateness.* With positive duties, goal orientations that require agents to intervene in the world with a view to consequences are imported into the moral sphere. Whereas it is always within the power of an agent to refrain from performing an action, the realization of an intended state of affairs is never solely dependent on the good will of the agent alone but also on the contingencies of available means, the causal connections with other events, and the limitations of a situation of action. Positive norms of action render prognostication indispensable, as well as a concrete expenditure of effort, energy, and attention; and with this there arise the problem of imputing responsibility for the consequences and side effects of action, the problem of the reasonableness of imposing moral demands (*Zumutbarkeit*) and of the division of moral labor between different agents, and in general the problem of assessing results in the light of goals that admit of greater and lesser degrees of fulfillment. Whether an act of providing assistance is appropriate, whether it can be reasonably required of someone, whether it should be regarded as sufficient in a given instance: these issues depend on the circumstances. The difficulties that must be dealt with in discourses of application increase as (more or less specific) ends are integrated into the content of norms.

Their *relative* freedom from the burden of problems of application establishes at most that negative duties enjoy a heuristic advantage, not that positive duties should be completely excluded from the sphere of what is morally justifiable, for problems of application can never be entirely ignored in the case of negative duties either. A categorical privileging of negative rights would call for a different justification. Let us consider, for example, the list of negative duties to which Bernard Gert accords privileged status:[52]

1. You should not kill anyone.

2. You should not cause pain to anyone.

3. You should not prevent anyone from developing his abilities.

4. You should not deprive anyone of freedom or opportunity.

5. You should not restrict anyone's possibilities of satisfying his needs.

6. You should not deceive anyone.

With such intuitively evident examples in mind, Charles Fried outlines corresponding categorical rights as the core of a universalistic morality. In his view negative basic norms are defined by precisely those duties that have as their content the protection of the integrity of a person as a freely acting being: "What we may not do to each other, the things which are wrong, are precisely those forms of personal interaction which deny to our victim the status of a freely choosing, rationally valuing, specially efficacious person, the special status of moral personality."[53]

Here Fried expresses an intuition deeply rooted in the liberal tradition: the integrity of the person seems to be adequately protected only by the general, unconditional, and negative duties that assure everybody the same zones of inviolability of subjective freedom by imposing obligations to refrain from certain actions. However, this conclusion follows only given Fried's underlying assumption of an individualistic concept of the person that privileges action guided by interests and informed by the rationality of choice, and hence a type of action that has in fact become dominant under modern social and economic conditions. Freedom of choice, rational determination of ends in the light of analytically clarified preferences, informed choice, and efficient employment of appropriate means—these notions circumscribe competences demanded by the success-oriented actions of an egocentric, self-regarding agent. Interestingly enough, these conditions are far from sufficient for defining the status of the person deemed worthy of protection from the moral point of view. For we encounter a person as essentially worthy of *moral* respect only when we adopt the performative attitude toward a second person. Only when at least two people encounter each other in the context of an intersubjectively shared lifeworld with the goal of coming to a shared understanding about something can—and must—they mutually recognize each other as *persons capable of taking responsibility for their actions* (*zurechnungsfähige Personen*). They then impute to each other the capacity to orient themselves to validity claims in their actions.

From this viewpoint the privileged status accorded basic duties such as "You should not lie" can be accounted for in a different way. To these core duties belong only those that can be understood as aspects of the general demand: "Act with an orientation to mutual understanding and allow everyone the communicative freedom to take positions on validity claims." They are fundamental because they are oriented to respect for the integrity of communicatively acting subjects. But these norms do not just have the force of purely negative duties. In behaving truthfully I do not merely *refrain* from deception but at the same time *perform* an act without which the interpersonal relation between performatively engaged participants in interaction dependent on mutual recognition would collapse. The norms that prescribe the fulfillment of the necessary pragmatic presuppositions of communicative action as a duty are strangely indifferent regarding the distinction between negative and positive duties: by showing respect for another person, I at the same time protect the vulnerable core of his person. Hence, it is no coincidence that other norms of this kind, (for example, those that oblige us to respect normative validity claims) are formulated in positive terms. Gert's ten rules also include such positive duties:

7. You should keep your promises.

10. You should do your duty.

The fundamental status of the kinds of commands that Gert includes in his catalog of duties cannot be explained in terms of the determinateness of norms prescribing omissions but only in terms of their self-referential character. These duties regulate precisely the necessary pragmatic presuppositions of communicative action from whose normative content discourse ethics derives the basic substance of morality by analyzing the universal and necessary communicative presuppositions of the practice of argumentation—that is, the reflective form of communicative action. Gert's ten rules are concerned immediately with the integrity of the person himself as a symbolic structure that is produced and reproduced through relations of reciprocal recognition; they are concerned mediately with the preservation and development of the bodily existence of the respect-worthy person. The constitutional susceptibility of a personality structure that is at the mercy of interpersonal relations is of even greater moment than the more tangible vulnerability of the integrity of body and life: the symbolic structure can disintegrate while the physical substrate remains intact. For this reason, we sometimes risk death rather than live a life devoid of freedom. This insight is indeed open to ideological misuse, but its truth is not thereby denied as such.

In regard to (c), because a person can be individuated only through socialization and because an individual's inner center develops only as he engages in communicative structures of reciprocity, morality, which counteracts this vulnerability, reflects the intersubjective structure of this vulnerable identity itself. Hence the integrity of the individual person, which calls for equal respect for all, cannot be safeguarded without simultaneously safeguarding the social fabric of relations of reciprocal recognition. Just as justice and solidarity are simply two sides of the same coin, so too negative and positive duties spring from the *same* source. If rights and duties are to foster the integrity of individuals who are by their very nature socialized, then the constitutive social context of interaction is not something secondary for those whose lives and identity are made possible and sustained by it. *Omissions* are no less a potential threat to personal integrity than injuries actively inflicted.

In complex societies, of course, claims to a fair share of scarce social resources—positive rights to basic goods such as food and housing, health care, education, and opportunities for work—can be satisfied only through organizations. In this context individual rights and duties are transformed into institutional rights and duties: the organized society as a whole is the subject of obligations—claims to positive rights are raised against it.

Society as a whole is an anonymous addressee, a fact that generates complications over and above the problems already mentioned. In the case of positive rights, problems of what can be reasonably expected and of accountability, which call for a moral "division of labor," are particularly pressing.[54] These problems become even more acute when the individual, as a member of an organized state, raises claims against institutions to benefits resulting from institutionally mediated positive duties, while at the same time fulfilling the role of an addressee of such claims. These problems cannot be solved at the level of moral rules; they call for mechanisms of coordination such as law and political power. What interests me here from the moral point of view is solely the fact that the relation between negative and positive duties is represented differently from the liberal tradition once we abandon the narrow, individualistic concept of the person.

The deontological force of normative validity claims cannot be explicated in terms of an abstract primacy of negative rights of freedom over positive rights of participation, for, as far as the integrity of essentially socialized individuals is concerned, these categories of rights are coeval. Fried too recognizes this: "Respect for our common humanity has provided the basis for the account of the categorical wrongs and the corresponding negative rights. Now, the same common humanity is the source of positive rights as well. . . . Common human nature is not merely something which each of us possesses singly. . . . It is also like a single thing we all share, like the common thread that runs through each bead in a string. There are aspects of common humanity which we share because of the efforts of others to produce them: the fruits of common labour, the security of civil society, the riches of culture and civilization, the fact of language."[55] If we take these reflections seriously and elaborate them through a theory of communication, we will no longer accord negative rights and duties privilege over positive rights and duties on account of their allegedly categorical character, the determinateness of their content, or the lack of ambiguity concerning their addressee and his undifferentiated duty. It is quite sufficient to appeal to a common process of discursive will formation that subjects *all* norms to the same standard—the capacity to command general assent—and secures the deontological force of their validity against an unlimited orientation to consequences by admitting only regulations that are equally in the interest of all. Only the universalistic privileging of what is equally good for all brings the moral point of view to bear in the justification of norms.

9. Thus far I have assumed that the deontological distinction between the right and the good, as well as the primacy of what is morally right or obligatory over what is ethically desirable or preferable, are unproblematic. But this involves a prior determination against the possibility of construing morality as one aspect of a more comprehensive ethics of the good and of grounding it within this framework. This decision may reflect a specifically modern prejudice—thus, at any rate, argue defenders of classical approaches. Charles Taylor, for example, claims that the modern morality of justice is based on a selective understanding of modern identity. Once we grasp the latter in its full complexity, the underlying ethical strata of competing fundamental goods, in which the modern principles of justice and solidarity are rooted in turn, will be uncovered.[56] From this perspective the right loses its primacy over the good; indeed, the deontological distinction between questions of justice and questions of the good itself becomes problematic. By endeavoring to revive the claims of an ethics of the good under modern conditions, Taylor is disputing not the universalistic claim of the morality of justice but the autonomy of rational morality. At the same time, he raises the issues of the

place of moral theory in philosophy as a whole and of the tasks to be accomplished by philosophy as such, for if it were open to philosophy to uphold its classical claim to make universally valid statements about the meaning of the good, or not unsuccessful, life, then it would also have to accept the task of privileging one particular way of life over others—for example, the classical project of living an examined life. It would not have to limit itself to a formal account of the moral point of view or of the ethical problematic but would clarify the concrete totality of the existential orientations within which the limited role, but also the existential significance, of morality first become comprehensible.[57]

Taylor's critique does in fact make explicit certain background assumptions of the modern morality of reason. Deontological approaches that take the normative validity of moral commands and norms as the phenomenon in need of explanation at the outset do indeed presuppose that moral prescriptions are oriented to the consensual resolution of conflicts of action. This involves at least four distinct assumptions. (1) Morality is tailored to interactive relations between subjects capable of action and not to goods—that is, things in the world that can acquire value and importance for individual agents. In this way morality is set apart from the beginning as a social phenomenon and is delimited from individual aspirations to happiness, existential problems, and sensuous needs. (2) Morality relates to interactions regulated by norms. These bind their addressees to fulfill reciprocally interconnected behavioral expectations by selecting a few possibilities from a broad spectrum of value orientations and making them generally binding. Morality is thereby restricted from the outset to what admits of normative validity and invalidity, and thus to rights and duties, and is demarcated from the axiological sphere of what is to be preferred and optimized. (3) Morality is understood as a peaceful alternative to violent resolution of action conflicts for which there is no equivalent. Moral commands must be capable of gaining the assent of the parties to the conflict and must themselves be shown to be legitimate or worthy of recognition in respect of what they impose as a duty. In this way morality is secured against all purely naturalistic interpretations. (4) From this assumption there follows, where recourse to collectively binding religious or metaphysical worldviews is no longer available, the more far-reaching

(as opposed to God, polis, etc.)

assumption that a consensual justification of rights and duties can be generated only through argument, that is, through the cogency of good reasons.

Taylor's critique is sparked by the question of the rationality of rational morality. Kant sought to ground morality in a postmetaphysical fashion, not by appeal to a totality higher than the human mind but from reason itself as the source of world-constitutive ideas. Taylor too does not want to fall back on traditional natural law; he wants to eschew any direct recourse to an objective realm of essences or values. At the same time, however, he regards an autonomous grounding of morality in reason to be impossible. A morality that rests solely on a rational procedure of impartial judgment must, in his view, alienate itself in a subjectivistic manner from sources of motivation and relinquish the possibility of illuminating the background in terms of which alone the existential meaning of moral life becomes comprehensible: "It has no easy way of capturing the background understanding surrounding any conviction that we ought to act in this or that way—the understanding of the strong good involved. And in particular, it cannot capture the peculiar background sense, central to much of our moral life, that something incomparably important is involved" (87). But if we cannot justify moral commands without first having experienced the relevance of the *whole* dimension through acquaintance with "higher-order goods," the differentiation between the right and the good, and above all the primacy of the right over the good, become problematic. Then the justice of the morality of justice and the rationality of rational morality are not ultimate but derive their inspiration, impulse, and pathos from antecedent commitments and affective states:

The more one examines the motives—what Nietzsche would call the "genealogy"—of these theories of obligatory action, the stranger they appear. It seems that they are motivated by the strongest moral ideals, such as freedom, altruism and universalism. These are among the central moral aspirations of modern culture, the hypergoods which are distinctive to it. And yet what these ideals drive the theorists towards is a denial of all such goods. . . . Impelled by the strongest metaphysical, epistemological, and moral ideas of the modern age, these theories narrow our focus to the determinants of action, and then restrict our understanding of these determinants still further by defining practical reason as exclusively procedural. They utterly mystify the priority of the moral by identifying it not with substance but with a form

of reasoning, around which they draw a firm boundary. They then are led
to defend this boundary all the more fiercely in that it is their only way of
doing justice to the hypergoods which move them although they cannot
acknowledge them. (88f.)

In what follows I will present the alternative Taylor proposes and
examine whether an ethics of the good consonant with the modern
identity, though universalistic in aspiration, can indeed be defended
with the cognitive resources available to postmetaphysical reflection.[58]

Taylor is neither a metaphysician in his theoretical orientation nor
an antimodernist in the conclusions he arrives at, but his Catholic
skepticism toward the potential self-sufficiency of a purely secular,
proceduralist ethics leads him to cling to the classical claim of philosophy. He wants to explicate the meaning of the fulfilled life at least
to the degree that it sheds light on the "modern identity." Taylor is
interested not merely in a descriptive cultural history of the configurations of values that have attained preeminence in the modern era
but in the justification of the self-understanding that has become
ineluctable for us in the modern age. This analysis is by no means
value neutral; on the contrary, it makes fundamental value orientations explicit and understands itself as an *ethics of the contemporary era.*
This accounts for the theoretical orientation to an ethics of the good:
goods are an objective matter and not merely a reflection of subjective
values and preferences. The systematic results of Taylor's historically
informed investigation can be summed up in four theses:

(a) The different ethical systems we encounter provide general
orientation concerning the meaning of life, the integrity of one's
fellow human beings, and one's own dignity; they provide standards
for strong evaluations, that is, an orientation to what has its end or
purpose within itself. We judge our own goals and purposes in the
light of such ultimate ends. This objectivity justifies us in speaking in
an ontologizing fashion of "higher-order goods": "these ends or
goods stand independent of our own desires, inclinations or choices"
(20). Strong evaluations belong to the ontological constitution of a
being who finds himself situated in a force-field of attractions and
repulsions and must seek the meaning of life through his orientation
to the highest goods.

(b) The ethics of the good presupposes that the good is something
objective and independent of the wills of particular subjects. How-

ever, the horizon of goods and values is disclosed only through a language in which subjects can articulate their ethical feelings and judgments in an appropriate fashion. Of course, the "vision of the good" can be made accessible to experience only through linguistic articulation and cannot be justified in a strict sense. We must be able to *say* what motivates us most deeply; we must be able to articulate what constitutes a fulfilled life as such. Taylor falls into an ontological mode of thought, posing the question of the Good underlying individual goods, of the "constitutive Good" that first confers on goods the motivating quality of what is binding and worthy of allegiance that infuses subjects with passion and moral pathos. The Platonic Idea of the Good, which we grasp through contemplation, the agape of the benign Christian God, or the wellspring of autonomy, the Kantian capacity of the subject to bind his own will through insight: these ideas are "moral sources" of which modern moral theories have lost sight.

(c) Modern identity draws on three different moral sources simultaneously: the Christian notion of the love of God, of whose goodness all creation partakes; the Enlightenment notion of the self-responsibility of the subject, who in virtue of his reason is capable of acting autonomously; and, finally, the romantic belief in the goodness of nature that finds expression in the creative accomplishments of the human imagination: in the work of art and in the self-realization of the individual (understood on the model of artistic production). There is indeed broad consensus concerning the fundamental values of freedom, justice, welfare, and the eradication of suffering, "but under this general agreement, there are profound rifts when it comes to the constitutive goods, and hence moral sources, which underpin these standards" (495). Taylor thinks that modern identity is prey to a shallow, unreflective, and, to that extent, false self-understanding that obstructs the sources of enthusiasm for the good. Today selective and deficient views of modernity compete against each another. This war of gods and demons can be resolved only by an ethic that makes explicit in a different fashion the existential tension between God's word, human reason, and the creative capacities of inner nature. Just this is what Taylor seeks to accomplish.

(d) It is one thing to make a diagnosis and elucidate it historically and quite another to administer the therapy. Taylor is caught in a dilemma and knows it. His goal is not merely to describe modern identity by exploiting the resources of the history of ideas but to justify the identity outlined as a formation of fundamental orientations that is ineluctable and authoritative for us (and for all other moderns). An ethics of the good that discloses the order of constitutive goods as a publicly accessible reality can realize this ambitious argumentative goal. But under the premises of postmetaphysical thinking, this route is closed to us. Arguments will not suffice to open the eyes of the "value-blind" children of modernity to the efficacy of the highest goods; that requires the world-disclosing power of an evaluative language that first lifts the scales from our eyes: "There is no coherent place left for an exploration of the order in which we are set as a locus of moral sources, what Rilke, Pound, Lawrence and Mann were doing in their radically different ways. . . . The order is only accessible through personal, hence 'subjective', resonance" (510). Thus philosophy must pin its hopes on art. Only in aesthetic experience, freed from the spell of anthropocentric thinking, do we encounter something objective capable of awakening our sense for the good: "The great epiphanic work actually can put us in contact with the sources it taps" (512).

The reflections summarized under (a) through (d) point to a division of labor among philosophical ethics, art, and aesthetics. But this *evasion* reveals the epistemological impasse in which a metaphysical ethics of the good finds itself. The aesthetic considerations that Taylor adduces are themselves problematic. In the wake of Adorno and Derrida, what can be accomplished by modern art can scarcely any longer be construed as "epiphany."[59] Moreover, Friedrich Schlegel already saw that what is distinctive of modernity is that the "aesthetic" tears itself loose from the good and the true. Modern art can no longer be tapped as a source of the moral. But even if we could accept an aesthetics that still believes in the ethical relevance of the world-disclosing power of modernism, its implications for philosophy would be of a *renunciatory* nature: it would either have to resign itself to the role of aesthetic criticism or itself become aesthetic. At any rate, it would have to abandon any pretension to convince on the basis of its *own* arguments. Adorno faced a similar conclusion and responded to it by developing a negative dialectics. But that does not accord with Taylor's philosophical goal of bringing a modern ethics of the good to bear *within* the discourse of experts.

Regardless of how we assess Taylor's proposed alternative, the fact that an ethics of justice has nothing to say concerning questions of motivation raises a problem. Thus far I have understood the question "Why be moral?" in such a way that it admits of a trivial answer: it makes no sense "to try to prove a 'good will' to someone through rational argumentation, that is, to conclusively compel him, as it were, to translate his cognitive grasp of moral obligation into a corresponding act of will."[60] But Taylor has given the question a different, less trivial meaning. Over and above the problem of weakness of will, the willingness to look at a matter from the moral point of view depends on both one's awareness of the moral dimension as such and one's taking it seriously. Hence philosophy should protect us from becoming blind or cynical toward moral phenomena. It should, Taylor believes, persuade us of the preeminent importance of the orientation to the good; it should *sensitize* us to the hidden dimension of the good and infuse us with the strength for passionate engagement in the cause of the good. But a postmetaphysical philosophy is too belated to perform the one task, the awakening of moral sensibility, and is overtaxed by the other, that of overcoming moral cynicism.

Philosophy is overtaxed by what Apel terms "the existential question concerning the meaning of being moral."[61] For moral despair demands an answer to the fundamental ethical question of the meaning of life as such, of personal or collective identity. But the ethical-existential process of reaching an individual self-understanding and the ethical-political clarification of a collective self-understanding are the concern of those involved, not of philosophy. In view of the morally justified pluralism of life projects and life-forms, philosophers can no longer provide on their own account *generally binding* directives concerning the meaning of life. In their capacity as philosophers, their only recourse is to reflective analysis of the procedure through which ethical questions *in general* can be answered. As to the propaedeutic task of awakening the faculty of moral perception, philosophy is not in a privileged position when it competes with the rhetorically moving, exemplary representations of the novelist or the quietly insistent intuitions of common sense. We learn what moral, and in particular immoral, action involves *prior* to all philosophizing;

it impresses itself upon us no less insistently in feelings of sympathy with the violated integrity of others than in the experience of violation or fear of violation of our own integrity. The inarticulate, socially integrating experiences of considerateness, solidarity, and fairness shape our intuitions and provide us with better instruction about morality than arguments ever could.

Theories are directed against other theories, but at least they can correct bad theories that tend to alienate us from our better moral intuitions. The demonstration that the moral point of view, as expressed by (U), is generally valid and does not merely express a culture-specific or class-specific evaluative orientation prevents us from succumbing to a relativism that robs moral commands of their meaning and moral obligations of their peculiar force. Hence moral theory is competent to clarify the moral point of view and justify its universality, but it can contribute nothing to answering the question "Why be moral?" whether this be understood in a trivial, an existential, or a pedagogical sense. While Apel shares this view, at the same time he interprets the question in yet another sense, as "the question of the ultimate rational ground of 'moral existence.'" Understood in *this* sense it supposedly calls for a philosophical answer and receive one in the form of an "ultimate justification" (*Letztbegründung*).

10. Apel proposes the following intuitive elucidation of the idea of an ultimate justification:

> It is mistaken to assume that questions such as "Why be moral?" or "Why be logical?" or "Why be rational?" must be answered either by a deductive justification or an irrational decision. In reality the situation in which the problem is supposed to arise does not even exist, that is, the situation in which we are faced with a decision for or against reason, logic, or morality and could nevertheless already engage in argument, or at least pose the why-question. . . . One who poses the why-question in earnest has thereby already entered the terrain of argumentative discourse, which means that he can assure himself through reflection on the meaning of his act that he has already necessarily recognized the rules of cooperative argumentation and hence also the ethical norms of a communication community.[62]

I have deployed a similar argument to justify (U) as a rule of argumentation.[63] The goal is to establish two nontrivial results: that questions of justice do admit of rational answers and how—that is, by

means of which rules of argumentation or which moral principle—
they can be answered. Transcendental-pragmatic arguments are designed to remind anyone who so much as enters into argumentation
that he is already participating in a normatively structured practice.

We must be careful not to read too much into this statement. The
normative content of the general presuppositions of argumentation
is appealed to in this way solely in response to the *epistemic* question
of how moral judgments are possible and not the *existential* question
of what it means to be moral. Contrary assertions notwithstanding,
Apel appears to saddle the demonstration of the moral principle with
the latter more ambitious claim. He regards the issue of whether we
can view ourselves as capable of moral insight as depending on
whether we are already in a certain sense moral. This is reminiscent
of a figure of thought familiar from religion and metaphysics: we
may regard ourselves as capable of "the truth" because we are already
"within the truth." This thought could be understood in an unob-
jectionable sense in the present context. Our argumentative praxis
belongs to a form of life that is completely structured by communication, and everyday language use oriented to reaching understanding is already tied to unavoidable pragmatic presuppositions that are
by no means morally neutral. In communicative action as such, we
always already move within the boundaries of a lifeworld saturated
with ethical value. However, what Apel has in mind cannot be moral
existence in this sense. Demonstrating the substantive normative presuppositions of argumentation is by no means sufficient to reveal the
foundational interrelation of discourse, action oriented to reaching
understanding, and the lifeworld; that is a matter for a formal pragmatic analysis of language, not for moral theory. Moreover, Apel's
notion of "moral existence" has the connotation of obligatoriness that
transcends the particularity of the concrete ethical substance of a
lifeworld—the universalistic standard of morality "cuts into the ethical substance of the lifeworld." In addition to an epistemic claim,
Apel invests practical reason with a more far-reaching existential
obligatoriness and elevates the justification of the moral principle to
the status of an "ultimate justification." Although Kant's practical
reason is not restored to its position of preeminence in the intelligible
realm, it nonetheless retains something of its omnipotence.

Let me first clarify what is involved in this existential claim. A cognitivist ethical theory understands the operation of practical reason in purely epistemic terms. It is content to point out that, in order to provide answers to moral questions of the type "What should I do?" that take the form of singular judgments, participants engage in discourses concerning application in particular cases and, when necessary, must engage in justificatory discourses. And it belongs to the normative sense of every moral judgment that it makes a duty of the action expressed in its propositional content. But a supernorm that made a duty of acting in accordance with duty could say no more than what is already contained in the normative import of an individual moral judgment. A supernorm that made the realization of justice *in general* a duty in a reflexive manner would be either redundant or meaningless and hence would not need to be justified. I suspect that Apel's "ultimate justification" would amount to just that: the justification of a supernorm that states that justice as such ought to exist. This is how we must understand Apel when he criticizes Rawls "for failing to offer a prior justification for why justice as such should exist."[64] Again he criticizes Kohlberg for failing to provide a justification for the claim that "postconventional conscience ... should make a moral rather than, for example, an egoistic-strategic use of the capacity for 'role-taking.'"[65] By insisting on this demand, Apel ultimately invests the question concerning morality with existential significance.

What more could this existential obligatoriness add to the epistemic function of practical reason? In everyday practice, we can indeed suspend the presuppositions of communicative action in a concealed or open manner; at any time we can switch from an orientation to reaching understanding to that of a strategically acting subject concerned with his own success. All agents to whom freedom of will is attributed must be capable of making such decisions. But it is quite another issue whether strategic action is permitted or should be forsworn in a given situation, and thus whether it is morally admissible. *That* morally inadmissible actions should be forsworn is already expressed by the relevant norms. There is no need for a supernorm that makes the observance of moral commands a duty in a self-referential fashion. It would not augment in the least the binding force of elementary duties. Since this is so obvious, those who seek an ultimate justification must have some other end in view. I suspect that the meaning of an "ultimate justification" cannot be explicated solely within the framework of moral-theoretical reflections but must be understood in terms of a lingering (though unacknowledged) foundationalism that still pervades the architectonic disposition of Apel's philosophy. Only when philosophy takes upon itself problems it can solve through neither self-reflection nor self-referential argumentation does the philosopher find himself constrained to offer "ultimate justifications."

For Taylor, as we have seen, the proper task of philosophy is an ethical one—specifically, the traditional task of clarifying the meaning of life. Apel, by contrast, views the deontological question concerning the principle of justice as the pivotal issue of philosophy, though he is aware that a justification of the moral does not of itself provide a solution to the problem of meaning and of realizing individual or collective happiness.[66] In his view there is a relation of complementarity between the standard of morality first articulated by Kant "and the problem of personal or communal ethical life in relation to the concrete universal of a whole form of life."[67] The general statements of philosophy, while they express quite well what is essential to morality, do not extend to the substantive ethical life embodied in traditional or utopian forms of life. But this declaration of abstinence is ambiguous, for philosophy is supposed to clarify the meaning of the moral not just in the sense that it makes intelligible what it means to judge something from the moral point of view. It is supposed to explain what it means to *be* moral—the unique significance of morality in life as a whole—and thereby provide the will with a rational incentive to justice as such. But Apel thereby seeks to "justify" philosophically something that cannot be achieved through argumentation. A good will is awakened and fostered not through argumentation but through socialization into a form of life that complements the moral principle. A comparable effect may also be produced by the world-disclosing power of prophetic speech and in general by those forms of innovative discourse that initiate better forms of life and more reflective ways of life—and also the kind of eloquent critique that enables us to discern these indirectly in works of literature and art. World-disclosing arguments that induce us to see things in a radically different light are not essentially philosophical arguments and *a fortiori* not ultimate justifications.

There is, of course, an internal relation between moral conscious-ness and ego identity. Postconventional moral consciousness needs to be supplemented by an enlightened existential self-understanding that entails that I can *respect* myself only as someone who as a general rule performs the actions he takes to be morally right. But while moral consciousness can "foster" this complementary structure in a weak sense, it cannot guarantee it. Whether I have sufficient resolve to act in accordance with my moral insights even when they are opposed by strong interests of a different kind does not depend primarily on my capacity for moral judgment or on the level of justification of moral judgments but on my personality structure and form of life. This problem of weakness of will cannot be solved through moral cognition.

Apel might cite this fact in support of the thesis that more must be accomplished by philosophy than is allowed by a crude cognitivist ethical theory; it must aim at philosophical enlightenment and trans-form the existential self-understanding and worldview of members of modern societies through its claim to universal validity. At first sight, this thesis is incompatible with the goal of providing only answers that do not depend on metaphysically privileging one of the irreducible plurality of interpretations of life that today have equal claim to our allegiance. I suspect that Apel hopes to avoid this con-tradiction, by construing communicative reason as in essence moral-practical reason and then, in virtue of this Fichtean primacy of prac-tical reason, according the philosophical-explanatory discourse distin-guished by self-referentiality a preeminent position in the hierarchy of scientific discourses. Discourse ethics is supposed to remain neutral over against the plurality of belief systems yet not pay the price of renouncing substantive sources of motivation entailed by its proce-duralism. Apel believes that he can find an Archimedean point of self-reflection for the sphere of philosophical reflection dealing with the discourse principle. From this vantage point, philosophy is sup-posedly able to provide an ultimate justification that encompasses both theory and practice through the self-clarification of argumen-tation as such.[68]

Apel's theoretical framework, as I see it, rests on two problematic assumptions. The *first premise*—the privileging of discourse ethics on the basis of fundamental-philosophical considerations—Apel adopts at the cost of assimilating communicative to practical reason. By drawing on the resources of the theory of argumentation, the concept of communicative reason can be developed in the direction of an analysis of validity claims and the conditions of their discursive redemption. This involves in part the analysis of general presuppositions of argumentation. The more ambitious task of investigating different forms, and corresponding rules, of argumentation leads to specialized theories. In this way, too, a moral principle can be grounded and what it means to regard something from the moral point of view explicated. This addresses a specific kind of question, a specific aspect of validity in general: one moment of an encompassing communicative reason.

The latter has normative import only in the broader sense that a communicatively acting subject must accept pragmatic presuppositions of a counterfactual kind. He must make certain idealizations—for example, ascribe identical meanings to linguistic expressions, make context-transcending validity claims for his utterances, or regard his addressees as accountable subjects. The communicative agent thereby becomes the subject of a "must" in the sense of weak transcendental necessitation, without encountering the prescriptive "must" of a rule of action, whether the latter is understood deontologically in terms of the normative validity of a moral command, axiologically in terms of a constellation of preferred values, or empirically in terms of the efficacy of a technical imperative. Communicative reason, unlike practical reason, is not itself a source of norms of right action. It spans the *full* spectrum of validity claims (of assertoric truth, subjective truthfulness, and normative rightness) and hence extends beyond the sphere of moral-practical questions. Normativity in the more restricted sense of a binding practical orientation is not identical with the rationality of action oriented to reaching understanding as a whole. Normativity and rationality *overlap* in the field of justification of moral insights that are attained in a hypothetical attitude and, as we have seen, generate only weak rational motivations and at any rate cannot sustain an existential understanding of self and world.

The *second premise*—the privileging of a foundational discourse in general—is directly related to Apel's project of reformulating the basic problems of the first two paradigms of first philosophy—ontology and the philosophy of consciousness—in terms of a third, that of a pragmatics of language. Underlying this "transformation of philosophy"[69] is the idea that the substantive contents of metaphysics can be preserved only in the form of global scientific hypotheses that have a fallible status, whereas transcendental reflection on the conditions of objectively valid experience and argument as such uncovers a realm of genuine philosophical knowledge, which, itself infallible, accounts for the presuppositions of fallibilism and thereby satisfies the conditions of an ultimate grounding.[70] It is supposed to be possible to perform this justification of validity "from above" in one fell swoop, so to speak, "in strict reflection" on the general presuppositions of argumentation, and to secure the presuppositionlessness of original philosophical reflection for a philosophy that clarifies the presuppositions of all possible knowledge. The notion of ultimate justification suggests a residual foundationalism limited to the analysis of transcendental conditions, which Apel defends by appealing to the unique status enjoyed by the philosophical determination of presuppositions of argumentation in general. On this account, philosophy goes beyond the autonomous, differentiated spheres of methodically secured knowledge and enjoys a special immunity; its preeminent position in the hierarchy of forms of knowledge makes it invulnerable to externally produced cognitive dissonances. Philosophy thereby becomes the final haven of certainties that are otherwise unavailable on the assumptions of a generalized fallibilism.

If this is the *import* of the claim to provide ultimate justifications, two objections immediately suggest themselves. First, the abstract opposition of philosophy and science is a carry-over from the theoretical framework of a philosophy of consciousness that posits the basic questions of epistemology as fundamental. After the turn to the pragmatics of language, the conditions of possible agreement instead become the focus of interest. But the objectifying sciences—as the reflective form of our knowledge of the objective world—thereby lose their special status. They take their place among the diverse forms of knowledge operative in everyday life and in expert cultures among which philosophy mediates in the role of an interpreter without needing to "ground" any of them. At the same time, philosophy is involved in diverse forms of cooperation within the system of scientific knowledge, not just as a contingent matter but for methodological reasons. It has already forfeited its role as judge and director for the simple reason that there is no hierarchical gradation between discourses and corresponding metadiscourses.[71] The metatheoretical interconnection between theoretical results of the now-autonomous disciplines and spheres of knowledge is henceforth assured only by coherence, not by "grounding."

Moreover, both the hermeneutical-interpretive approach to symbolically prestructured objects and the rational reconstruction of the pretheoretical knowledge of competent judging, speaking, and acting subjects suggest a close kinship between philosophy, on the one side, and the humanities and the social sciences, on the other. The abstract opposition between philosophy and "science" (conceived on the model of the nomological empirical sciences) can no longer be sustained.[72] The distinctiveness of philosophy consists in neither its preoccupation with conceptual analysis nor the universalistic character of its questions. What sets philosophy apart is the self-referentiality of *some* of its arguments. But the self-referentiality of the undoubtedly central analysis of general presuppositions of argumentation that can be made only by participants in argument does not secure the philosophical enterprise the independence and infallibility Apel associates with the notion of an ultimate justification.

This second objection relates to the status and meaning of transcendental arguments, a topic I cannot here go into in detail. I will simply recall that thus far no equivalent has been found for Kant's transcendental deduction of the categories of the understanding, and there is little prospect that one will be found. Without it we are left with weak transcendental arguments in Strawson's sense.[73] These can establish only the factual inescapability of the general and necessary presuppositions of a nonreplaceable discursive order, such as the language game of argumentation. Because we do not in fact have a functional equivalent for rational discourses, we are left with no choice: we *unavoidably* accept the pragmatic presuppositions of this demanding form of communication because there is no alternative. This demonstration of the factual inescapability of substantive normative presuppositions of a practice *internally* interwoven with our sociocultural form of life is indeed conditional on the constancy of this life-form. We cannot exclude a priori the possibility of its undergoing changes. But that remains an empty possibility since—science fiction scenarios that transform human beings into zombies aside— we cannot even imagine a fundamental alteration in our form of life. The weak transcendental proof, if we can indeed carry it out as I assume in agreement with Apel, suffices to ground the universalistic validity claim (valid for all subjects capable of speech and action) of a moral principle conceived in procedural terms. If this principle can be deduced from the normative content of factually inescapable presuppositions, it would be shown that it cannot be meaningfully placed in question *as such* but only in some particular interpretation or other. But we do not need an ultimate justification to show this. An explanation of the moral point of view that rests on fallible reconstructions of the normative content of factually unavoidable presuppositions of argumentation by no means signifies renouncing moral universalism and tying the moral principle to elements of the background knowledge of a particular lifeworld.[74]

An ultimate justification of ethics is neither possible nor necessary. One can, of course, speculate whether a philosophy developed from such an Archimedean point could provide ready answers to questions that a rigorously cognitivist version of discourse ethics must leave unanswered. I am thinking, for example, of problems resulting from the fact that a rational morality must reflect on the limits beyond which adherence to its demands cannot be reasonably required or on the legal-institutional arrangements through which the imposition of special duties is mediated. A hierarchical philosophy that posited a privileged reflective standpoint would offer better preconditions for moral theory's once again overtaking and reflectively transcending itself.

Apel presents what he calls "Part B" of his ethics as a process of reflective self-transcendence. There he adopts the perspective of a politician acting on the basis of an ethics of responsibility and takes his orientation from cases where strict adherence to moral requirements would lead to irresponsible consequences because a strategically acting adversary does not accept the preconditions for the consensual resolution of an acute practical conflict. To prevent this solitary representative who shoulders political responsibility for the interests of the state from falling back into the sphere of unrestrained power politics, Apel supplies him with a principle by which choices between alternative strategies can be justified in accordance with an ethics of responsibility. He must orient himself to the more long-term goal of producing the conditions under which general observance of moral rules and consensual principles first becomes a reasonable demand and then the current dilemma of power politics disappears. Apel defines the goal of a cosmopolitan order, which Kant outlined in terms of a *philosophy of history,* as a morally grounded political goal of individuals who act in a representative capacity, and summarily elevates this goal of realizing the indispensable conditions of life under which moral action would also be a viable political duty to the status of an auxiliary principle *to be justified by moral theory.* He postulates the duty "to strive for moral progress and to regard its historical realization as conceivable in relation to the historical preconditions and—through ever renewed hypothetical reconstructions of history—to show it to be such."[75] I will not here go into Apel's paradoxical subordination of thought to the imperatives of morality; at present I am concerned with the undesirable consequences that result from Apel's *preempting* issues *within* moral theory that can be meaningfully addressed only *after* the transition to the normative problematic of political and legal theory.

Apel's auxiliary principle introduces a teleological perspective into deontological moral theory, as he himself remarks: the realization of morality itself is elevated to the highest good. But he thereby explodes the conceptual framework of a deontological ethics. In the first place, it must be asked on what level the auxiliary principle is to be justified. If on the same level as the moral principle itself, then one would have to be able to offer some analogue of the analysis of the content of general presuppositions of argumentation, which is not the case. Again, the fact that the auxiliary principle is formulated as a *special* duty addressed to holders of specific positions creates problems. An analogous translation of the moral principle into a concrete duty would take the form: "Always act in accordance with correctly applied valid norms," which amounts to nothing more than the redundant demand, "Act morally." If the auxiliary principle is to be viewed as a special duty, it must, like all other norms, be treated on a different level; that is, it must be subjected to generalization by participants in action and those affected themselves in justificatory discourses. However, that means that the principle would be tested under precisely the presuppositions of argumentation whose sufficient fulfillment it implicitly disputes. I cannot see how a form of argumentation that thematizes itself in such a contradictory manner could be possible.

Aside from this, the auxiliary principle calls for a structurally incoherent mode of action, one that is both morally required and *at the same time* to be pursued in a purposive manner. Although an ethics of the good can enjoin a course of action oriented to values in a normative fashion, deontological positions cannot make a duty of action oriented to success. With his auxiliary principle Apel wants to introduce something like a moral competence-competence and preempt *in abstracto* something that can be judged situationally only at the level of political will formation in the light of concrete possibilities of action. Apel clearly allows himself to be misled by the hierarchical structure of his theory into immediately addressing questions of political ethics "directly from above" through a superprinciple, although these questions are not situated on the same level as the justification of the moral principle. Behind the solitary politician of Apel's imagination there lurks the philosopher king who wants to put the world in order, not the citizen of a democratic state. In a democratic state, political will formation—even reforms with far-reaching political ramifications—is always pursued *within* the institutions of a legally constituted social and political order. Politicians are holders of democratically sanctioned positions of power whose decisions are contingent on legally institutionalized processes of opinion and will formation.

Relations between states too are so closely regulated by supranational institutions, treaties, and norms of international law that classical foreign politics is gradually becoming transformed into a worldwide internal politics that (fortunately) leaves increasingly little room for the heroic initiatives of solitary politicians. Questions of political ethics constitute an especially complicated application problem for which considerations in legal and perhaps even social theory are indispensable.

With the initial differentiation between "Part A" and "Part B" of his ethical theory, Apel already moves in a false direction by contrasting an ethics of conviction indifferent to consequences with an ethics of responsibility oriented to consequences. For within moral discourses, the principle of universalization necessitates the weighing of consequences and demands in general that all relevant features of the given situation be taken into account already in the justification of norms, but most especially in their application, as is explicitly required by the principle of appropriateness. And self-referential reflections on the reasonableness of moral demands already play a role within moral discourses.

In extreme cases, a tension may develop between moral insight and ethical self-understanding that cannot be uniformly resolved in favor of what is morally required, even when viewed morally, as would be the case if it were merely a problem of weakness of will.[76] Thus, in the case of an existential conflict, the single applicable norm might demand an action that the individual concerned indeed acknowledged to be morally required but could not perform without ceasing to be the person he is and wants to be—the burden imposed by this obligation might be too much for him to bear. In an exceptional case such as this, the preconditions of moral self-respect cannot be harmonized with one's relation to oneself as a person who endeavors to pursue his life project in an authentic fashion. A moral theory that insists on the primacy of the right over the good will not dispute this phenomenon as such but will describe it differently. *One* proposal is the familiar move of introducing duties toward oneself that can compete with other duties. But the concept of duties toward oneself cannot be reconciled with the requirement of symmetry between rights and duties. Hence a more plausible solution is to admit the possibility of a reflective turn in discourses of application; once we have established which norm is the only appropriate one in the particular case, it *may* be necessary to examine whether the singular judgment that follows from it requires an action that cannot be reasonably expected from an existential point of view.

Generally the problem of which moral actions can be reasonably enjoined first arises with the transition from moral to legal theory. Modern rational law makes the transition from morality to law by way of specific reflections on the reasonableness of imposing obligations. Norms are judged to be valid in the light of the moral principle only under the presupposition—explicitly stated in (U)—of *general* observance of norms. If this precondition is not met, norms cannot be reasonably imposed, regardless of whether they are valid. Kant uses this fact to justify the state monopoly on the exercise of legal coercion. Legal institutionalization alone can ensure general adherence to morally valid norms. That amounts to a moral reason for law in general. Conversely, there are moral considerations relevant to the justification of particular legal norms that the democratic legislative process must take into account. Since problems of application must be distinguished from problems of justification also in the case of legal norms, there arises the additional demand for institutionalization of discourses of application in the shape of an independent judiciary. In this way, the contours of a constitutional state, which Kant consistent with these determinations treated in his doctrine of law, become discernible; here the moral point of view is no longer applied *directly* to modes of action but to legal and political institutions. Finally, this normative approach can be pursued to the point where the classic problem of the limits of obedience to the law, and hence the preconditions for civil disobedience, legitimate resistance, and a "right to revolt," is raised. Then it is a question of the conditions under which a politically motivated violation of positive law would be morally justified or legitimate.[77] These remarks are intended only to lend plausibility to the view that the normative relations between morality, law, and politics are better explained by discourse theory in a step-by-step manner, without recourse to a false hierarchy of forms of discourse.

11. In laying the moral-theoretical foundations of a philosophical theory of justice, it is important to undertake the normative justification of the transition from morality to law in the proper manner. I propose (a) to take an objection of Thomas McCarthy as an occasion to point at least to some new perspectives in the theory of law and politics opened up by discourse ethics. Since underlying this objection is a doubt concerning the priority of the right over the good, I will also discuss (b) the concept of an "overlapping consensus" developed by John Rawls in his more recent writings.

(a) McCarthy grounds the need for legal regulation of behavioral expectations, and in particular for legal institutionalization of the opinion and will formation of a political legislator, in the indeterminacy of discursive procedures where different worldviews and a multiplicity of evaluative languages are competing with one another: "Disagreements of these sorts are likely to be a permanent feature of democratic public life. They are in general not resolvable by strategic compromise, rational consensus or ethical self-clarification, in Habermas's sense of these terms. All that remains in his scheme are more or less subtle forms of coercion, e.g. majority rule and the threat of legal sanctions."[78] Interestingly enough, McCarthy introduces the claim that morality must be supplemented by law with an argument that, were it sound, would undermine the very core of the discourse-ethical concept of morality. On his account, legal compulsion is supposed to compensate for the motivational weaknesses and cognitive indeterminacy of a moral discourse that rests on abstraction and idealization; however, he conceives the legally institutionalized processes of opinion and will formation through which legislation must legitimate itself not merely as a more complex network of discourses and negotiations but as an alternative to the discourse model: "We have to *modulate the* idea of rationally motivated agreement beyond Habermas's basic distinction between a strategically motivated compromise of interests and an argumentatively achieved consensus on validity."[79]

By contrast, a discourse theory of law *grounded in* discourse ethics holds fast to the discourse model. It explains the difference between the normative validity claim of moral rules and the claim to legitimacy of legal norms in terms of the fact that not just moral (and ethical) considerations enter into a presumptively rational process of political will formation of a legislator, but, in the first instance, programs and goals that are the result of more or less fair compromises, as well as information and predictions resulting from more or less controversial discussions among experts. A process of collective will formation along these lines would have the presumption of rationality in its favor to the extent that it could be realized in general in forms of discourse. The idea of the constitutional state can then be understood in terms of the endeavor to institutionalize the demanding communicative presuppositions and procedures of a network of forms of argumentation and negotiation differentiated in terms of the problem areas, for the political power employed in executing the requirements of the principle of discourse must itself be tamed through discourse.

I will address this theoretical proposal in detail in another place; here I am interested only in why McCarthy regards the alternative between force and rationally motivated agreement as incomplete. In his view, a third element comes into play with the will formation of a pluralistic society, the legitimate compulsion that he illustrates only by reference to the legal form of an institutionally regulated majoritarian process of decision making. As grounds, he cites primarily the incommensurability of standards of evaluation, worldviews, evaluative languages, and traditions that set narrow limits to the generalization of interests undertaken in justificatory moral discourses:

The success of Habermas's universalization principle in getting from multifarious "I want's" to a unified "we will" depends on finding "universally accepted needs." The argument just sketched suggests that this may not be possible when there are fundamental divergences in value orientations. The separation of formal procedure from substantive content is never absolute: we cannot agree on what is just without some measure of agreement on what is good. But practical discourse is conceived by Habermas to deal precisely with situations in which there is an absence of such agreement, that is, when there is a need to regulate matters concerning which there are conflicting interests and values, competing conceptions of the good.[80]

McCarthy knows how this objection could be met within the framework of discourse ethics. Need interpretations are not an ultimate given but depend on intersubjectively shared evaluative languages and traditions that are not anybody's personal property. Hence, critical revision of the vocabulary in terms of which we interpret our needs is a public and, where appropriate, discursively negotiable affair. In modern societies, we are confronted with a pluralism of forms of life—and a progressively greater individualization of life projects—that is not only unavoidable but even desirable; and this makes it ever more improbable, as McCarthy emphasizes, that we will agree on shared interpretations in such disputes. We can draw less and less on experiences and straightforward examples that have the *same* significance for *different* groups and individuals. We can count less and less on the same reasons having the same weight for different individuals and groups within different systems of relevance.

This fact, however, supports rather than undermines the universalistic approach of discourse ethics. The more that principles of equality gain a foothold in social practice, the more sharply do forms of life and life projects become differentiated from one another. And the greater this diversity is, the more abstract are the rules and principles that protect the integrity and egalitarian coexistence of subjects who are becoming increasingly unfamiliar with one another in their difference and otherness. To be sure, the sphere of questions that can be answered rationally from the moral point of view shrinks in the course of the development toward multiculturalism within particular societies and toward a world society at the international level. But finding a solution to these few more sharply focused questions becomes all the more critical to coexistence, and even survival, in a more populous world. It remains an empirical question how far the sphere of strictly generalizable interests extends. Only if it could be shown in principle that moral discourses must prove *unfruitful* despite the growing consensus concerning human rights and democracy—for example, because common interests *can no longer even* be identified in incommensurable languages—would the deontological endeavor to uncouple questions of justice from context-dependent questions of the good life have failed.

These reflections bring us back to a theme already broached in discussing Taylor's universalistic ethics of the good. The priority of the right over the good is also the main bone of contention in the disputes between communitarians and liberals.[81] The *socio-ontological* aspects of this involved debate need not concern us here, since the objections raised by communitarians against individualistic concepts of the person or instrumentalist concepts of society do not apply to the basic concepts of discourse ethics derived from the theory of communicative action. Discourse ethics occupies an intermediate position, sharing with the "liberals" a deontological understanding of freedom, morality, and law that stems from the Kantian tradition and with the communitarians an intersubjective understanding of individuation as a product of socialization that stems from the Hegelian tradition.[82] But the priority of the right over the good is disputed primarily on *epistemological* grounds. In this respect discourse ethics is as vulnerable as liberal theories of justice to objections that appeal to the contextuality and the rootedness in tradition of *all* conceptions of justice and practical reason, including the procedural. The contextualists insist that behind the allegedly general and neutral explanations of the moral point of view and the perspective of justice there are *always* concealed particular world interpretations informed

by specific evaluative languages and traditions. This context dependency contradicts the asserted independence of the general from the
particular and the consequent priority of the right over the good.

(b) Rawls responded in the course of the 1980s—most concisely in
the brief "Restatement" of his theory[83]—to the contextualist criticism
in both a defensive and an offensive manner. He has, on the one
hand, retracted the claim to justify a universally valid concept of
justice that had come under attack as foundationalist. He now presents the theory of justice merely as a systematic reconstruction of the
best normative intuitions of the Western tradition in political thought.
Rawls leaves open the question of whether the reconstructively
grounded principle of justice should be regarded as valid only for
societies shaped by *our* political-cultural traditions and not for modern conditions of life in general, and thus for *all modern* societies
irrespective of their cultural orientation and tradition. On the other
hand, Rawls accords the context of our traditions only the status of
an informative background. This intuitive background determines
the hermeneutic point of departure for the description of a hypothetical original position under whose normative constraints the parties can justify principles of justice neutral between different forms
of life. These constraints compel them to abstract from all comprehensive views of self and the world in which the different conceptions
of the good are articulated. Through the specification of the views
of justice built into the conditions of the original position, our tradition remains effective in an unthematized fashion in the consciousness of the parties. But neither our own nor alien traditions can be
thematized within the original position, unless it be in terms of the
anonymous concept of "comprehensive doctrines" in general. This is
the substantively indeterminate, complementary concept to the concept of justice, which Rawls terms "political, not metaphysical" because of its indifference over against all such worldviews.

In a further step Rawls examines whether this abstraction is possible and whether it proves to be fruitful. The principles of justice
justified in the original position should not be left hanging in the air
but must also be capable of being acted upon, of falling under "the
art of the possible." It belongs to the design of a "well-ordered
society" that its *ideal* citizens are also loyal to the institutions that they,
by hypothesis, recognize as legitimate, especially as just practices

constitute an experiential context in which the sense of loyalty is renewed with each successive generation. But the *real* citizens of contemporary liberal societies are flesh and blood individuals who have grown up in different traditions and forms of life and owe their self-understanding to competing worldviews. The political public sphere in which they come together to form a public body of citizens is characterized by a plurality of belief systems and interest structures and the coexistence and confrontation of cultural life-forms and individual life projects on which McCarthy bases his objection. Thus, the theory of justice first takes on a realistic shape by reflecting on itself as a whole and clarifying the conditions of its own acceptability. It must render plausible through a self-reflexive turn in argumentation the belief that its justification of principles of justice can expect to meet with agreement in the public arena of an *existing* body of citizens: "Justice as fairness is not reasonable unless in a suitable way it generates its own support by redressing each citizen's reason, as explained in its own framework" (141).

After all that has been said about the abstraction from comprehensive views of self and the world imposed by the structure of the original position, Rawls's response will come as no surprise: a concept of justice developed in ignorance of the content of competing worldviews will be an intersection set comprising normative statements on which the divergent value orientations of the comprehensive doctrines agree. An "overlapping consensus" in regard to the theoretically justified principles of justice will emerge in the public discourse of citizens who try to convince each other of the rightness of their respective political views.

To this the contextualist could object that Rawls prejudices the point at issue between them by making two assumptions specifically connected with the concept of a "modern" society. One of these assumptions is empirical in nature. In modern societies not just a *political order* has emerged that is perceptibly independent of other social action systems; *value spheres* specifically concerned with questions of political justice have also emerged. This assumption is empirically well confirmed, though it also has controversial implications: "Taking the political as a distinctive domain, let's say that a political conception formulating its basic characteristic values is a *freestanding* view. This means two things: first, that it is framed to apply in the first instance to the basic structures of society *alone;* and second, that it formulates the characteristic political values independent of non-political values and indeed of any *specific* relationship to them" (133). The other presupposition is of a conceptual nature and in this context deserves special consideration. A postmetaphysical concept of justice is not compatible with all comprehensive doctrines, only with non-fundamentalistic worldviews: "While an overlapping consensus may obtain between not unreasonable comprehensive doctrines, when is a comprehensive doctrine not unreasonable or simply reasonable? A reasonable doctrine must recognize the burdens of reason" (139).

Modern worldviews must accept the conditions of postmetaphysical thought to the extent that they recognize that they are competing with other interpretations of the world within the same universe of validity claims. This reflective knowledge concerning the competition between equally valid warring "gods and demons" creates an awareness of their fallibility and shatters the naiveté of dogmatic modes of belief founded on absolute truth claims. Recognizing the "burdens of reason" entails knowing that proponents and opponents in the contest between substantive worldviews may (for the time being) have equally good grounds for their inability to reach a consensus and for leaving contentious validity claims undecided. This fallibilism is grounded in the indeterminacy of discursive procedures, in local limitations on available information and reasons, and, in general, in the provinciality of our finite minds regarding the future. Under these conditions there is no guarantee that a rationally motivated consensus could always be attained. The idea of "reasonable disagreement" permits us to leave truth claims undecided while simultaneously upholding their unconditional character. One who, with this in mind, accepts the coexistence of competing worldviews by no means resigns himself to a mere *modus vivendi;* while upholding his own validity claims, he simply postpones the possibility of consensus, kept open in principle, to an indefinite future.

The model that Rawls has in mind is not that of competing paradigms governed by the standards of scientific rationality, and thus not the fallibility of the empirical sciences, but the uncoupling of religious creeds from the sanctioning power of the state and their coexistence under conditions of religious tolerance. But although this principle can indeed be justified in the original position, it is not the one that Rawls must presuppose. What Rawls in fact prejudges with the concept of an "overlapping consensus" is the distinction between modern and premodern forms of consciousness, between "reasonable" and "dogmatic" world interpretations. Modern forms of consciousness do not involve renunciation of interpretations of the world as a whole, and thus of "comprehensive doctrines" as such. They are set apart by a form of reflexivity that enables us to adopt an external perspective toward our own traditions and bring them into relation to other traditions. Whether we can in this way *transcend* the tradition in which our identity has been formed depends on a strong premise that is far from trivial and affords the contextualist an occasion to make his objection more pointedly. There must be a common basis on which mutual understanding among alien cultures, belief systems, paradigms, and life-forms is possible—that is, a translation *between* different evaluative languages and not merely communication among members of *the same* language group relying on reciprocal observation of alien cultures. The languages and vocabularies in which we interpret our needs and communicate our feelings must be mutually permeable; they should not be so deeply rooted in monadically self-enclosed contexts that cannot be transcended from within that they *imprison* the subjects who have been born and socialized into them.

Rawls can defend the thesis of the primacy of the right over the good with the concept of an overlapping consensus only if it is true that postmetaphysical worldviews that have become reflexive under modern conditions are epistemically superior to dogmatically fixed, fundamentalistic worldviews—indeed, only if such a distinction can be made with absolute clarity. Otherwise the disqualification of "unreasonable" doctrines that cannot be brought into harmony with the proposed "political" concept of justice is inadmissible. This differentiation between a modern and a traditional understanding of the world is possible only if competing interpretations of the world are not utterly incommensurable, if we at least intuitively accept context-transcending assumptions concerning rationality that first make possible translations from one context into another. But this is precisely what is disputed by a strong contextualism for which there is no single "rationality." On this conception, individual "rationalities" are correlated with different cultures, worldviews, traditions, or forms of life. Each of them is viewed as internally interwoven with a particular understanding of the world.

This touches on a debate concerning rationality that has been carried on for the past two decades by anthropologists, sociologists, and philosophers and to which Rorty, Davidson, and Putnam have also made contributions. I will limit myself to a discussion of the most recent book of Alasdair MacIntyre who draws upon different concepts of justice developed in the philosophical tradition to argue for his version of strong contextualism.

12. MacIntyre examines the concepts of justice of the three philosophical traditions that have their origins respectively in Aristotle, in Augustine and Aquinas, and in Scottish moral philosophy and contrasts these classical concepts with the specifically modern conceptions of morality and politics he associates, somewhat globally, with "liberalism."[84] Liberalism adopts a critical attitude not just toward rival traditions but toward tradition as such in an attempt to represent its own concepts of rationality and its own principles as generally valid. In MacIntyre's view, this abstract universalism obscures the fact that liberalism itself has by now become a tradition, though it refuses to acknowledge this. Each of these traditions is so intimately interwoven with a particular language and local form of life that practical reason and political justice can be understood only from the perspective that structures one of the different traditions. There is no standpoint outside the context of any particular tradition from which a rational evaluation of these theories and explanatory schemas could be undertaken.

Obliviousness of this fact is constitutive of modern forms of consciousness, as MacIntyre attempts to show in the case of liberalism. He attributes this bias to the structure of a language-game that generates the transcendental illusion of a universalistic self-misunderstanding on the part of a philosophical tradition that repudiates tradition as such. One of the so-called international languages forms the grammatical ground of this boundless universalism. These languages have established themselves—after the fashion of American scientific prose—as *lingua franca* and create the impression of a medium into which any utterances whatever, regardless of how alien the traditions from which they derive, can be translated without further ado. International languages of this kind exert grammatical pressure on their users to appropriate alien traditions in a context-neutralizing manner. MacIntyre also regards as a grammatical illusion the historical consciousness that Nietzsche denounced in his second "Untimely Meditation" as antiquarian historiography: "When texts from traditions with their own strong, substantive criteria of truth and rationality, as well as with a strong historical dimension, are translated into such languages, they are presented in a way that neutralizes the conceptions of truth and rationality and the historical context. . . . The distortion by translation out of context—from the standpoint of those who inhabit the traditions from which the distorted texts are taken—is of course apt to be invisible to those whose first language is one of the internationalized languages of modernity" (384f.). International languages prejudice the self-understanding of the forms of life of which they are constitutive. Hence, the reflexivity of modern worldviews does not establish their superiority over the traditional understanding of the world, as Rawls assumes in accordance with the liberal tradition. Because they are parasitic on *unacknowledged* traditions, they are themselves degenerate forms of world interpretation. They impose a false ontological preunderstanding on the rootless heirs of modernity, a "boundless cosmopolitanism" that leads them to absolutize their own standards of rationality and assimilate everything alien without regard to context. The liberal inhabitants of the modern world have no sense for what is ultimately inaccessible in alien traditions and precisely for this reason fail to recognize the possibility of actually *learning* something from alien cultures. Abstract universalism is merely the obverse side of a globally objectifying historicism.

But MacIntyre fails to mention that this diagnosis of the contemporary scene follows in the footsteps of the cultural criticism of the German mandarins. If the diagnosis is to express something more than the mere distaste of the educated European for "Americanism" and "shallow" Enlightenment culture, it stands in need of systematic grounding. MacIntyre offers an interesting proposal to this effect in the last three chapters of his book. His argument proceeds on two fronts. Against the alleged abstract universalism of the Enlightenment, MacIntyre defends (a) the thesis that there is no such thing as a context-transcending rationality, only different forms of rationality rooted in traditions. And against a performatively self-contradictory relativism, he upholds (b) the thesis that productive communication between such self-centered traditions is no less feasible than learning from alien traditions. From the perspective of our own culture, we maintain steadfastly the unconditionality of validity claims; we take our forms of argumentation and investigation seriously and do not have to regard our practices of justification and criticism as merely arbitrary social conventions, as Rorty would have it. In what follows I will examine whether the contextualist thesis can be reconciled with the antirelativist one.

MacIntyre's argument involves two steps. First, he shows how we can speak of the rationality of a particular tradition without having to renounce the moment of unconditionality we unavoidably associate with fundamental concepts in every tradition. Then he seeks to demonstrate how communication between alien cultures is possible without postulating an underlying context-transcending rationality. MacIntyre portrays the competition between comprehensive views of self and world in a *different* light from Rawls. The coexistence of equally strong doctrines, with conceptions of the good that can overlap in a postmetaphysical concept of justice on condition that they submit themselves, as products of modern culture, to the conditions of reflexivity—this idea is now superseded by the model of a dispute, oriented to truth, concerning the hegemony of the most cogent tradition, the one that proves to be *superior* in its concept of practical reason, its ideals of life, and its interrelated conceptions of the good and the just. A tradition will prove to be rationally superior only if, like all historically rooted traditions, it possesses the power of substantive interpretations of the world and adopts a critical stance toward modern forms of consciousness.

In regard to (a), the rationality embodied in an inherited context is articulated in an endogenous tradition of inquiry of the kind investigated by MacIntyre, who takes as his examples the four philosophical movements mentioned. It is only at the third stage in the process of a tradition's becoming reflexive, however, that traditions of inquiry first arise. During the first stage, the authority of learned opinions and texts is not yet placed in question, while at the second stage, the processes of dogmatic articulation and systematization have advanced to a level where contradictions and unsolved problems come to light but cannot yet be methodically resolved. Only at the third stage are problem solutions construed as learning processes, so that one's own earlier conceptions can now be criticized as errors in the light of the corrected conceptions. From the perspective of the clarification of one's own errors there emerges a coherence concept of truth: that is true which serves within the context of our traditions to correct errors. Although this concept of truth reflects only the experience of tradition-immanent learning processes, from within our respective traditions we raise truth claims that have absolute validity for us; they confirm the dissolution of the only form of cognitive dissonance to which we are subject. In this way standards of truth have determinate meaning only within the context of a particular tradition of investigation, but for their adherents they do not (as a result) have merely local significance. Like the basic concepts of the language game of argumentation itself, they preserve a con-text-transcending sense: "The concept of truth is timeless" (363).

The concept of truth is crucial to the interesting limit cases in which epistemological crises can no longer be resolved by a renewal of the basic conceptual vocabulary that draws on the resources of one's own tradition but only by learning another tradition recognized as superior. If the claim concerning the dependency of forms of rationality on traditions is to hold good in this case too, the instruction derived from alien traditions must be described as both an internally motivated paradigm shift and at the same time as a *paradigm leap* from one tradition to the other.

The *endogenous* resolution of an epistemological crisis must satisfy three conditions. First, it makes possible an explanation in terms of the new paradigm of the problems that could not be solved in the old vocabulary; second, it will make clear retrospectively the obstacles that hindered the tradition from finding a productive solution to problems prior to the innovation; and, finally, it will ensure certain continuities within the tradition through the paradigm shift and beyond: "these first two tasks must be carried out in a way which exhibits some fundamental continuities of the new conceptual and theoretical structures with the shared beliefs in terms of which the tradition of inquiry had been defined up to this point" (362) But precisely this third condition cannot be fulfilled by an *exogenously* induced learning process: "Derived as it is from a genuinely alien tradition, the new explanation does not stand in any sort of substantive continuity with the preceding history of the tradition in crisis. In this kind of situation the rationality of tradition requires an acknowledgment by those who have hitherto inhabited and given their allegiance to the tradition in crisis that the alien tradition is superior in rationality and in respect of its claims to truth to their own" (365). This account turns on the fact that the rational discrediting of one's own tradition still proceeds according to its own standards of rationality, whereas learning a rationally superior alien tradition presupposes a process of conversion, namely, the adoption of *new* standards of rationality. If different forms of rationality inhere in different traditions, there can be no bridge between them. The shift between mutually exclusive totalities requires a transformation in the identities of learning subjects. The latter must alienate themselves from themselves in the moment of transition and in the course of a conversion in their understanding of self and world must learn to understand their own past in the light of another tradition acknowledged to be superior.

But this model of what is involved in learning alien traditions is open to at least three objections. In the first place, the description is too selective. The model holds at best for learning processes in which the transition to a new level of justification signifies global, categorial devaluation of the sort of grounds valid up to that point—as happens, for example, in the transition from mythical narratives to monotheistic or cosmological explanations from first principles, or in the dissolution of religious and metaphysical worldviews in postmetaphysical thought. But all of the ethical systems MacIntyre has in mind compete *within* the same universe of discourse of Western philosophy. They interpenetrate to a sufficient degree that they can learn something from each other without compromising their identity. Furthermore, MacIntyre cannot uphold his own learning theory—modeled on the ideas of recent postempiricist philosophy of science—without falling into a performative self-contradiction. Either his metatheoretical claims about stages of increasing reflexivity hold for any tradition whatsoever, in which case they could not have been developed from within the context of a particular research tradition, which contradicts the presupposition on which they rest; or these claims lose their context-transcending meaning and have only local validity, but then MacIntyre becomes entangled in precisely the relativism he tries to avoid by means of his learning theory. Finally, the proposed concept of learning through conversion is not internally consistent. The recognition of the rational superiority of an alien tradition can be sufficiently motivated from the perspective of one's own tradition only if the learning subject can compare the explanatory power of both traditions in relation to the *same* problems. But precisely this is denied him, because in the absence of a zone of rational overlap the two traditions are incommensurable.

In regard to (b), MacIntyre attempts to counter this last objection with a theory of "thicker" though less than complete translation. If learning from an alien tradition is to be possible, the two traditions must be capable of communicating with one another without assuming common standards of rationality. Now "good" translations cannot limit themselves to literal correlation of expressions of the one language with expressions of the other; rather, they must conform to the model of acquisition of a "second first language" to the extent that they take into account the internal intermeshing of communicative expressions with the totality of a life practice. Understanding a language presupposes at the very least virtual participation in the native language games, if not a secondary socialization into the indigenous forms of life. The meaning of a communicative utterance is revealed from the contexts in which it is uttered. Hence, the understanding of a communicative utterance becomes deeper with access to the context-constitutive horizons of the linguistically structured lifeworld in which the utterance is situated.

This way of distinguishing between good and bad translations draws on well-worn hermeneutic insights. It loses its triviality only with the additional assertion that the better the interpreter learns to master his second language, the more clearly he recognizes the *untranslatability* of its central components: "The characteristic mark . . . is to be able to recognize where and in what respect utterances in the one [language] are untranslatable into the other" (375). With the acquisition of at least two "first," that is, actually spoken, languages and by becoming accustomed to the corresponding practices of an extended form of life, the "good" translator gradually gains a stereoscopic perspective from which he is supposed to be able to perceive "zones of untranslatability." He learns to move back and forth between both contexts and experiences the failure of attempts to transpose *adequately* constitutive expressions of the one language into the other: "You cannot express some of Plato's key thoughts in the Hebrew of Jeremiah or even of the Wisdom literature, but you also cannot express them in Homeric Greek" (375). With this intuitive appeal to "zones of untranslatability," MacIntyre *clarifies*, on the one hand, how those who belong to different traditions, each crystallized around its own rational core, can at all communicate with one other; and, on the other, he wishes to *explain* thereby why, if they enter such zones, they can recognize the rational superiority of another tradition. When an interpreter experiences the failure of attempts at translation, he must be capable of adopting both irreconcilable perspectives and yet of understanding the meanings that cannot be mutually transformed into one another.

The inconsistency of this account becomes apparent once we reflect on what MacIntyre must think he can accomplish if he is even to find examples to illustrate his thesis of untranslatability. Equal mastery of two essentially incommensurable language worlds—let us say, biblical Hebrew and classical Greek—enables him to paraphrase examples from both languages with the help of English in such a way that the difficulty of an exact or literal translation becomes plausible for the reader. Of course, MacIntyre cannot understand such paraphrasing *as* translation, since the circumscribing explications of inaccessible meanings are supposed instead to demonstrate the untranslatability of central expressions. Under the precondition of genuine bilingualism, MacIntyre presumably experiences essential inaccessibility, which he nevertheless communicates to readers in a third language. But in doing this, the interpreter has assuredly found a language for his experience of the "absolutely other" in zones where the mutually exclusive forms of rationality inhering in the different traditions no longer overlap. The fact that the experience of untranslatability is *not* inexpressible should raise our suspicions.

MacIntyre himself anticipates the obvious objection "that only insofar as we can come to understand what it is that is allegedly inaccessible to us could we have grounds for believing in such inaccessibility, and that the acquisition of such understanding is of itself sufficient to show what we alleged to be inaccessible is in fact not so." He responds to his own objection in the following manner: "If it is the case . . . that a condition of discovering the inaccessible is in fact a matter of two stages, in the first of which we acquire a second language-in-use as a second first language and only in the second of which can we learn that we are unable to translate what we are now able to say in our second first language into our first first language, then this argument loses all its force" (387). The ad hoc irreversibility built into *this* description has an air of arbitrariness about it; the fact, contingent in itself, that MacIntyre in his own example makes use of a third language—English—to paraphrase the presumably untranslatable meanings of expressions of the first and second languages already betrays the conceptual necessity of a *tertium comparationis* that enables us bring the two language worlds *into relation to each other*.

How would a subject have to be constituted who comes upon something absolutely untranslatable in communicating with the adherents of an alien tradition? Let us suppose to begin with that the speaker's identity, which has been constituted through primary socialization and becoming habituated to the traditions and life-forms of his mother tongue, remains essentially unaltered by the acquisition of a second first language. His identity, we might say, is inflexible. As soon as a speaker of this kind advances into regions where the rationalities of different languages and traditions prove to be mutually impervious, he is faced with an alternative: either he changes his identity by converting to an avowedly rationally superior language, tradition, and life-form, or he acquires a second identity but one he cannot bring into relation with his first identity rooted in the past. In short, he suffers a split personality. In either case there would no longer be a subject to whom the *experience* of change of identity or of fragmentation of identity could be *ascribed*. Something analogous holds for the experience of incommensurability of language worlds and the untranslatability of their constitutive expressions; we could not attribute such an experience to a speaker with an inflexible identity essentially rooted in a tradition. For in the course of the experience ascribed to him, this referent would change; hence, if the referent is to remain constant, we must abandon the assumption of a *rigid identity*. In its place we make the more realistic assumption that a subject who learns to master two languages ideally well emerges from the process of acquiring the second first language with a *bilingually extended identity*. The speaker has so broadened his understanding of self and world that he is sufficiently flexible to remain identical with himself when he makes the transition from one language world to the other—and to escape the fate of conversion or even of a split personality. A flexibly maintained identity enables him to bring the languages and rationalities of *both* of his past worlds, the primary and the secondary, into relation in such a way that both are fused into a broadened horizon of possible understanding. And after this fusion of horizons in his own person, the bilingual speaker can express the difficulties of translating from one tradition into another by *reciprocal* paraphrasings of each language in the other—and also in a third language. The problem—or, better, apparent problem—of complete untranslatablility must have already been solved before we can even identify zones of more or less radical *difficulties* of translation. This has been shown in a different way by Davidson in his critique of the notion of a conceptual scheme. MacIntyre's rehabilitation of a strong concept of tradition is inspired by culture-critical motives. He wants to make students—who live betwixt and between traditions—aware that they cannot live an authentic life without the critical appropriation of the substantive contents of a tradition with which they identify. This pedagogical intention does not account for his radically contextualist position, for which the insights Gadamer articulated in his philosophical hermeneutics, for example, would be sufficient. Against this MacIntyre not only emphasizes the ties of an interpreter to the conditions of his hermeneutic point of departure but maintains in addition the peculiar asymmetry of a communicative situation in which one side is viewed as capable of learning from the other only from a perspective that remains bound to its own context (or, alternatively, through subjection to an alien perspective). MacIntyre seems to restrict all interpretive procedures to *processes of self-understanding*. He is misled by his pedagogical intention into assimilating the understanding of arbitrary symbolic expressions to the clarification of an existential self-understanding. This ethical curtailment of his concept of interpretation explains the ethnocentric self-centeredness from which alone traditions that satisfy MacIntyre's description can encounter one another.

Even in exemplary instances of intercultural understanding where not just rival conceptions but conflicting standards of rationality clash, unprejudiced communication between "us" and "them" nevertheless necessitates a *symmetrical relation*. The fusion of interpretive horizons at which, on Gadamer's account, every communicative process aims should not be understood in terms of the false alternative between an assimilation "to us" and a conversion "to them." It is more properly described as a convergence between "our" perspective and "theirs" guided by learning processes, regardless of whether "they" or "we" or both sides must reform the practices of justification thus far accepted as valid. Concepts such as truth, rationality, and justification play the *same* role in *every* language community, even if they are interpreted differently and applied in accordance with different criteria. And this fact is sufficient to anchor the same universalistic concepts of morality and justice in different, even competing, forms of life and show that they are compatible with different conceptions of the good—on the assumption that the "comprehensive doctrines" and "strong traditions" enter into unrestricted dialogue with one another instead of persisting in their claims to exclusivity in a fundamentalistic manner. In this sense Rawls's concept of an overlapping consensus represents one possible interpretation of the principle that the general and the particular reciprocally presuppose each other.

13. A deontological moral theory that concentrates on questions of justice pays for the presumptive general validity of moral judgments with a narrow concept of morality. But it does not thereby banish questions of the good or unfailed life from the pale of rational treatment. It need only maintain that ethical discussions, in contrast to moral arguments, are always already embedded in the traditional context of a hitherto accepted, identity-constituting form of life. Moral judgments differ from ethical judgments only in their degree of contextuality.

The implications of a narrow concept of the moral for issues in ecological ethics are of greater moment. The anthropocentric profile of theories of the Kantian type seems to render them blind to questions of the moral responsibility of human beings for their nonhuman environment. These theories proceed on the assumption that moral problems arise only within the circle of subjects capable of speech and action because we, in Günther Patzig's words, "as members of a community of human beings count and depend on the cooperation and consensus of others."[85] But our moral feelings, judgments, and actions are directed not only to subjects capable of speech and action but also to animals. Patzig has the merit of confronting pressing ecological questions of the protection of animals and the preservation of species without overstepping the limits of an "ethics without metaphysics." As with the extension of the spectrum of issues of justice to include questions of the good life, here it is also a matter of supplementing moral questions in the narrow sense—limited to rational, or at least potentially rational, subjects—with questions of another kind. Is there such a thing as responsibility toward nature independent of responsibility for present and future humanity? What, in particular, is the nature of our obligation to protect animals?[86]

Patzig describes the predicament in which an anthropocentric moral theory finds itself when it attempts to justify the protection of animals, for example: "Is it possible to extend the sphere of validity of moral obligations beyond the human realm to encompass all living creatures who are capable of experiencing pain and suffering but also pleasure? Here we run up against a clear barrier. . . . For animals cannot enter into relations of principled reciprocity with us of the kind that govern our conduct toward other human beings."[87] On the other hand, our moral intuitions speak an unambiguous language. We have an unmistakable sense that the avoidance of cruelty toward all creatures capable of suffering is a moral duty and is not simply recommended by prudential considerations or even considerations of the good life. And we cannot settle the matter, following Kant, by saying that whereas we have duties in relation to animals, we do not have duties *toward* them. Animals confront us as vulnerable creatures whose physical integrity we must protect *for its own sake*.

The founder of utilitarianism, Jeremy Bentham, had little difficulty in answering the question of the scope and sphere of application of moral duties: "The question is not, Can they reason? nor, Can they talk? but, Can they suffer?"[88] Yet how is this utilitarian response to be reconciled with an anthropocentric approach if duties in the strict sense can only follow from rules that rational beings impose upon themselves through insight? Valid norms deserve the intersubjective recognition of all potentially affected because the latter, were they to engage in argumentation, could convince themselves that these norms are equally in the interest of all. Now animals are not creatures of a kind that "could enter into a relation of principled reciprocity with us." But what, then, is the status of duties that impose a determinate responsibility on us as addressees of valid norms, not only *for* or *in respect of* animals but toward these animals themselves, if animals for their part do not belong to the domain of possible addressees of norms?

Patzig summarily dispenses with the symmetry between duties and rights that is a conceptually necessary consequence of the reciprocal recognition of at least potentially free and equal subjects and defines the status of duties toward animals in an asymmetrical manner: "Animals do not have duties toward humans, but humans have duties toward animals."[89] At the same time he opens up the possibility of a gradation of duties incompatible with the binary encoding of the mode of validity of strict duties. The greater the sensitivity to pain of the animals, the more onerous duties should be. But this amounts to a transformation of the concept of duty; it is no longer a question of duties in the deontological sense but of the relative preferability of goods. This suggests that questions of environmental ethics, as well as ethical questions of how to live one's life, should be treated from a different perspective—a teleological one—and that only questions of the well-ordered coexistence of persons should be treated in a deontological manner.

Now the exclusion of ethical questions from the sphere of moral questions or questions of justice no doubt makes sense because the question of what is good for me or for us, all things considered, is already formulated in such a way that it invites an answer whose claim to validity is relativized to prior life projects and forms of life. Identity-constitutive values and ideals cannot *obligate* us in the same sense as moral norms; they lack the *unconditionality* of a categorical ought. But we have a sense of being under categorical obligations toward animals. The horror inspired by the torment of animals is, at any rate, more closely related to outrage at the violation of moral demands than to the pitying or condescending attitude toward people who, as we are wont to say, have made nothing of their lives or are failures by their own standards of authenticity. We "ought" not to neglect animals callously, much less cruelly torment them.

In an attempt to do justice to these intuitions, Patzig tries to *connect* the injunction to protect animals, grounded initially in utilitarian terms, to the deontological theory: "Our theory of rational morality suggests a different explanation of the norm forbidding the infliction of unnecessary suffering on animals. Each of us knows what pain and suffering are and we expect all other human beings to respect our vital interest in avoiding them as much as possible. But it would be irrational to make a radical distinction between human and non-human creatures where the latter behave in such a way that we are compelled to assume that they are capable of experiencing pain and suffering. *Thus* the prohibition on arbitrarily inflicting suffering and callous neglect is extended beyond the human domain to include non-human creatures."[90] Regrettably, the "thus" here masks a non sequitur, for the principle of generalization does not entail that the norm of refraining from inflicting pain on others should be extended to encompass *all* creatures sensitive to pain, so long as this principle demands only equal consideration of the interests of all those we may assume are capable of adopting the perspective of all others. Apart from their potential "yes" or "no" responses it cannot be determined whether such a norm could meet with the agreement of all and hence is valid. Animals, as Patzig correctly emphasizes, simply do not belong "to the parties to the contractual reciprocity that underlies human morality."[91]

Otherwise we would be at a loss to explain why the command to refrain from inflicting suffering on animals does not encompass—as in the case of human beings—the further duty to respect animal life, that is, not to kill animals. If animals had a moral claim of the *same* kind as human beings to be protected from suffering inflicted on them by human beings, it would unavoidably appear paradoxical that they should not have an even more emphatic claim not to be killed by human beings. But the discussion concerning the qualified permissibility of animal experiments with fatal results has already shown us that we do not regard the rationally justified and painless killing of animals as an act of murder. Moreover, nonvegetarians seem to have few scruples about eating meat. This paradox can at least be brought closer to resolution if we take the discourse-ethical interpretation of rational morality as our starting point and recall that the feeling of duty has its roots in the fundamental relations of recognition we always already presuppose in communicative action.

Social interactions mediated by the use of language oriented to mutual understanding are constitutive for sociocultural forms of life.

This kind of communicative socialization through which persons are simultaneously individuated generates a deep-seated vulnerability, because the identity of socialized individuals develops only through integration into ever more extensive relations of social dependency. The person develops an inner life and achieves a stable identity only to the extent that he also externalizes himself in communicatively generated interpersonal relations and implicates himself in an ever denser and more differentiated network of reciprocal vulnerabilities, thereby rendering himself in need of protection. From this anthropological viewpoint, morality can be conceived as the protective institution that compensates for a constitutional precariousness implicit in the sociocultural form of life itself. Moral institutions tell us how we should behave toward one another to counteract the extreme vulnerability of the individual through protection and considerateness. Nobody can preserve his integrity by himself alone. The integrity of individual persons requires the stabilization of a network of symmetrical relations of recognition in which nonreplaceable individuals can secure their fragile identities in a *reciprocal* fashion only as members of a community. Morality is aimed at the chronic susceptibility of personal integrity implicit in the structure of linguistically mediated interactions, which is more deep-seated than the tangible vulnerability of bodily integrity, though connected with it.

Clearly this difference between personal and bodily integrity disappears in the animal world because we do not attribute personality to creatures with whom we cannot speak and cannot come to an understanding about something in the world. Nevertheless, we communicate with animals in a different way once we involve them in our social interactions, in however asymmetrical a fashion. Such interactions take on a measure of continuity in our association with domestic animals: our conscience is particularly insistent "concerning species with which we can communicate with particular ease."[92] Like moral obligations generally, our quasi-moral responsibility toward animals is related to and grounded in the potential for harm inherent in all social interactions. To the extent that creatures participate in our social interactions, we encounter them in the role of an alter ego as an other in need of protection; this grounds the expectation that we will assume a fiduciary responsibility for their claims. There exists a quasi-moral responsibility toward animals that we encounter in the role (if not *completely* filled) of a second person, one whom we look upon as if it were an alter ego. We can adopt a performative attitude toward many animals, though not toward plants. In that case, they are no longer objects to be observed by us, or even just objects of our empathy, but beings who, in their interaction with us, make their distinctive mode of being felt in a manner different than a rock does its mineral hardness or a plant does the osmotic interaction of an organism with its environment. To the extent that animals participate in our interactions, we enter into a form of contact that goes beyond one-sided or reciprocal observation because it is *of the same kind* as an intersubjective relation.

In making such statements, we must be wary of mystifications. Interactions between humans and animals are mediated by nonlinguistic gestures, and the injuries that human beings are capable of inflicting on an animal do not affect anything resembling a personal identity—rather, they are a direct assault on its psychophysical integrity. Again, an animal does not experience its pain reflexively like a human being, who in suffering is cognizant of the fact that he is in pain. These and similar asymmetries characterize the way in which animals participate in our interactions. At the same time, the interactions must satisfy the condition that we should not confront animals in the objectifying attitude of a third person, nor just communicate about animals but *with* them. We must be able to ascribe characteristics of agents to animals, among others the ability to initiate utterances and to address them to us. Then we have duties that are *analogous* to our moral duties, because like the latter they are rooted in the presuppositions of communicative action. Of course, they are analogous to moral duties only to the extent that the asymmetries in the interactions admit comparison with relations of recognition between persons.

If this justification of interactive duties toward animals by appeal to a theory of intersubjectivity is not completely wide of the mark, we can also explain why animals, on the one hand, are rendered particularly dependent on human beings and in need of protection by the asymmetrical structure of possible interactions, but why, on the other, they can enjoy this moral protection only within the intersubjective horizon of *our* modes of interaction. Human beings always find themselves already within this horizon and as persons can never leave it, whereas animals belong to other species and other forms of life and are integrated into our forms of life only through participation in our interactions. The limits of our quasi-moral responsibility toward animals are reached once humans, in their role as members of one species, confront animals as exemplars of another. However, it is a tricky moral question to determine in which situations this is permissible. I do not wish to preclude a priori that some vegetarians exhibit a moral sensibility that may prove to be the correct moral intuition under more auspicious social circumstances. In that case animals would come to be recognized in all situations as possible participants in interaction, and the protection to which we feel obligated in our interactions with animals would be extended to include protecting their existence.

Human responsibility for plants and for the preservation of whole species cannot be derived from duties of interaction, and thus cannot be *morally* justified.[93] Nevertheless, I am in accord with Patzig in believing that, aside from prudential considerations, there are good *ethical reasons* that speak in favor of the protection of plants and species, reasons that become apparent once we ask ourselves seriously how, as members of a civilized global society, we want to live on this planet and how, as members of our own species, we want to treat other species. In certain respects, *aesthetic reasons* have here even greater force than ethical, for in the aesthetic experience of nature, things withdraw into an unapproachable autonomy and inaccessibility; they then exhibit their fragile integrity so clearly that they strike us as inviolable in their own right and not merely as desirable elements of a preferred form of life.

3

Lawrence Kohlberg and Neo-Aristotelianism

I

Among my American friends Larry Kohlberg was always the one who for me embodied most convincingly the distinctively American tradition that stretches back from Mead and Dewey via Royce and Peirce to the transcendentalists—from Chicago to Concord, so to speak. It is hardly a coincidence that Kohlberg came of age academically in the place where Charles Morris, among others, kept alive the spirit of pragmatism. I recall one evening at his house in Cape Cod, as we sat beside the fireplace with a view of the ocean shortly after sunset. Larry took a battered volume from the shelf and began to recite an ode of Walt Whitman, rather haltingly, running the syllables together, with a strange mixture of understatement and deep involvement. At that time I scarcely understood a word of the poem, but the sound of his voice, the rhythmic flow of the free verse, the whole scene spoke eloquently enough: here we were witnessing one of the roots from which this man's life drew its nourishment. During my last visit to Harvard, he took me to William James Hall and pointed out the inscription that expresses the essential intuition of pragmatism:

The community stagnates without the impulse of the individual, the impulse dies away without the sympathy of the community.
—William James

These words are deeply embedded in the American tradition. But is this also true of the proposition the sentence expresses, of the insight the maxim encapsulates? To put it more pointedly: Is this statement true for Americans alone? Or does it also embody a truth for those who are not the fortunate heirs to the political thought of a Thomas Paine and a Thomas Jefferson? It might be objected that it was easy for a German of the younger generation like myself, who graduated from high school after World War II under the influence of "reeducation," to distance himself from the elitism of the German *Gymnasium* and to open himself unreservedly to the universalistic, egalitarian values of the radical democratic tradition. Yet the crucial issue is to what extent the genesis of such convictions compromises their validity.

In what follows I will defend a thesis that does not sit well with the spirit of the times: that anyone who has grown up in a reasonably functional family, who has formed his identity in relations of mutual recognition, who maintains himself in the network of reciprocal expectations and perspectives built into the pragmatics of the speech situation and communicative action, cannot fail to have acquired moral intuitions of the kind articulated in propositions such as that of James. The maxim asserts the reciprocal dependence of socialization and individuation, the interrelation between personal autonomy and social solidarity, that is part of the implicit knowledge of *all* communicatively acting subjects; it does not merely express a more or less subjective opinion concerning what some person believes is the good life.[1] That proposition articulates an intuition we acquire in various different contexts on the condition that we grow up in surroundings that are not completely undermined by systematically distorted communication.

Kohlberg defends the thesis that moral judgments exhibit the same structure in all cultures and societies in the following way: "We claim that there is a universally valid form of rational moral thought process which all persons could articulate, assuming social and cultural conditions suitable to cognitive-moral stage development. We claim that the ontogenesis toward this form of rational moral thinking occurs in all cultures in the same stepwise, invariant stage sequence."[2] Each of these sentences contains two theses that need to be defended independently—the first with the resources of moral philosophy, the

(margin, handwritten) What constitutes a reasonably functional family? X

second in the field of developmental psychology. However, the invalidity of the one assertion would not be without implications for the truth of the other.

Philosophers engage in the controversy surrounding the question of moral universalism on normative grounds without drawing on empirical theories. But the relevant empirical theories must at least be in accord with the rational reconstructions of the intuitive knowledge of competent speaking, acting, and judging subjects proposed by philosophy. Einstein's theory of relativity was a challenge to Kant's "Metaphysical Foundations of Natural Science." In another sense Kohlberg's theory, as we shall see, represents a touchstone against which Kant's "Foundations of the Metaphysics of Morals" must be tested. A developmental theory of the Piagetian kind can function at best as an *indirect* test of the theories the psychologist has relied upon in his description of the cognitive operations of the highest stage of moral-psychological development. This amounts only to a test of the coherence of different theories that cannot be brought into direct relation to one another but must not contradict one another at the metatheoretical level where we piece together the different theoretical elements. On the other hand, cognitive psychology is clearly dependent on the philosophical theories it employs in constructing its empirical theory. Kohlberg's theory furnishes a good example of this interdependence. He uses arguments from Hare, Frankena, and Rawls, among others, to delimit the domain of "judgments of justice." In addition, he relies on moral theories of this sort to provide a structural description of the postconventional judgments of Stage 6, which are not adequately supported by empirical evidence, for considerations of logical completeness of the sequence of developmental stages demand that a highest stage be postulated.[3]

In what follows, I will concentrate on the philosophical aspects of the universality thesis. A moral-philosophical defense of the universalistic position is crucial for Kohlberg's research program for at least two reasons:

(1) Kohlberg himself was well aware of the fact that his "metaethical assumptions" stand in need of justification within the framework of philosophical discourse. Were there already compelling moral philosophical reasons against universalistic approaches as such, a universalistically oriented theory of moral development would also be

subverted. Yet Kohlberg's use of the term "metaethical" to characterize his categorial framework is misleading,[4] for we cannot delimit the object domain of moral judgments independently of the normative theories that already inform the description of the highest stage of moral judgment, nor can we make clear what is to be understood by problems of justice and their corresponding solutions. Moreover, the fundamental philosophical assumptions of psychological theories have to be clarified if we are to be able to counter objections against reconstructive research projects based on an erroneous philosophy of science.

(2) In addition, differentiations and alterations in moral philosophical foundations have implications for the construction of the empirical theory extending to the details of experimental design. At the metatheoretical level, moral-philosophical and moral-psychological programs are implicated in a hermeneutic circle in which they must complement each other. Thus, changes in the philosophical explanation of the moral point of view shed new light on how to conduct empirical surveys of moral judgments and how to select instruments and evaluate data.

In recent years universalistic theories such as those of Rawls, Dworkin, Apel, and myself have been sharply criticized by philosophers such as Alasdair MacIntyre, Bernard Williams, Charles Taylor, Michael Sandel, and David Wiggins. From these involved discussions I will first extract three serious objections. Then I will reverse the direction of criticism and discuss some difficulties in the neo-Aristotelian position on which these objections are based. This discussion should put us in a position, finally, to revise the fundamental premises of Kantian moral theory in such a way that neo-Aristotelian objections can be accommodated within a deontological framework.

II

Classical ethics, which achieved its mature form in the work of Aristotle, is inspired by the ambition to find a philosophical answer to *one* fundamental question: "How should I live?" or "How should one live?" In virtue of this prior orientation, practical questions are invested with teleological significance. The question "What ought I to do?" or "What is right for me?" is subordinated to a more encompassing question, "What is the good life?" A consequence of this turn toward an ethics of the good is the uncoupling of practical reason from theoretical cognition. Practical reason is identified with prudence, *prudentia* or *phronesis,* and thus as a faculty that always operates within the horizon of established customs and practices and consequently renounces the claim to knowledge reserved by Aristotle exclusively for science or theory in the strict sense. With the emergence of the modern empirical sciences, however, philosophical theory also had to give up the strong claim to knowledge grounded ultimately in metaphysics. But *phronesis,* as the Aristotelian counterpart of *episteme,* was also affected by the latter's altered status and weakened claim. With the unsettling of theoretical reason, the status of practical reason also becomes problematic.[5]

Practical reason needed to be reconsidered in the light of the modern ideas of theory and science. The path of ethics now branched out in three directions. The capacity for moral judgment was either excluded from the sphere of reason altogether in an empiricist manner, thereby giving rise to a long series of noncognitivist positions; or moral reflection was reduced to instrumental calculations of consequences of action, as in the case of utilitarianism. Kant alone reserved a place for moral judgment in the realm of practical reason and thereby upheld its status as genuine knowledge. In Kant's view all judgments—empirical, normative, even aesthetic—raise a claim to validity that can be supported or criticized by appeal to good reasons. These theoretical determinations entail at the same time that the concept of morality henceforth stands in need of mediation by a theory of knowledge. What one understands by morality becomes a matter of how one answers the question concerning the possibility of rationally resolving practical questions in general.

Aristotle could still construe the claim to knowledge of his ethics, which was embedded in a metaphysical worldview, in the sense of a weak cognitivism. Because he took his orientation from the situation of the citizen in the polis, understood as the proper *telos* of human existence, his ethics could still provide orientation concerning the ontological conditions and the institutional framework of the good life. Without such a metaphysical background on which to draw, Kant confronted the task of first explaining the possibility of moral insight as such and then of situating practical reason within the theoretical framework of a tripartite, though only formally unified, reason. The categorical imperative can be understood as an explication of the viewpoint of impartial judgment formation.

The moral point of view is the perspective from which we can decide among controversial normative claims impartially, solely on the basis of reasons. Kant had to pay a price for this move to a postmetaphysical concept of autonomous morality, and this is the issue on which the dispute between philosophers still turns today. The proponents of Aristotelian ethics are convinced that modern directions in moral theory have come at too high a price; these theories have renounced the proper goal of ethics—that of answering the existential question of the wherefore of our lives—but have gained nothing worth speaking of in return. Even the categorical imperative demands an exercise of abstraction with far-reaching consequences—disregarding everyday practices and hence the very context in which moral judgment and action takes place. Here I set aside questions of interpretation and accept for the sake of argument the concept of morality the neo-Aristotelians ascribe to Kant. They admonish deontological positions in the Kantian tradition for detaching practical reason from the context of ethical life and restrict it to a narrow moral outlook defined by one or other formulation of the principle of universalization. The intuitive meaning of the categorical imperative is clear: moral questions should be decided with regard to what all could will. Only those norms and modes of action are morally valid or obligatory that could meet with the justified assent of all involved (or all affected). In fact, the moral point of view requires a threefold abstraction: (1) abstraction from the motives required of those involved, (2) abstraction from the particular situation, and (3) abstraction from existing institutions and forms of life.

(1) The moral point of view involves a shift in the focus of practical reason from questions of the form, "What is good *for me/for us?*" to questions of justice of the form "What should *one* do?" With this change in perspective, the significance of the once-canonical orientation to happiness and well-being also changes. The question concerning *eudaimonia* originally encompassed the sphere of all possible goods, including justice, as well as all of the virtues, including the sense of justice. But under the deontological aspect of the question of what all could will, justice and autonomy (that is, the capacity to

act in accordance with self-imposed laws) are singled out as the sole morally relevant determinations. The moral point of view necessitates differentiating between the right and the good. All goods, including the highest good of my life project or of the form of life to which we collectively aspire, are deprived of their moral status and are lumped together with things designed to satisfy contingent needs and wants; henceforth, goods fulfill only subjective preferences. In contrast to the ethics of the good, the morality of justice sets duty and inclination in conflict with one another. From this opposition there follow two disturbing consequences:

(a) Viewed from the perspective of classical ethics, practical reason completely loses its point if moral judgment is restricted to interpersonal obligations, so that the question of how we should live—as individuals and members of a community—must be left up to blind decision or sheer impulse. It was precisely these issues of individual life projects and collective ways of life that philosophy once promised to illuminate through reflection. What was held to be essential to philosophy was that it should help us to lead a reflective life. Must philosophy now renounce this preeminent task in favor of that of submitting just one subset of practical questions, questions of justice, to a more clear-cut standard of judgment?

(b) Second, once the bond between the right and the good is broken, the question of why one should act morally at all can no longer be answered satisfactorily. Classical ethics sought to demonstrate that striving for the highest good is compatible with both our obligations and our true interests. But in Kant's view, free will is constituted by moral insight alone; he conceives of autonomy as a subject's capacity to bind his will and to be guided in action by moral judgment alone. However, motivation by insight into what is morally required extends no further than the motivating power of good reasons. Hence Kant must invest practical reason with the higher authority of an intelligible world. But if we reject Kant's metaphysical background assumptions concerning the noumenal and the phenomenal realms, the question of why we should make the moral point of view our own, even when it is not in our interest, becomes unavoidable. The question "Why be moral?" remains open: "The *I* that stands back in rational reflection from my desires is still the *I* that has those desires. . . . It cannot, just by taking this step, acquire the motivations of justice."[6]

(2) From the moral point of view, practical reason focuses its attention on the justification of norms while problems of application recede into the background. Practical reason is thereby transformed from a context-dependent faculty of prudent deliberation that operates within the horizon of an established form of life into a faculty of pure reason operating independently of particular contexts. While Aristotelian *phronesis* focuses on specific alternative courses of action and links normative considerations with empirical observations and questions of rational choice in a nonperspicuous manner, practical reason in the Kantian sense, by contrast, is restricted to questions of normative justification in such a radical fashion that no tradition or way of life, however deeply rooted in our everyday praxis, can escape problematization. No normative validity claim raised in the lifeworld is immune to challenge; *everything* counts as a hypothesis until it has regained its validity through the authority of good reasons.

This focus on questions of justification in abstraction from problems of application is characteristic of the posttraditional level of moral judgment. But the way in which Kant makes the break with conventional thought leaves him vulnerable to the charge of context insensitivity. Because he explicates the moral point of view in terms of the "moral law" and construes the question "What should I do?" exclusively in terms of the justification of maxims, he seems to restrict the exercise of practical reason to assessing alternative courses of action in the light of the moral law. Moral justification seems to amount to nothing more than the deductive application of an abstract basic principle to particular cases, with the result that the specific context of the given situation loses its *peculiar* relevance. Abstraction from the particular constellation of the individual case also has the effect of excluding the consequences of action from normative consideration. For this Kant pays the price of the rigidity of an ethics of conviction. The model of moral judgment tailored to questions of justification overlooks the fact that the choice between competing norms of action and their application gives rise to problems of its own. As a general rule, problems of applying implicitly presupposed norms are even more exigent than those of justification.[7]

(3) Seen from the moral point of view, issues of moral cognition take precedence over questions of practical orientation; problems are shifted from the existential plane of the concrete practical concern of socialized individuals regarding their individual and collective lives to the abstract level of the reflection of isolated subjects on what *all* could accept as a law governing their actions. Kantian practical reason transcends the sphere of validity of traditions and institutions that are constitutive of the particular life-form of a given collectivity with its specific practices and customs and concrete virtues and duties. From this abstraction there follow in turn two unfortunate consequences:

(a) First, an atomistic conception of the person is presupposed, since each individual who examines his maxims from the moral point of view finds himself compelled to go beyond the context of his own form of life *in foro interno* if he is to encounter all others as Others, that is, as isolated individuals. Free will operates in a vacuum, disengaged from the social bonds that first invest ethical life with meaning. To the atomistic concept of the person who relates to himself as his own private property there corresponds a contractualist concept of society that denies any inherent moral quality to a life reduced to calculations of self-interest: "For a society to be a community in this strong sense, community must be constitutive of the shared self-understandings of the participants and embodied in their institutional arrangements, not simply an attribute of certain of the participants' plans of life."[8]

(b) Furthermore, from a contextualist perspective, it is doubtful whether *any* concept of justice can claim universal validity. Lifeworlds are totalities that exist only in plural form. But if ethical life is tied to the specific characteristics of a certain form of life, then every concept of good and evil, however abstract, is affected and shaped by the intuitive preunderstanding embodied in the concrete totality of moral conceptions dominant in a particular place. Concepts of justice cannot be separated from the complex totality of a concrete ethical life and a *particular* idea of the good life. This is why in MacIntyre's view "the Enlightenment project of justifying morality" had to fail.[9] The conceptions of an autonomous morality developed by Rousseau and Kant in the eighteenth century also seem to remain tied to the period from which they arose. Already in their basic core we can discern traces of the possessive individualism that would become dominant in the course of capitalist modernization.

III

The objections leveled against moral theories of the Kantian type may be summarized as follows. The *deontological* privileging of what one ought to do as the basic moral phenomenon makes the abstract separation between the right and the good unavoidable. This leads to abstraction from the requisite motivations, with the result that the question of why we should act morally at all no longer admits of a plausible answer. The *cognitivist* privileging of the posttraditional level of moral judgment gives prominence to questions of normative justification. This leads to abstraction from particular situations and neglect of questions of the application of norms. The *formalist* privileging of the general over the particular, finally, goes hand in hand with an atomistic concept of the person and a contractualist concept of society. This leads to abstraction from an ethical life that can assume concrete form only within particular forms of life. This interrelation raises doubts about the possibility of a strict separation between form and content and of a context-independent conceptualization of justice as such.

The outcome of our reflections leaves us with two alternatives: either we return to the Aristotelianism underlying these criticisms, or we modify the Kantian approach to take account of legitimate objections. Only those who are ready to restore a metaphysical mode of thinking could unhesitatingly embrace the first alternative. Contemporary neo-Aristotelians are not willing to do this. But their attempts to develop a practical philosophy in an Aristotelian spirit without drawing on metaphysical premises run up against difficulties that are, in my view, insurmountable.

(1) In modern societies we encounter a pluralism of individual lifestyles and collective forms of life and a corresponding multiplicity of ideas of the good life. As a consequence we must give up one of two things: the claim of classical philosophy to be able to place competing ways of life in a hierarchy and establish at its acme one privileged way of life over against all others or the modern principle of tolerance according to which one view of life is as good as any other, or at least

has equal right to exist and be recognized. MacIntyre wants to have his cake and eat it. On the one hand, he wants to uphold the classical cognitive claim: "In what does the unity of an individual life consist? . . . To ask 'What is the good for me?' is to ask how best I might live out that unity and bring it to completion. To ask 'What is the good for man?' is to ask what all answers to the former question must have in common."[10] On the other hand, given the premises of postmetaphysical thought, MacIntyre can no longer appeal directly to what he calls Aristotle's "metaphysical biology." On this was founded the thesis that "man" can actualize his nature and attain "the good" only within the privileged context of one particular form of life: the polis. MacIntyre, by contrast, has to work his way through a proliferating multiplicity of practices, traditions, and biographical patterns of life without being able to reach any single privileged complex of distinguishing characteristics of "the" good life. As Richard Bernstein remarks: "While there are constraints on how I can answer the question 'What is good for me?' this does not prevent a wide variety of answers, each of which may clash, and be incompatible with others—may require participation in practices incompatible with others, and even may require incompatible virtues. This (modern) conception of *a* human good does not limit 'the subversive arbitrariness' that can invade 'the moral life.'"[11]

(2) If we take modern pluralism seriously, we must renounce the classical philosophical claim to defend one uniquely privileged mode of life—for example, the *vita contemplativa* in opposition to the different forms of the *vita activa*. Bernard Williams nevertheless wants to secure the cognitive status of moral consciousness under these premises. But practical reason then begins to look suspiciously like *phronesis*. Once its metaphysical underpinning has been removed, the latter must either be assimilated to everyday knowledge or elevated to the status of reflective knowledge. In moral consciousness Williams sees the possibility of a form of ethical cognition that qualifies as knowledge and yet remains below the level of reflection of objectifying science and philosophy. Thus, on the one hand he stresses the limits of philosophy: "How truthfulness to an existing self or society is to be combined with reflection, self-understanding, and criticism is a question that philosophy, itself, cannot answer. It is the kind of question that has to be answered through reflective *living*."[12] But then

he must, on the other hand, specify criteria in terms of which a reflective form of life can be distinguished from an unreflective one: "Ethical reflection becomes part of the practice it considers, and inherently modifies it." But it is thereby faced with a paradoxical task. Although practical reason eschews the objectifying procedure of empirical inquiry into moral behavior no less than the theoretical constructions of philosophy, yet it is supposed to produce a form of practical knowledge "that would help us to find our way around in a social world which . . . was shown to be the best social world for human beings."[13] Williams is compelled to attribute to practical reason a form of rationality that goes beyond sheer common sense but whose difference from scientific rationality remains to be determined.

If practical reason can inform members of a social lifeworld concerning what is best for them and how they should regulate their common life, it makes possible a form of practical knowledge that is undoubtedly secured from within the lifeworld and yet points beyond its horizon. The horizon of every form of life is fluid, its boundaries permeable. There is no absolute barrier to the "desire for as much intersubjective agreement as possible."[14] Practical knowledge can all the more readily claim to be knowledge the more radically we open ourselves to others and expand our local knowledge and ethnocentric outlook—indeed, extend our community in a virtual manner such that our discourse ultimately includes *all* subjects capable of speech and action. But this process would yield the perspective Kantians call the moral point of view. Certainly, "if the agreement were to be uncoerced, it would have to grow from inside human life."[15] However, this qualification also holds for an intersubjective construal of the concept of practical reason that preserves intact its universalistic core: what "we" agree about coincides with what all could possibly assent to, provided we respond in a sufficiently radical fashion to Rorty's pragmatist call for the most comprehensive possible extension of the sphere of application of the word "we." If each individual community can achieve "knowledge" (in not just a metaphorical sense) concerning what is good for it, it is far from obvious why this practical knowledge should not be extended in an intercultural direction and become so thoroughly emancipated from provincial limitations that it orients itself to what is *equally good for all*. Without metaphysical backing, what Aristotle called *phronesis* must either dissolve into mere common sense or be developed into a concept of practical reason that satisfies the criteria of procedural rationality.[16]

(3) By contrast, if we wish to remain faithful to the Aristotelian conviction that moral judgment is bound to the ethos of a particular place, we must be prepared to renounce the emancipatory potential of moral universalism and deny so much as the possibility of sub-jecting the structural violence inherent in social conditions character-ized by latent exploitation and repression to an unstinting moral critique. For only the transition to the posttraditional level of moral judgment liberates us from the structural constraints of familiar dis-courses and established practices.[17] Charles Taylor counters this charge with a universalistic ethics of the good that appeals to supreme goods transcending all particular forms of life. The examples he proposes, however, derive from Plato, the Stoics, and Christianity, that is, from traditions that appeal to the authority of reason, uni-versal natural law, or a transcendent deity.[18] These are the forerun-ners of moral universalism but are grounded in cosmological and religious worldviews that are even more difficult to reconcile with postmetaphysical thought than the teleological worldview of Aristotle.

Contemporary neo-Aristotelianism has played quite different po-litical roles in Germany and the United States. Similar lines of ar-gument take on a different significance in the two political cultures— in Germany a conservative, in America a critical. But as Herbert Schnädelbach has shown, the conservative bent of neo-Aristotelian-ism is not altogether accidental:

> For the neo-Aristotelian turned conservative, *autonomy is the same as funda-mental opposition.* ... The neo-Aristotelian ethic of prudence, with its weak foundationalism and its refined relativization of the principle of autonomy, is in its implications an eminently *political* ethic. The hermeneutic linking of ethics with ethos engenders not just a habitual bias in favour of the existing state of affairs, it also generates a systematic mistrust of the individual who can only *exemplify,* but never himself be *the bearer of,* an ethos. ... The fact that the ethos already embodied in the political must always take precedence over the moral individual accounts for the tendency of neo-Aristotelians *to collapse the difference between politics and morality from the perspective of politics,* while at the same time *warning against the moralization of politics.*[19]

In sum, all attempts at a historicist revival of Aristotelian ethics on a postmetaphysical footing are beset with insuperable difficulties.

Hence I propose to explore the other alternative left open to us and examine whether the misgivings concerning the deontological, cognitivist, and formalist abstractions can be accounted for *within* the framework of a moral theory of the Kantian kind, though reinterpreted in intersubjective terms.

IV

I will now take up once again with particular reference to Kohlberg's theory the objections discussed in the second section.

Abstraction from the Requisite Motives

Kohlberg consistently made a sharp distinction between moral dilemmas and questions of the good life. He illustrates what I have called the deontological abstraction with the responses of a young woman talking about a critical decision in her life: "I've had a personal decision, my decision to divorce . . . but I didn't view it as a moral problem. It wasn't. There weren't any moral issues involved really. The issues involved were—was it the right thing *for us?* . . . I knew that I'd be giving up my entire life and I'd have to begin again because it involved a geographical change and a change in work." When asked to say what *would* constitute a moral problem, she imagined the following situation: "Usually where two principles that I consider valuable look as though they may be clashing, then it's very hard to make a decision about things. When I think about things like child abuse, for example, there is the principle of family unity and the principle of the welfare of the child . . . although in this case I would always look out for the welfare of the child." Concerning this Kohlberg remarks: "Her resolution of the dilemma of child abuse vs. family unity can claim to be universalizable, impartial and agreed upon as right by all human beings. The decision of her own divorce . . . cannot be resolved from the 'moral point of view', whereas the dilemma of child abuse can be."[20]

Ethical questions of the good life can be distinguished from moral questions by a certain self-referentiality. They refer to what is good *for me* or *for us*—in this case, to what was best for the woman, her husband, and others directly affected by the divorce. This egocentric—or, as in the case of political questions, ethnocentric—reference is a sign of the internal relation between ethical questions and problems of self-understanding, of how I should understand myself (or we ourselves as members of a family, community, nation, and so forth). The question "What is the best thing for me (or us) in this situation?" must be answered in the light of the underlying question: "Who am I, and who would I like to be?" ("Who are we, and who do we want to be?") It is one's own identity that is here at stake. The fact that ethical questions are implicitly informed by the issues of identity and self-understanding may explain why they do not admit of an answer valid for everyone. But the logic of such questions does not completely exclude the possibility of rational answers in this dimension. Ethical problems need not be abandoned to subjective decisions or preferences. Contrary to what is often alleged, the latter is not a consequence of the deontological approach: "Personal decisions are understood to be culturally, historically and individually relative, though some degree of empathy, sensitivity and communication is required to resolve such problems."[21]

The hermeneutical clarification of one's identity also appeals to reasons; a self-referential interpretation must satisfy the precondition that it admits of assessment in terms of authenticity and inauthenticity. This kind of interpretation depends on a descriptive grasp of one's own processes of development—"Who am I?"—as much as on life projects and ego ideals—"Who would I like to be?" Hence, an understanding of self interpreted in this way can claim validity only for persons with determinate histories and specific life projects. The relativization of the validity of ethical statements does not constitute a deficiency but is the result of the logic of a question directed to me (or us) alone and *ultimately* can be answered only by me (or by us), though authentic interpretations must, of course, be compatible with valid moral norms.

This differentiation does not yet solve the problem of how the deontological chasm between moral judgment and factual conduct can be bridged. But this motivational problem can be posed only within the framework of a philosophy that is still confident of providing general answers to questions of the good life. A moral theory that no longer claims to know the telos of "the" good life must leave the question "Why be moral?" unanswered. On the premises of postmetaphysical thought, there is no reason why theories should have the binding power to *motivate* people to act in accordance with their insights when what is morally required conflicts with their interests. The disposition to act responsibly is contingent on processes of socialization and the degree of success in identity formation. But an identity cannot be produced by arguments. Thus, the fact that moral theory does not aspire to anything over and above the task of reconstructing the moral point of view and justifying its general validity does not amount to a deficiency. It can only show the participants the procedure they must follow if they want to solve moral problems and must leave all *concrete* decisions up to them. To think that one has the right answer is to know that one does not have good reason to act *otherwise*. The capacity of moral judgments to motivate agents to act stands in direct proportion to the rationally motivating force of the reasons on which they are grounded. The extent to which rational motives actually influence action depends on the individuals, the circumstances, the interest positions, and the institutions involved.

Abstraction from the Given Situation

Kant did not effect the transition to autonomous morality in a *sufficiently consistent* fashion. He presented the categorical imperative as a response to the concrete question "What ought I to do?" and did not fully realize that the shift in focus to problems of justification also entailed a strict separation of issues of justification of norms from those of their application. The categorical imperative must not be understood as a moral law that can be applied *directly* to maxims and actions. The categorical imperative is, rather, a proposal concerning how the viewpoint of impartiality, from which the validity of norms can be judged, should be understood. We cannot justify norms and defend concrete actions *in the same breath*. In justificatory discourses we appeal to the constellation of individual situations only by way of illustrating the conditions of application of a norm by means of examples. This is not a matter of correctly deciding a concrete case that permits different courses of action in a particular situation but of establishing the validity of norms that could be appealed to in such decisions. Knowledge of valid norms does not extend to knowing how one ought to decide in a *particular* situation. Discourses of application require different data and principles from discourses of justification. Kohlberg's substages A and B may have something to do with this differentiation, at least at the postconventional level.

If the employment of practical reason is no longer conceived as an operation in the mind of a solitary individual but is instead opened up to public argumentation, then the empirical consequences of normatively regulated action can also be submitted to the tribunal of norm-testing reason. Hence an ethics of conviction must yield to an ethics of responsibility. The notion of ideal role taking, which Kohlberg borrowed from G. H. Mead, is realized in the form of a shared practice of argumentation or deliberation that compels each participant to take the perspectives of all others. This idea has only recently attracted attention in analytic philosophy. David Wiggins, for example, interprets the procedure of universalization in terms of uniting the perspectives of the agent, the object of action, and the observer in a specific form of communication: "What is envisaged here is a public scene . . . in which moral agents are at once actors and spectators. . . . Actors here are persons doing things and persons having things done to them. Spectators are not strangers to these roles. Nor are actors strangers to the role of spectators. For everyone plays each of these three roles at some point, and his direct and indirect knowledge of the other roles constantly informs his playing of each."[22] This description at least comes close to the interweaving of perspectives produced under the communicative presuppositions of moral argumentation. Here what concerns me is that a communication-theoretical interpretation of the moral point of view should liberate the intuition expressed in the categorical imperative from the burden of a form of moral rigorism that is deaf to the consequences of actions. A norm can command the rationally motivated assent of all only if everyone involved or potentially affected has taken into consideration the consequences and side effects of the general observance of the norm for himself and others.

The same liberating consequence follows from the logic of discourses of application.[23] The principle of universalization that regulates discourses of justification does not exhaust the normative sense of the impartiality of a just judgment. A further principle must be adduced to guarantee the correctness of singular judgments. An impartial judge must assess which of the competing norms of action—

whose validity has been established in advance—is most appropriate to a given concrete case once all of the relevant features of the given constellation of circumstances have been accorded due weight in the situational description. Thus, principles of appropriateness and the exhaustion of all relevant contextual features come into play here. And practical reason thereby also comes into play in discourses of application.

Abstraction from Concrete Ethical Life

Neo-Aristotelians have a valid point when they criticize the atomistic concept of the person and the contractualist concept of society that have informed virtually every modern approach in moral and legal theory. But Hegel, who was among the first to spell out this criticism, was equally aware that there is also an element of truth in these modern abstractions. Individualistic approaches give expression to the notions of autonomy and freedom of conscience that are indissociable from the self-understanding of the modern period. Thus, Kant too grounded moral consciousness in the intelligible ego of the individual subject. What he had in view were the limit situations in which moral insights have to be defended against the prejudices of the majority or even of a prejudiced society as a whole. Idealist thought was influenced by Luther's Protestant maxim, "Here I stand, I can do no other." American Pragmatism, also a child of the Protestant spirit, must be credited with the achievement of overcoming the individualism of contract theories without sacrificing the moral contents that had previously been situated in the conscience of the individual. Peirce, Royce, and Mead developed the ideas of an unlimited communication community and a universal discourse that represent an alternative to abstract internality because they transcend all existing states of affairs while retaining the character of a *public* court of appeal. Already the notion of "ideal role taking" preserves the characteristics of a transcendental socialization and invokes the social bond that unites humanity as a whole.

With the notion of an ideally extended communication community as its point of reference, moral theory also leaves behind all presocial concepts of the person. Individuation is merely the reverse side of socialization. Only in relations of reciprocal recognition can a person constitute and reproduce his identity. Even the innermost essence of a person is internally connected with the outermost periphery of a far-flung network of communicative relations. Only in the aggregate of his communicative expressions does a person become identical with himself. The ego is also rendered vulnerable by the social interactions through which it is formed—by the dependencies in which it becomes implicated and the contingencies to which it is exposed. Morality serves to counterbalance this susceptibility implicit in the very process of socialization.

But in that case it is not possible to deduce a substantive normative concept of autonomy from the necessary presuppositions of the teleological action of isolated subjects.[24] To achieve this goal we must take the model of action oriented to reaching understanding as our point of departure. In communicative action speaker and hearer assume that their perspectives are interchangeable. By entering into an interpersonal relation in the performative attitude, they commit themselves to recognizing each other symmetrically as responsible subjects capable of orienting their actions to validity claims. And their behavioral expectations remain reciprocally interconnected in the normative context of the lifeworld. In this way the necessary presuppositions of communicative action constitute an infrastructure of possible communication constructed around a moral core—the idea of unforced intersubjectivity. Since argumentative praxis is merely a reflexive form of communicative action, it transmits the normative force of its presuppositions to the communicative presuppositions of argumentation. Only at this level do the perspectives, relations of recognition, and normative expectations built into communicative action become *completely reversible* in all relevant respects, for participants in argumentation are credited with the ability to distance themselves temporarily from the normative spectrum of all existing forms of life.

The foregoing prefigures an ethics of discourse that can explain how Kohlberg can postulate an internal connection between cognitive abilities and moral consciousness. Robert Selman, for example, has extended research on perspective taking into the field of interpersonal negotiation strategies.[25] These and similar investigations[26] provide empirical confirmation of the underlying intuition that an intersubjective interpretation of the moral point of view can be pursued as far as the presuppositional analysis of action oriented to reaching understanding. This coheres in turn with the Aristotelian insight that we acquire our moral intuitions not through philosophical instruction or other explicit communications but in an implicit manner through socialization. Because they must take place in the medium of communicative action, all socialization processes are shaped by the structure of this type of action, but the presuppositions of communicative action already carry within themselves the germ of morality.

V

From his dissertation onward, Kohlberg held steadfastly to his theoretical program. He repeatedly analyzed the same data and elaborated in an ever more precise fashion the same fascinating ideas. This attitude contrasts impressively with the latent opportunism of institutionalized research. His bearing made Kohlberg a philosopher among scientists, though one who never deviated from the standards of a true researcher. He was, on the other hand, so much a philosopher that his conception of how his theory should be implemented in educational praxis bordered on the Platonic. He walked a stretch of the road that led a disillusioned Piaget from philosophy to psychology, but in the opposite direction. In the role of psychologist, he embodied more completely the classical self-understanding of philosophy than the majority of his philosopher colleagues who are intimidated by the authority of the sciences.

4

To Seek to Salvage an Unconditional Meaning Without God Is a Futile Undertaking: Reflections on a Remark of Max Horkheimer

Max Horkheimer's late philosophy, scattered throughout various notes and essays, takes the form of reflections from a damaged life. Alfred Schmidt has deciphered in them the outline of a systematic intention. His proof is an indirect one, using Horkheimer's tools as a key to unlock the door to Schopenhauer's philosophy of religion.[1] These illuminating reconstructions have impressed upon me the reasons and motives that induced Horkheimer to look to Schopenhauer in his quest for a religion that could satisfy the longing for perfect justice. Horkheimer's interest in the doctrines of Judaism and Christianity was spurred less by a concern with God as such than with the redemptive power of God's will. The injustice that comes to pass in a suffering creature should not be permitted to have the last word. At times it seems as if Horkheimer wanted to put the religious promise of redemption directly at the service of morality. At one point he explained the prohibition of images in terms of the notion that "in the Jewish religion what is important is not how things stand with God, but how they stand with men."[2] Schopenhauer's metaphysics seemed to offer a resolution of an aporia in which Horkheimer had become involved in consequence of two equally strong convictions. For him too, the critical task of philosophy consisted essentially in salvaging the truth in religion in the spirit of the Enlightenment; nevertheless, it was clear to him that "one cannot secularize religion without giving it up."[3]

This aporia has haunted Greek philosophy like a shadow from the moment of its initial encounter with the Jewish and Christian tradi-

metaphysics – 1) div. of philosophy incl. ontology + epistemology 2) philosophy of ontology + cosmology

Metaphysical – of or relating to the transcendent or supernatural

ontology – relations of being to things – nature +

Reflections on a Remark of Max Horkheimer

tion onward. In Horkheimer's case, it is made even more acute by his profound skepticism concerning reason. What for him is the essential substance of religion—morality—is no longer tied to reason. Horkheimer praises the dark writers of the bourgeoisie for having "trumpeted far and wide the impossibility of deriving from reason any fundamental argument against murder."[4] I have to admit that this remark irritates me now no less than it did almost four decades ago when I first read it. I have never been altogether convinced of the cogency of the skepticism concerning reason underlying Hork-heimer's ambivalence toward religion. The idea that it is vain to strive for unconditional meaning without God betrays not just a metaphys-ical need; the remark is itself an instance of the metaphysics that not only philosophers but even theologians themselves must today get along without.

Before I attempt to back up this objection, I want to clarify the fundamental moral intuition that guided Horkheimer throughout his life; I will then turn to the kinship between religion and philos-ophy that Horkheimer never lost from sight and, finally, reveal the premises on which he based his appropriation of Schopenhauer's negative metaphysics. In what follows I draw on notes and essays that Alfred Schmidt made available to the public[5] and to whose systematic import he was first to draw attention.[6]

I

Once the rationality of the remorse experienced by a religiously tutored conscience is rejected by a secularized world, its place is taken by the moral sentiment of compassion. When Horkheimer expressly defines the good tautologically as the attempt to abolish evil, he has in view a solidarity with the suffering of vulnerable and forsaken creatures provoked by outrage against concrete injustices. The re-conciling power of compassion does not stand in opposition to the galvanizing power of rebellion against a world devoid of atonement and reparation for injustice. Solidarity and justice are two sides of the coin; hence, the ethics of compassion does not dispute the legitimacy of the morality of justice but merely frees it from the rigidity of the ethics of conscience. Otherwise the Kantian pathos expressed in Horkheimer's injunction "to proceed into the desert in spite of everything, even if hope were lost" would be incomprehensible.[7] And under the banner "necessary futility," Horkheimer does not shrink from drawing the almost Protestant conclusion: "It is true that the individual cannot change the course of the world. But if his whole life is not a gesture of wild despair that revolts against it, he will fail to realize that infinitely small, insignificant, futile, nugatory modicum of good of which he is capable as an individual."[8] The shared fate of exposure to the infinitude of an indifferent universe may awaken a feeling of solidarity in human beings, but among the community of the forsaken, the hope of solidarity and pity for one's neighbor must not undermine equal respect for everyone. Moral feelings imbued with a sense of justice are not just spontaneous impulses; they are more intuitions than impulses. In them a correct insight, in an emphatic sense of "correct," comes to expression. The positivists "have not the faintest inkling that hatred of the decent and admiration for the depraved are inverted impulses not just before the tribunal of custom, but of truth, and that they are not merely reprehensible in an ideological sense, but are objectively debased experiences and reactions."[9]

Horkheimer is so secure in his fundamental moral intuitions that he can qualify them only as "correct insights." This moral cognitivism seems to place him firmly in the Kantian camp. Nevertheless, he is so profoundly influenced by the dialectic of enlightenment that he repeatedly disputes the role Kant still accorded practical reason. What remains is only a "formalistic reason" that is no "more closely allied to morality than to immorality."[10] Material investigations alone could overcome this sterile formalism, though indeed only in a paradoxical manner. Unable to specify the good, a critical theory of society should reveal specific injustices in given cases. Because this theory, in its skepticism toward reason, no longer maintains a positive relation to the normative contents it uncovers step by step in the criticism of unjust conditions, it must borrow its normative orientations from a cultural ethos that has already been superseded—that of a metaphysically grounded theology. The latter preserves the legacy of a *substantive* reason that has since been rendered impotent.

Horkheimer is under no illusions about the vertiginous nature of this theoretical undertaking. Social theory "has superseded theology but has no new heaven to which it can point, not even a mundane one. Of course, social theory cannot completely efface [heaven's] traces and hence is repeatedly questioned about how it is to be attained—as though it were not precisely the discovery of social theory that the heaven to which one can point the way is no heaven."[11] No theory could possibly accommodate itself to this Kafkaesque figure of thought, at least not without embracing an aesthetic mode of expression and becoming literature. Hence, the thoughts of the late Horkheimer circle around the idea of a theology that *must* be "displaced" by the critical and self-critical activity of reason, yet which, in its capacity as justifying morality's claim to unconditionality, *cannot* be replaced by reason. Horkheimer's late philosophy may be understood as wrestling with this dilemma and his interpretation of Schopenhauerian metaphysics as a proposal for resolving it.

In the essay entitled "Theism-Atheism," Horkheimer traces the development of the Hellenistic notion of an interrelation between theology and metaphysics up to the great metaphysical systems in which theology and natural philosophy converged. He is interested above all in the militant atheism of the eighteenth century that "was able to promote rather than to stifle interest in religion."[12] Even the materialistic antithesis to Christianity that substituted "Nature" for "God" and merely readjusted the fundamental concepts accordingly still remained caught up in the metaphysical framework of worldviews. Kant's critique of metaphysics opened the door to the mystical and messianic currents that, from Baader and Schelling to Hegel and Marx, found their way into philosophy. Horkheimer was aware of the theological current in Marxist theory from the beginning: with the idea of a just society, the Enlightenment opened up the prospect of a new beyond in the here and now; the spirit of the Gospel was now to reach worldly fulfillment through the march of history.

The secular sublation (*Aufhebung*) of ontotheology by the philosophy of history has profoundly equivocal implications. On the one hand, philosophy becomes disguised theology and salvages the latter's essential content. The very meaning of atheism itself ensures the enduring relevance of theism: "Only those who employed the word in a derogatory sense understood it as the opposite of religion. Those who professed atheism at a time when religion still had power were wont to identify themselves more sincerely with the theistic precept of devotion to one's neighbor and other creatures as such than most of the adherents and fellow travelers of the various religious confessions."[13] On the other hand, philosophy can recover the idea of the unconditioned only in the medium of a reason that has in the interim sacrificed the infinite on the altar of historical contingency and has abjured the unconditioned. A reason that can appeal to no authority higher than that of the sciences is a naturalized faculty that has regressed to intelligence in the service of pure self-affirmation; it measures itself by the yardstick of functional contributions and technical successes, and not by a mode of validity that transcends space and time: "With God dies eternal truth."[14] *In the wake of* the Enlightenment, the truth in religion can be salvaged only in a way that annihilates truth. A critical theory that sees itself as the "successor" to theology finds itself in this unhappy predicament because everything to do with morality ultimately derives from theology.

II

The rational sublation of theology and its essential contents: how can this still be accomplished in the present day, in the light of the irreversible critique of metaphysics, without destroying the import of religious doctrines or of reason itself? With this question Horkheimer, the pessimistic materialist, appeals to Schopenhauer, the pessimistic idealist. On Horkheimer's surprising interpretation, Schopenhauer's enduring importance lies in the fact that his thoroughgoing negativism salvages the "spirit of the Gospels." According to Horkheimer, Schopenhauer accomplished the improbable feat of providing an atheistic justification of the morality underlying theology, and thus of preserving religion in the absence of God.

In the world as will and representation, Horkheimer discerns, first, the sterile Darwinian operation of instrumental reason degraded to a tool of self-preservation, which—up to and including a globally objectifying scientific intellect—is dominated by a blind and indefatigable will to life that pits one subject against another. On the other hand, precisely this reflection on the abysmally negative ground of being is supposed to awaken in subjects who seek remorselessly to dominate one another some inkling of their *common* fate and an awareness that all manifestations of life are pervaded by an *identical* will: "If the realm of appearances, sensible reality, is not the work of positive divine power, an expression of inherently good, eternal Being, but of a will that affirms itself in everything finite, that is mirrored in a distorted fashion in multiplicity, and yet that remains at a profound level identical, then everyone has reason to view himself as one with all others, not with their specific motives, but with their entanglement in delusion and guilt, their drivenness, joy and decline. The life and fate of the founder of Christianity becomes a model, no longer based on commands but on insight into the inner constitution of the world."[15]

What fascinated Horkheimer in Schopenhauer is the prospect of a metaphysical justification of morality through insight into the constitution of the world as a whole, yet in such a way that this insight is at the same time directed against central assumptions of metaphysics and coheres with postmetaphysical skepticism concerning reason. Negative metaphysics upholds the distinction between essence and appearance only with an inversion of the order of priority between them—inverted Platonism. This in turn grounds the expectation that insight into the "pitiless structure of infinitude" could produce "a community of the forsaken." However, Horkheimer is aware of the shadow of performative self-contradiction that has haunted all negative metaphysics since Schopenhauer and Nietzsche. Even if we prescind from epistemological misgivings about intuitive, bodily access to the thing-in-itself, it remains mysterious how the turning of the irrational world-will against itself that constrains it to continual reflection will come about: "The metaphysics of the irrational will as the essence of the world must lead to reflection on the problematic of truth."[16] In Schmidt's formulation of the dilemma, "If the essence of the world is irrational, then that cannot remain incidental to the truth claim of precisely this thesis."[17] In the light of this result, the statement that it is futile to seek to salvage unconditional meaning without God can also be understood as a criticism of Schopenhauer, as a critique of the "last great philosophical attempt to rescue the essential core of Christianity."[18]

In the final analysis, Horkheimer's ambiguous formulations vacillate between Schopenhauer's negative-metaphysical justification of morality and a return to the faith of his forefathers. This unresolved argumentative impasse leads me to reexamine the premise from which Horkheimer's late philosophy begins: that "formalistic" reason, or the procedural reason that remains under conditions of postmetaphysical thought, is equally indifferent to morality and immorality. As far as I can discern, Horkheimer's skeptical assertion rests primarily on the contemporary experience of Stalinism and on a conceptual argument that presupposes the ontological concept of truth.

III

Horkheimer's thought is influenced even more than Adorno's by the harrowing historical fact that the ideals of freedom, solidarity, and justice deriving from practical reason, which inspired the French Revolution and were reappropriated in Marx's critique of society, led not to socialism but to barbarism under the guise of socialism: "The vision of instituting justice and freedom in the world which underlay Kant's thought has been transformed into the mobilization of nations. With each revolt that followed in the wake of the great revolution in France, it seems, the humanistic elements atrophied while nationalism thrived. In this century it was socialism itself that orchestrated the supreme farce of perverting the pledge to humanity into an intransigent cult of the state. . . . What Lenin and the majority of his comrades aspired to before assuming power was a free and just society. In reality they prepared the way for a totalitarian bureaucracy under whose sway there was no more freedom than in the tsarist empire. That the new China is entering on a phase of barbarism is plain to see."[19] From this experience Horkheimer drew consequences for the reconstruction of the architectonic of reason announced in the concept of "instrumental reason." There is no longer any difference between the operation of the understanding in the service of subjective self-assertion, which imposes its categories on everything and transforms it into an object, and reason as the faculty of ideas whose place understanding has usurped. Indeed, the ideas themselves have been caught up in the dynamic of reification; elevated to absolute ends, they retain merely a functional significance for *other* ends. But by exhausting the supply of ideas in this way, every claim that points beyond instrumental rationality loses its transcending power; truth and morality forfeit their unconditional meaning.

Thinking that is sensitive to historical changes, even down to its fundamental concepts, submits itself to the tribunal of new experience. Thus, it is not inappropriate to ask whether the bankruptcy of state socialism that has in the interim become apparent does not offer *other* lessons, for this bankruptcy is partly the doing of ideas that the regime, while distancing itself from them ever further, misused for the purposes of its own legitimation because—which is more important—it *had* to appeal to them. A system that collapsed despite its brutal Orwellian apparatus of oppression because social conditions eloquently contradicted everything prefigured by its legitimating ideas, manifestly cannot *dispose of the inner logic of these ideas as it wishes.* In the ideas of the constitutionally embodied republican tradition, however egregiously abused, there persists the element of existing reason that resisted the "dialectic of enlightenment" by eluding the leveling gaze of the negative philosophy of history.

The controversy surrounding this thesis could be resolved only by recourse to material analyses. As a consequence, I will limit myself to the conceptual argument that Horkheimer develops from the critique of instrumental reason.

Horkheimer's assertion that the difference between reason and understanding has *become obsolete* in the course of the world-historical process still presupposed, in contrast to contemporary poststructuralism, that we can *recall* the emphatic concept of reason. The critical import of "instrumental reason" is first thrown into relief by this act of recollection. And through anamnetic retrieval of the substantive reason of religious and metaphysical worldviews, we can reassure ourselves of the unconditionality that concepts such as truth and morality once carried with them before they succumbed to positivistic and functionalistic disintegration. An Absolute or Unconditional becomes accessible to philosophy only together with justification of the world as a whole, and hence only as metaphysics. But philosophy remains true to its metaphysical beginnings only as long as it attempts "to imitate positive theology" and proceeds on the assumption that cognizing reason rediscovers itself in the rationally structured world or itself actually confers a rational structure on nature and history. As soon as the world "in its essence, by contrast, does *not* of necessity cohere with the spirit, philosophical confidence in the being of truth dissipates completely. Then truth is henceforth sublated only in transient human beings themselves and becomes as transient as they are."[20]

It never occurred to Horkheimer that there might be a difference between "instrumental" and "formal" reason. Moreover, he unceremoniously assimilated procedural reason—which no longer makes the validity of its results dependent on the rational organization of the world but on the rationality of procedures through which it solves its problems—to instrumental reason. Horkheimer assumes that there cannot be truth without an Absolute, without a world-transcending power "in which truth is sublated." Without ontological anchoring, the concept of truth is exposed to the inner-worldly contingencies of mortal men and their changing situations; without it, truth is no longer an idea but merely a weapon in the struggle of life. Human knowledge, including moral insight, can lay claim to truth, he believes, only if it judges itself in terms of relations between it and what is as these relations are manifested to the divine intelligence alone. In contrast to this strangely traditional conception, in the final section I will argue for a modern alternative—a concept of communicative reason that enables us to recover the meaning of the unconditioned without recourse to metaphysics. But first we must clarify the true motive that causes Horkheimer to hold fast to the classical concept of truth as *adaequatio intellectus ad rem*.

Decisive for Horkheimer's persistence in maintaining an ontological anchoring of truth are the ethical reflections he attributes to Schopenhauer: only insight into the identity of all life, into a unitary ground of being, even if it be irrational, in which all individual appearances are brought into harmony with one another, "can ground solidarity with all creatures long before death."[21] The unified thought of metaphysics renders plausible why it should be that the effort to overcome egoism would find a sympathetic response in the constitution of the world. For this reason alone, unity takes precedence over multiplicity for philosophers, the unconditional occurs only in the singular, and the one God has greater importance for Jews and Christians than the multiple deities of antiquity. It is the peculiar fate of bourgeois culture that individuals entrench themselves in their particularity and thereby reduce individualism to a falsehood. Horkheimer so emphatically regards this societal state of nature of competitive society as the fundamental problem of morality that for him justice and solidarity become synonymous with "renouncing the self-assertion of the isolated ego." Egoism has congealed to such an extent into an inverted condition of things that the transition from self-love to devotion to others is unthinkable without metaphysical assurance of the prior unity of an unfathomable world-will that provokes us to insight into a possible solidarity of the destitute: "Schopenhauer drew the necessary consequences: the insight into the baseness of one's own life which cannot be separated from the suffering of other creatures is correct; the identification with those who suffer, with man and animal, is correct, the renunciation of self-love, of the drive to individual well-being as the ultimate goal; and the induction after death into the general, the non-personal, the nothing is desirable."[22] The individuated will is base only when it turns itself against others; it becomes good when, through compassion, it recognizes its true identity with all other beings.

IV

Already in *The Dialectic of Enlightenment* Horkheimer credits de Sade and Nietzsche with the recognition that "after the formalization of reason, compassion still remained, so to speak, as the sensual consciousness of the identity of the general and the particular, as naturalized mediation."[23] On the Schopenhauerian interpretation, of course, compassion cannot assume the role of dialectical *mediation* between individual and society, between equal respect for all and the solidarity of each with all. Here it is solely a matter of the abstract self-overcoming of individuality, of the dissolution of the individual in an all-encompassing oneness. But with this the very idea in which the moral substance of Christianity consists is abrogated. Those who at the Last Judgment come, one after the other, before the eyes of God as unrepresentable individuals stripped of the mantle of worldly goods and honors—and hence as equals—in the expectation of receiving a fair judgment, experience themselves as *fully individuated beings* who must give an account of their life histories in full responsibility for their actions. Together with this idea, however, the profound intuition that the bond between solidarity and justice must not be severed must also be given up.

Admittedly, in this respect Horkheimer does not follow Schopenhauer without misgivings. His interpretation of the Ninety-first Psalm reveals his struggle to overcome a certain dissonance. The doctrine of the individual soul, he writes, has an additional significance in Judaism, one unadulterated by the expectation of an afterlife: "The idea of continued existence signifies in the first instance, not the after-life, but the identification with the nation so crassly distorted by modern nationalism, which has its prehistory in the bible. By conducting his life in accordance with the Torah, by spending days, months, years in obedience to the Law, the individual becomes so much one with others despite personal differences that after his death he continues to exist through those who survive him, in their observance of tradition, of love for the family and the tribe, in the expectation that at some time things may still become better in the world. . . . Not unlike the figure of Jesus in Christianity, Judaism *as a whole* bore witness to redemption."[24] Horkheimer tries to circumvent the problem of superseding the individual, of repudiating inalienable individuality, by changing the question. The issue is not whether the kingdom of the Messiah is of this world but whether the fundamental moral intuition of Judaism and Christianity to which Horkheimer unwaveringly adheres can ultimately be adequately explained without reference to the unrestricted *individuation* possible in a *universal* confederation.

The moral impulse of unwillingness to resign oneself to the force of circumstances that have the effect of isolating the individual and to secure the happiness and power of one person only at the cost of the misfortune and powerlessness of another—this impulse confirms Horkheimer in the view that the reconciling potential of solidarity with those who suffer can be realized only if individuals renounce themselves as individuals. He fails to see that the danger of a nationalistic distortion of the identificatory bond with the nation arises precisely at the moment when false solidarity permits individuals to be subsumed into the collectivity. Unified metaphysical thought—however negatively accented—transposes solidarity, which has its proper place in linguistic intersubjectivity, communication, and individuating socialization, into the identity of an underlying essence, the undifferentiated negativity of the world-will.

Quite a different, dialectical unity is produced in communication in which the structure of language inscribes the gap between I and Thou. The structure of linguistic intersubjectivity makes harmony between the integration of autonomy and devotion to others possible for us—in other words, a reconciliation that does not efface differences. Horkheimer is by no means deaf to this promise of reconciliation inherent in language itself. At one point he puts it trenchantly: "Language, whether it wants to or not, must lay claim to truth."[25] He also recognizes that we have to take into account the pragmatic dimension of language use, for the context-transcending truth-claim of speech cannot be grasped from the blinkered perspective of a semantics that reduces utterances to propositions: "Truth in speech is not properly predicated of detached, naked judgments, as though printed on a piece of paper, but of the conduct of the speaker toward the world that is expressed in the judgment and concentrates itself in this place."[26] What Horkheimer has in mind is clearly the theological tradition, extending from Augustine through logos mysticism to radical Protestantism, that appeals to the originary character of the divine Word and to language as the medium of the divine message to man: "But theological metaphysics is in the right against positivism, because no proposition can avoid raising the impossible claim, not merely to an anticipated result, to success, as positivism maintains, but to truth in the proper sense, regardless of whether the speaker reflects on it or not."[27] Prayer, in which the believer seeks contact with God, would lose its categorial difference from incantation and regress to the level of magic if we confused the illocutionary force of our assertions with their perlocutionary effects, as does the unrealizable program of linguistic nominalism.

But these insights remain sporadic. Horkheimer fails to treat them as clues to a language-pragmatical explanation of the *unconditional* meaning associated with *unavoidable* truth claims. His skepticism toward reason is so thoroughgoing that he can no longer see room for communicative action in the world as it is now constituted: "Today talk has become stale and those who do not want to listen are not altogether wrong. . . . Speaking has had its day. Indeed so has action, at least insofar as it was once related to speech."[28]

V

His pessimistic diagnosis of the times is not the only reason that Horkheimer refrains from seriously entertaining the question of how something we accomplish on a daily basis—orienting our action to context-transcending validity claims—is possible. In fact, a profane answer to this question, such as the one proposed by Peirce, for instance, could not have *sufficiently* satisfied Horkheimer's metaphysical need for religion.

Horkheimer equated Kant's formalistic reason with instrumental reason. But Peirce reinterprets Kantian formalism in the direction of a pragmatics of language and construes reason in procedural terms. The process of sign interpretation achieves self-awareness at the level of argumentation. Peirce now shows how this nonquotidian form of communication is commensurate with the "unconditional meaning" of truth and of context-transcending validity claims in general. He conceives of truth as the redeemability of a truth claim under the communicative conditions of an ideal community of interpreters— that is, one extended ideally in social space and historical time. The counterfactual appeal to an *unlimited* communication community of this kind replaces the moment of infinitude or the supratemporal character of "unconditionality" with the idea of an open yet goal-directed process of interpretation that transcends the boundaries of social space *from within* from the perspective of an existence situated *in the world. In time,* learning processes are to form an arch bridging all temporal distance; *in the world,* the conditions we assume are at least sufficiently fulfilled in every argument are to be realized. We are intuitively aware that we cannot rationally *convince* anyone, not even ourselves, of something if we do not accept as our common point of departure that all voices that are at all relevant should be heard, that the best arguments available given the current state of our knowledge should be expressed, and that only the unforced force of the better argument should determine the "yes" and "no" responses of participants.

The tension between the intelligible realm and the realm of phenomena is thereby shifted to general presuppositions of communication, which—despite their ideal and only approximately realizable content—participants must in every case actually accept if they wish to thematize a controversial truth claim. The idealizing force of these transcending anticipations penetrates into the very heart of everyday communicative praxis, for even the most fleeting speech-act-offer, the most conventional "yes" or "no," *point* to potential reasons, and hence to the ideally extended audience they must convince if they are valid. The ideal moment of unconditionality is deeply rooted in factual processes of communication because validity claims are Janus faced: as universal, they outstrip every given context; at the same time, they must be raised and gain acceptance here and now if they are to sustain an agreement capable of coordinating action. In communicative action, we orient ourselves to validity claims that we can raise only as a matter of fact in the context of *our* language, of *our* form of life, whereas the redeemability implicitly co-posited points beyond the provinciality of the given historical context. Whoever employs a language with a view to reaching understanding lays himself open to a transcendence from within. He is left without any choice because he masters the structure of language through the intentionality of the spoken word. Linguistic intentionality outstrips subjects but without *subjugating* them.

Postmetaphysical thought differs from religion in that it recovers the meaning of the unconditional without recourse to God or an Absolute. Horkheimer's dictum would have been justified only if by "unconditional meaning" he had meant something different from the notion of unconditionality that also belongs to the meaning of truth as one of its moments. The significance of unconditionality is not to be confused with an unconditional meaning that offers consolation. On the premises of postmetaphysical thought, philosophy cannot provide a substitute for the consolation whereby religion invests unavoidable suffering and unrecompensed injustice, the contingencies of need, loneliness, sickness, and death, with new significance and teaches us to bear them. But even today philosophy can explicate the moral point of view from which we can judge something impartially as just or unjust; to this extent, communicative reason is by no means equally indifferent to morality and immorality. However, it is altogether a different matter to provide a motivating response to the question of why we should follow our moral insights or why we should be moral ar all. In *this* respect, it may perhaps be said that to seek to salvage an unconditional meaning without God is a futile undertaking, for it belongs to the peculiar dignity of philosophy to maintain adamantly that no validity claim can have cognitive import unless it is vindicated before the tribunal of justificatory discourse.

5

Morality, Society, and Ethics: An Interview with Torben Hviid Nielsen

Torben Hviid Nielsen: The main topic of discussion will be your views on moral theory and ethics, particularly in the form they have assumed since the publication of *Theorie des kommunikativen Handelns* in 1981.[1] In the first part we will concentrate on the concept of morality and the relation between justice, law, and care. The second part will deal with questions concerning the universal-pragmatic justification of discourse ethics. The focus will be on the validity of norms, the status of the so-called ideal speech situation, and the differentiation between the justification of norms and the procedure of democratic will formation. And in the third part we will discuss morality and ethics in relation to the notions of system and lifeworld.

I

THN: How should we understand the development that has led you from the sociological critique of the pathologies of modernity in *The Theory of Communicative Action* to the moral theory developed in *Moral Consciousness and Communicative Action*[2] and the subsequent series of articles and lectures? Can discourse ethics be seen as a philosophical answer, from the perspective of the individual, to the sociological question of the proper, nonpathological relation between system and lifeworld in the modern world? Why have you concentrated since 1981 on issues in philosophical ethics rather than on this sociological question left open in *Theory of Communicative Action*?

Jürgen Habermas: I see this differently. What was of primary importance for the philosophical foundations of *The Theory of Communicative
Action* was the introduction of the linguistic-pragmatic concept of
communicative rationality. Granted, I did deal with legal and moral
development following Weber and Durkheim, but the two theoretical
approaches I drew upon in my discussion, discourse ethics and Kohlberg's theory of stages of moral consciousness, remained in the background at that time. Only in subsequent years did I turn my attention
directly to these matters that had been left to one side. The title essay
of *Moral Consciousness and Communicative Action* dates back to my time
at the Max Planck Institute at Starnberg and reflects the kind of
research undertaken there. The essay on discourse ethics is the result
of seminars I held directly after my return to Frankfurt, and hence
in a philosophy department. Since 1983 I have been working in
different professional surroundings, which tends to influence the
direction of research.

Your assumption is also mistaken in that this concern with questions
of moral theory simply takes up again a number of problems I had
already discussed in 1973 in the final part of *Legitimationsprobleme im
Spätkapitalismus.*[3] At that time I proposed a model of "suppressed
generalizable interests" in order to clarify the sense in which it is
possible to distinguish between "general" and "particular" interests.
Later, in *The Theory of Communicative Action* I did not return to this;
rather, as you correctly point out, I attempted to describe social
pathologies by means of a two-level concept of society, that is, as
deformations that can be traced back to disruptions in the reproduction of the lifeworld (2:142ff.). There I was particularly interested in
pathologies that arise when systemic imbalances that are symptomatic
of crisis in the economy or the state apparatus are displaced onto the
lifeworld and interfere with its symbolic reproduction (2:385ff.). Had
I wanted to analyze more closely this phenomenon of reification of
communicative relationships through monetarization and bureaucra-
tization—that is, the phenomenon to which Marx attached the global
term *alienation*—moral-theoretical considerations would have been
completely out of place. Rather, a more careful definition of the
concept of systematically distorted communication would have been
needed. This I considered—on the basis of empirical research on
pathologies within the family—as the interpersonal counterpart of

the intrapsychical disturbances that psychoanalysis traces back to the unconscious avoidance of conflict and explains in terms of corresponding defense mechanisms. But since 1974 I have not returned to these ideas on communication pathologies that arise at the level of elementary interactions.[4] I still consider my suggestions relevant, by the way, and I think that this is confirmed by the interesting work of Jim Bohman and Martin Löw-Beer.

THN: You present discourse ethics as both the continuation and completion of your earlier theoretical work on ethics and a response to the political agenda of the public discussions of the 1980s. Do you feel a certain tension between these two concerns, between your own theoretical development, which points back to questions raised in the 1960s, and the political themes of the 1980s? Have these themes contributed to your shift of emphasis from a more social, "Hegelian" ethics to a more individual, "Kantian" conception of morality?

JH: Actually, my research program has remained the *same* since about 1970, since the reflections on formal pragmatics and the discourse theory of truth first presented in the Christian Gauss Lectures.[5] On the other hand, anyone who is at all sensitive to politics and the political impact of theories is bound to react to changed contexts. In the 1960s it was necessary to engage the theories of technocracy of one group and in the early 1970s the crisis theories of another. And since the mid-1970s I have felt the pressure of the neoconservative and the poststructuralist critiques of reason, to which I responded with the concept of communicative rationality. This constellation remained unchanged in the 1980s, and it was for this reason that I continued to work on a critique of the philosophy of consciousness and sought to lend it greater philosophical precision. In *Der Philosophische Diskurs der Moderne* (1985) I tried to show that "representational thinking" can be replaced by something other than the defeatism of the deconstructionists or the contextualism of the neo-Aristotelians.[6]

It was in connection with this intersubjective self-criticism of reason that I also reacted to the rather suspect popularity enjoyed by philosophical ethics at present and proceeded to work out the issues raised by Mead's communicative ethics, which had always interested me.[7] Hence discourse ethics, like Mead's work, takes its lead from intuitions underlying Kantian moral theory while eschewing the latter's individualistic premises.

THN: Discourse ethics refers specifically to modern conditions of life, as do *The Theory of Communicative Action* and *The Philosophical Discourse of Modernity.* They defend the Enlightenment and modernity against traditionalism, on the one hand, and postmodernism, on the other. Thus, both you and one of your main opponents, the neo-Aristotelian Alasdair MacIntyre, agree that the concept of virtue, for instance, is incompatible with modern life. Why is it that all traditional, substantive moralities have become obsolete? And what is your response—a nonsubstantive morality that is better warranted than MacIntyre's answer, better, that is, than the proposed return to traditional virtues?

JH: In my opinion, *After Virtue* has two principal weaknesses. First, MacIntyre makes things too easy for himself from a critical perspective by selecting in Alan Gewirth an untypical and rather easily criticizable example of a universalistic position instead of dealing with Rawls or Dworkin or Apel. Second, his appeal to the Aristotelian concept of praxis gets him into trouble as soon as he tries to extract a universal core from the pluralism of equally legitimate forms of life that is unavoidable in modernity. Where can he find an equivalent for what Aristotle could still fall back on—I mean a substitute for the metaphysical preeminence of the polis as the exemplary form of life in which people (all those, that is, who do not remain barbarians) could realize the goal of a good life? Under modern conditions, philosophy can no longer stand in judgment over the multiplicity of individual life projects and collective forms of life, and how one lives one's life becomes the sole responsibility of socialized individuals themselves and must be judged from the participant perspective. Hence, what is capable of commanding universal assent becomes restricted to the *procedure* of rational will formation.

THN: Discourse ethics offers a view of ethics that is narrow or minimal in two respects: its approach is deontological, cognitivistic, formalistic, and universalistic, and it focuses on issues of justice as its primary subject matter. Thus, the traditional concern with the good or happiness (or a combination of both) is excluded. Why this exclusive focus on justice? Do you regard this as a necessary feature of all modern ethical theories?

JH: Under modern conditions of life none of the various rival traditions can claim prima facie general validity any longer. Even in answering questions of direct practical relevance, convincing reasons can no longer appeal to the authority of unquestioned traditions. If we do not want to settle questions concerning the normative regulation of our everyday coexistence by open or covert force—by coercion, influence, or the power of the stronger interest—but by the unforced conviction of a rationally motivated agreement, then we must concentrate on those questions that are amenable to impartial judgment. We can't expect to find a generally binding answer when we ask what is good for me or for us or for them; instead, we must ask what is *equally good for all.* This "moral point of view" throws a sharp, but narrow, spotlight that picks out from the mass of evaluative questions practical conflicts that can be *resolved* by appeal to a generalizable interest; in other words, questions of justice.

In saying this, I do not mean that questions of justice are the only relevant questions. Usually ethical-existential questions are of far more pressing concern for us—problems, that is, that force the individual or group to clarify who they are and who they would like to be. Such problems of self-clarification may well be of greater concern to us than questions of justice. But only the latter are so structured that they can be resolved equitably in the equal interest of all. Moral judgments must meet with agreement from the perspective of all those possibly affected and not, as with ethical questions, merely from the perspective of some individual's or group's self-understanding or worldview. Hence moral theories, if they adopt a cognitivist approach, are essentially theories of justice.

THN: Why is it that the sphere of "justice" cannot be further differentiated? Why should the fragmentation of modernity come to a halt before the three Kantian critiques and the corresponding spheres of value, so that questions of justice can be treated only under a single aspect? Michael Walzer's book *Spheres of Justice* may be read as an extended argument for dividing justice into different spheres (of membership, welfare, the economy, education, and so on); in this way he seeks to defend pluralism and equality: "the principles of justice are themselves pluralistic in form . . . different social goods ought to be distributed for different reasons, in accordance with different procedures, by different agents."[8]

JH: I agree entirely with this statement though not with the consequences Walzer wishes to draw from it.

That a norm is just or in the general interest means nothing more than that it is worthy of recognition or is valid. Justice is not something material, not a determinate "value," but a dimension of validity. Just as descriptive statements can be true, and thus express what is the case, so too normative statements can be right and express what has to be done. Individual principles or norms that have a specific content are situated on a different level, regardless of whether they are actually valid.

For example, different principles of distributive justice exist. There are material principles of justice, such as "To each according to his needs" or "To each according to his merits" or "Equal shares for all." Principles of equal rights, such as the precepts of equal respect for all, of equal treatment, or of equity in the application of the law, address a different kind of problem. What is at issue here is not the distribution of goods or opportunities but the protection of freedom and inviolability. Now all of these principles of justice can be justified from the perspective of universalizability and can claim prima facie validity. But only in their application to particular concrete cases will it transpire *which* of the competing principles is the most appropriate in the *given* context.

This is the task of discourses of application. Within the family, for instance, conflicts of distribution will tend to be decided on the principle of need rather than on the principle of merit, whereas the situation may well be the reverse in cases of conflicts of distribution at the level of society as a whole. It depends on which principle *best fits* a given situation in the light of the most exhaustive possible description of its relevant features. But I find the idea of a universal correlation of principles of justice with spheres of action highly problematic. The kinds of considerations Walzer entertains could be accommodated in discourses of application, but then they would have to prove themselves in each particular instance in its own right.

THN: The limitation of moral theory to questions of justice leads you to make a sharp distinction between "moral questions" (which can in principle be decided rationally in terms of a principle of universalization) and "evaluative questions" (which are questions of the good life and as such admit of rational treatment only within the horizon of a concrete historical form of life or an individual life history). But do you in fact exclude the possibility of congruence between justice and the good life? John Rawls, who also maintains the priority of the right over the good, presupposes the possibility of such congruence at least under the conditions of a "well-ordered society." He takes the view that a moral theory should specify how the right and the good are related to each other.[9]

JH: Yes, in a society that possessed all of the resources of a modern society and was in addition well ordered—that is, just and emancipated—socialized individuals would enjoy not only autonomy and a high degree of participation but also relatively broad scope for self-realization, that is, for the conscious projection and pursuit of individual life plans.

THN: While you separate justice from the good life, you also include elements of care and responsibility in your concept of justice. But how can Carol Gilligan's notions of "care" and "responsibility" be integrated into your discourse-theoretical conception of justice?[10] The ethics of care is oriented to the concrete other, not the generalized other; it calls for a contextual, rather than an abstract, formal, mode of thought; it focuses on social relationships, not fixed roles, and traces moral questions back to conflicting interests instead of competing rights. How can these differences be subsumed under a formal concept of justice?

JH: Let me address the first two points together and then turn to the second two.

The impression that deontological ethical theories such as Kantian ethics compel us to overlook the concrete other and his or her particular situation is created only by an avoidable one-sided preoccupation with questions of justification. Kant conceived of morality in general from the Rousseauean perspective of a legislator who reflects on how some matter can be regulated in the common interest of all citizens, hence from the perspective of universalizability. In this way, the problem of application is lost sight of. The unique disposition of a particular case that calls for regulation, and the concrete characteristics of the people involved, come into view only *after* problems of justification have been resolved. It is only when it has to be established which of the prima facie valid norms is the most *appropriate* to the given situation and the associated conflict that a maximally complete description of all the relevant features of the particular context must be given. Thus Klaus Günther entitled his excellent study of discourses of application *Der Sinn für Angemessenheit* (The sense of appropriateness) (Frankfurt, 1988). Practical reason is not fully realized in discourses of justification. Whereas in justifying norms practical reason finds expression in the principle of universalization, in the application of norms, it takes the form of a principle of appropriateness. Once we grasp the complementarity of justification and application, it becomes clear how discourse ethics can address the misgivings you share with Carol Gilligan and also with Seyla Benhabib.[11]

Let us now turn to the other objection: that deontological ethics concentrates on rights to the exclusion of needs and in addition neglects the significance of membership relations in favor of institutionally defined roles. Viewed historically, in the light of the individualism of the Kantian tradition, this objection is justified, but it does not apply to discourse ethics. The latter adopts the intersubjective approach of pragmatism and conceives of practical discourse as a *public* practice of *shared,* reciprocal perspective taking: each individual finds himself compelled to adopt the perspective of everyone else in order to test whether a proposed regulation is also acceptable from the perspective of every other person's understanding of himself and the world. Justice and solidarity are two sides of the same coin because practical discourse is, on the one hand, a procedure that affords everyone the opportunity to influence the outcome with his "yes" or "no" responses and thereby takes account of an individualistic understanding of equality; on the other hand, practical discourse leaves intact the social bond that induces participants in argumentation to become aware of their membership in an unlimited communication community. It is only when the continued existence of this communication community, which demands of all its members an act of selfless empathy through ideal role taking, is assured that the networks of reciprocal recognition, without which the identity of each individual would necessarily disintegrate, can reproduce themselves.

THN: How should we understand the division between morality and law? According to Durkheim and Weber, they are two distinct spheres that result from the dissolution of traditional ethics, but somehow they also remain bound to one another through a common center. Must morality and law be conceived in the modern period merely as different ways of institutionalizing procedures that serve the same purpose?

JH: Positive law and postconventional morality complement each other and together overlay traditional ethical life. From a normative point of view, it is easy to see that universalistically grounded moral norms are in need of supplementation. A precondition of the general acceptance of any norm that passes the generalization test is that it should also be actually adhered to by everyone. It is precisely this condition that a reflexive morality which breaks with the certainties of a concrete ethical life cannot itself guarantee. Thus, the very premises of an ambitious postconventional mode of justification generate a *problem of what can be reasonably expected* (*Problem der Zumutbarkeit*): adherence to a valid norm is to be expected only of an individual who can be sure that all others will also follow the norm. Kant already justified the transition from morality to state-sanctioned law in this way. But Kant also recognized the problem generated by the recourse to the medium of state power. Political power is not a neutral medium; its use and organization must themselves be subjected to moral constraints. The idea of a state governed by the rule of law is the response to this demand.

Kant and early liberalism share a conception of the rule of law to the effect that the legal order is itself exclusively moral in nature or at least is one form that the implementation of morality assumes. But this assimilation of law to morality is misleading. The political aspect of law brings quite different factors into play. Not all matters that call for and admit of legal regulation are of a moral nature. Even if legislation were to approximate sufficiently to the ideal conditions of discursive belief formation and will formation, the decisions of the legislator could not be based solely on moral grounds—and most certainly not those of a legislator in a welfare state. *Pragmatic* reasons always play a considerable role in reaching a (more or less) fair balance of nongeneralizable interests, as do *ethical* grounds in the accepted self-understanding and preferred form of life of a group in which different traditions, grounding different identities, come together and have to be harmonized with one another. For this reason, the claim to legitimacy of positive law could not be assimilated to the claim to moral validity, even if it were based on rational will formation. Together with the introduction of pragmatic and ethical reasons, other factors come into play in the question of the legitimacy of law: *legitimacy* rests on a broader range of aspects of validity than the normative validity of moral norms of action.

Moreover, legal validity has two distinct components: the empirical component of the enforcement of law and the rational component of the claim to legitimacy. Legal validity requires that both components be justifiable simultaneously to the addressees: the cognitive expectation that, if necessary, force may be brought to bear to ensure that everyone adheres to the individual legal norms (for which reason legality of behavior, that is, behavior that merely conforms to the law, is *sufficient* for the law). At the same time, it must warrant the normative expectation that the legal system merits recognition on good grounds (for which reason the law must at all times *make possible* more than mere legality, namely, obedience based on insight into the legitimacy of the legal order).

II

THN: Let us turn to the topic of your linguistic-pragmatic justification of discourse ethics, in particular your development of Toulmin's analyses in *The Uses of Argument,* Wittgenstein's "language-games," and Chomsky's "universal grammar" into a formal pragmatics. Already at this methodological level, I would like to know how you would respond to a new variation on the old objection to the alleged Eurocentrism of your defense of the Enlightenment and your concept of evolution.

One might wonder whether the whole notion of a formal pragmatics is merely the result of a dubious generalization from Indo-European languages. Whorf compared "Standard Average European" with non-European languages and found that such central features as the function of verbs, the tense structure, and the grammatical relation between subject and predicate in the latter languages were fundamentally different from the characteristics you take to be universal.[12] I cannot go into the details here, but there seem to be abundant linguistic data that raise serious doubts about the whole program of a universal pragmatics or that even refute it. Perhaps you could argue that the non-European languages are less developed, but then you would have to show how development of grammatical deep structures is even possible.

JH: The Sapir-Whorf hypothesis was discussed at length in the 1950s, by and large with negative results. Clearly the surface structures of individual languages may differ radically, without the agreement between the underlying semantic structure of simple assertoric statements or the pragmatic structure of the speech situation (such as personal pronouns, spatial and temporal indices) being thereby diminished. What Whorf had in mind were, rather, the differences between linguistic worldviews, which had already interested Humboldt though it did not lead him to draw conclusions in favor of linguistic relativism. Avoiding relativism by no means forces us to fall back on the notion of an evolution of language systems. In the case of natural languages, an evolutionary hypothesis is manifestly inappropriate, since the grammatical complexity of languages scarcely changes over time.

Whorf's intuition has recently found resonance again on a different level, in the rationality debate initiated by anthropologists, which has developed in a number of different directions. I think the crucial point in *this* debate is whether we must take account of an asymmetry that arises between the interpretive capacities of different cultures in virtue of the fact that some have introduced "second-order concepts" whereas others have not. These second-order concepts fulfill necessary cognitive conditions for a culture's becoming self-reflective, that is, for its members' adopting a hypothetical stance toward their own traditions and on this basis grasping their own cultural relativity. This kind of decentered understanding of the world is characteristic of modern societies. What the argument is about, therefore, is whether such cognitive structures represent a threshold that demands *similar* processes of learning and adaptation of *any* culture that crosses it.

According to the contextualists, the transition to postmetaphysical concepts of nature and posttraditional conceptions of law and morality is characteristic of just one tradition among others and by no means signifies that tradition as such becomes reflexive. I don't see how this thesis could be seriously defended. I think that Max Weber was fundamentally right, especially in the careful universalistic interpretation that Schluchter has given his thesis of the universal cultural significance of Occidental rationalism.[13]

THN: Your moral theory takes the form of an examination of moral argumentation. The only moral principle you lay down is a principle of universalization, which is supposed to play a role in moral argumentation similar to that played by the principle of induction in deciding empirical-theoretical questions. It specifies that a norm is valid only if it could be accepted by all potentially affected in a real process of argumentation, meaning that the norm must be capable of satisfying the interests of each participant. But why should the participants agree to the consequences of the general observance of the norm? Often they merely arrive at a consensual determination of their disagreement. That would be similar to the procedure of political will formation resulting in a consensus that certain issues and controversies must be left to *other* forms of discussion.

JH: Argumentation is not a decision procedure resulting in *collective decisions* but a problem-solving procedure that generates *convictions.* Of course, argumentative disputes concerning the truth claims of assertoric statements or the rightness claim of normative statements may remain undecided and no agreement be reached; then the questions are left open for the time being, though on the assumption that only one side can be right. In practical discourses, however, it may transpire that the conflict at issue is not a moral one at all. It may be an ethical-existential question affecting the self-understanding of a given individual or group, in which case any answer, however rational, will be valid only relative to the goal of my or our good, or not unsuccessful, life and cannot claim to be universally binding. Or perhaps it is a pragmatic question of balancing opposed but nongeneralizable interests, in which case the participants can at best reach a fair or good compromise. Thus, the breakdown of attempts at argumentation in the sphere of practice may also reflect the realization that self-interpretive discourses or negotiations are called for rather than moral discourses.

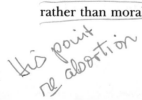

Parliamentary processes of will formation also have a rational core, for political questions admit of discursive treatment either from empirical and pragmatic or moral and ethical points of view. There is a definite time frame within which decisions must be reached in legally institutionalized processes of belief formation such as these. The standard procedures combine elements of belief formation oriented to truth with majoritarian will formation. From the perspective of a theory of discourse that seeks to sound out the normative potential of such procedures, majority rule must retain an internal relation to the cooperative search for truth. Ideally, then, a majority decision must be reached under discursive conditions that lend their results the presumption of rationality: the content of a decision reached in accordance with due procedure must be such as can count as the rationally motivated but fallible result of a discussion provisionally brought to a close under the pressure of time. Hence, one should not confuse discourse as a procedure for making moral or ethical *judgments* with the legally institutionalized procedures of political *will* formation (however much the latter are mediated by discourse).

THN: You defend cognitivism in moral theory by maintaining an analogy between truth claims and normative validity claims. However, this analogy can be upheld only by identifying the norms that underlie the principle of universalization with normative validity as such. How can, and why must, moral theory neglect norms that have de facto social currency but are not valid in the strict sense? And is this exclusion possible without severing the dialectical connection between abstract morality and social ethics?

JH: Viewed from the performative perspective of their addressees, norms claim to be valid in a manner analogous to truth. The term "analogous" indicates, of course, that the mode of validity of norms should not be assimilated to the truth of propositions. The differences can be seen even prior to divergences at the level of rules of argumentation and in the specific nature of the arguments admissible in either case; they already begin with the fact that normative validity claims are embodied in norms, that is, in structures that are on a higher level than individual moral actions and regulative speech acts, whereas truth values are ascribed only to individual assertoric statements and not to theories. In the latter case, the higher-level structures—the theories—owe their validity to the set of true propositions derivable from them, whereas particular commands and prohibitions obtain their validity from the norms underlying them.

One interesting difference, is that taking propositions to be true has no impact on what is essential to the truth of sentences, the existence of states of affairs. By contrast, the fact that norms are taken to be right has immediate consequences for the regulation of action essential to norms. As soon as a norm governing action gains sufficient recognition among, and is adhered to by, its addressees, a corresponding practice is generated, regardless of whether the norm can be justified and *deserves* recognition or whether it is merely *de facto* recognized for the wrong reasons, for example, or is adhered to out of sheer habit. For this reason, it is important to distinguish between the validity of a norm and its social currency, the fact that it is generally held to be valid. I can agree with you thus far.

However, I am not sure that I understand the meaning of your question. The *moral theorist* adopts a normative point of view; he shares the attitude of an addressee of the norm who participates in discourses of justification and application. From this perspective, we must begin by abstracting from existing traditions, customary practices, and present motives, in short, from the established ethical life of a society. On the other hand, it is primarily this ethical life that must interest the *sociologist*. But the latter adopts the objectifying attitude of a participant-observer. We cannot simultaneously adopt the second-person attitude of an addressee of a norm and the third-person attitude of a sociological observer. What you have in mind is presumably the complicated case where knowledge acquired in the one attitude is interpreted in the other. That is the situation of the sociologist who assesses a descriptively formulated belief in the legitimacy of an observed, socially valid order in terms of the reasons that could be adduced in support of its legitimacy from the perspective of *potential* addressees. The participant in argumentation (or the moral theorist, as his philosophical alter ego) switches his role accordingly the moment he views the empirical aspects of matters in need of regulation through the spectacles of a legislator and takes account in his reflections of the reasonableness or acceptability of regulations. These different ways of viewing things and their different objects must be clearly distinguished from one another, but such differences yield no arguments in support of a fallacious sociologization of moral theory.

You spoke of empirically valid norms that do not have (normative) validity. Strictly speaking, this formulation applies only to conventions such as table manners, that is, to customary rules that are followed for the most part without needing, or being amenable to, rational justification.

THN: The preconditions of an ethics of discourse are fulfilled at the ontogenetic level only at Kohlberg's final, postconventional stages of moral-psychological development. But only a minority of the adult population ever reaches these stages (if we can rely on the relevant longitudinal studies).[14] Then we are faced with the paradox of a society with postconventional social institutions while a majority of the population languish at the preconventional or conventional stages of moral consciousness. How is this possible? And how can it be reconciled with your claim that normative structures function as the pacemaker of social evolution?[15] If the answer is that postconventional morality is embedded in legal structures, then you must give a plausible explanation of how such a situation can be stabilized.

JH: Social innovations are often initiated by marginal minorities, even if they are later generalized to the whole of society at the institutional level. This may explain why positive law in modern societies must be understood as the embodiment of postconventional structures of consciousness, although many members are found to have reached only a conventional stage of moral consciousness. Nor does a conventional understanding of a postconventional legal system necessarily lead to instabilities; for example, it sometimes prevents radical interpretations that lead to civil disobedience.

What's more, findings concerning the moral consciousness of the general population are problematic; it is a matter of considerable controversy whether Kohlberg's methods of collecting data do not in fact lead to artificial results in the definition of stages. For instance, children master the moral judgments of a given stage long before they have the verbal resources to articulate this knowledge in response to the familiar dilemmas.

THN: The question about the analogy between normative validity and truth is merely a variation on a question that was originally put to you in an interview with the *New Left Review* and that has remained unanswered: "How do you conceive the relation between philosophical and scientific truth-claims? Are philosophical truth-claims cognitive claims, and would a rational consensus ultimately guarantee the truth of a consensus theory of truth itself?"[16]

JH: I think that philosophy today plays two roles simultaneously: the role of an interpreter who mediates between the lifeworld and expert cultures and a more specialized role within the scientific system in which it cooperates with various reconstructive sciences. In so doing, it generates statements that claim to be true in the same way as other scientific statements. The discourse theory of truth also contains assertions that must be defended against rival theories of truth within the relevant universe of discourse.

But your question expresses another doubt. You seem to suggest that the self-referentiality of philosophical statements—in this case, the assertions of a theory of truth—necessarily land the discourse theory of truth in a vicious regress. I disagree. Of course, the reconstruction of our intuitive understanding of truth in terms of a theory of discourse that I propose might well turn out to be wrong, or at least inadequate. But the practice, whether in everyday life or in science, which depends on the correct use of this intuitive knowledge remains unaffected by these attempts at philosophical reconstruction and by their possible revisions. It is impossible to refute this practical knowledge itself, only an incorrect description of it.

THN: The concept of a performative contradiction, which you have appropriated from Karl-Otto Apel (though stripped of its transcendental connotations), plays a decisive role in your justification of morality.[17] The argument underlying your employment of performative contradictions seems convincing in the narrow sense that nobody can systematically dispute the necessary presuppositions of communicative action while engaging in it without placing his own rationality or responsibility in question. But how can one establish in this way that one type of ethical theory is better than another?

JH: The demonstration of performative contradictions in particular cases serves to refute skeptical counterarguments. This casuistic practice can also be developed into a method that serves, as in Strawson, to identify unavoidable presuppositions of a practice for which there is no functional equivalent in our form of life. Apel and I employ this method to discover universal pragmatic presuppositions of argumentation and to analyze their normative content. In this way I attempt to justify a principle of universalization as a moral principle. The initial intention is simply to demonstrate that moral-practical questions can indeed be decided on the basis of reasons. These general presuppositions of argumentation have the same status in discourse ethics as the construction of the original position in Rawls's theory of justice. It must then be left to discussion between such theoretical positions to show which version of Kantian ethics is the best. This professional dispute will involve many different aspects and certainly cannot be resolved by direct appeal to performative self-contradictions.

THN: What is the status of the "ideal speech situation"? Is it partially *counterfactual,* or is it part of a *society fictionally represented as a lifeworld,* or is it a *hypostatization?* Or are all three theses somehow interrelated? The first you adopt explicitly in *Moral Consciousness and Communicative Action.*[18] The second follows from an understanding of discourse ethics as a further development of the third of the fictions posited in *The Theory of Communicative Action* as necessary to conceptualize society as lifeworld—I mean the assumption of complete transparency of communication.[19] The third is attributed to you by Wolfgang Schluchter, who claims that the logic of your argumentation compels you to transform the ideal speech situation from a necessary presupposition of communication into an ideal of reality, and hence to hypostatize it as such.[20]

JH: For present purposes, we can ignore the second position because the passage cited deals with a concept of the lifeworld that I reject as idealistic. The first position implies only that the unlimited communication community (unlimited, that is, in social space and historical time) is an idea that we can approximate in real contexts of argumentation. At any given moment we orient ourselves by this idea when we endeavor to ensure that (1) all voices in any way relevant get a hearing, (2) the best arguments available to us given our present state of knowledge are brought to bear, and (3) only the unforced force of the better argument determines the "yes" and "no" responses of the participants. Unfortunately, I once dubbed the conditions under which these idealizing presuppositions would be fulfilled the "ideal speech situation," a term whose concretistic connotations are misleading. It suggests the kind of hypostatization that Schluchter, albeit with reservations, mistakenly attributes to me. Schluchter bases his argument, among other things, on the formula *"Vorschein einer Lebensform"* ("prefiguration of a form of life"), from which I distanced myself a decade ago.[21] However, at no time did I "hypostatize the unlimited communication community from a necessary presupposition into an ideal of reality," as Schluchter, citing Wellmer, would have it.

As a matter of fact, I hesitate to call the communication community a regulative idea in the Kantian sense, because the notion of an "unavoidable idealizing presupposition of a pragmatic kind" cannot be subsumed under the classical opposition between the "regulative" and the "constitutive."

From the participant perspective, the idea of the truth of fallible statements we make here and now is regulative. On the one hand, all reasons available here and now warrant us in claiming truth for 'p'; on the other, we have no assurance that 'p' will be able to withstand all future objections—we have no way of knowing whether it will be among the valid statements that would *repeatedly* command assent in the unlimited communication community *ad infinitum*. But the general pragmatic presuppositions of argumentation as such are by no means merely regulative, for these conditions must be satisfied to a sufficient degree here and now if we want to engage in argument at all, where that degree of satisfaction counts as "sufficient" which qualifies our actual argumentation as a spatiotemporally localizable component of the universal discourse of the unlimited communication community. But this does not mean that the latter is thereby transformed into an idea that constitutes a reality. The conceptual schema of world constitution is inapplicable here. The point is, rather, that if we want to enter into argumentation, we must make these presuppositions of argumentation *as a matter of fact*, despite the fact that they have an ideal content to which we can only approximate in reality.

With the validity claims raised in communicative action, an ideal tension is imported into social reality itself, which comes to conscious awareness in participating subjects as a force that explodes the limits of the given context and transcends all merely provincial standards. To put it paradoxically, the regulative idea of the validity of utterances is constitutive for the social facts produced through communicative action. To this extent I go beyond Kant's figures of thought, as Schluchter remarks, though without embracing the totalizing viewpoint of Hegel. Already in Peirce the idea of the unlimited communication community serves to replace the moment of infinitude or timelessness of the unconditionality of truth with the idea of a procedure of interpretation and communication that transcends the limits of social space and historical time *from within the world*. The learning processes of the unlimited communication community should form an arch *in* time bridging all temporal distances, and *in* the world they should realize the conditions whose fulfillment is a necessary presupposition of the unconditionality of context-transcending validity claims.

While it is introduced in the context of a theory of truth, this notion also structures a concept of society grounded in communicative action, since communicative interactions are regulated by intersubjectively recognized validity claims. These unconditional validity claims introduce into the lifeworld a moment of transcendence that permeates its symbolic structures. For this reason, even the counterfactual assumptions of communicatively acting subjects can expect to meet with support from the side of social reality; every factually raised claim to validity that transcends the limits of a given lifeworld generates a new fact with the "yes" and "no" responses of its addressees. Mediated by this cognitive-linguistic infrastructure of society, the results of the interplay between inner-worldly learning processes and world-disclosing innovations become sedimented [in social reality]. This is the Hegelian element detected by Schluchter, which he can see from his Kantian perspective (in my opinion erroneously) only as the illicit objectification of a regulative idea.

III

THN: You understand discourses as a reflective form of communicative action, which for its part is situated in the lifeworld. By contrast, all normative elements disappear at the level of the social subsystems steered by the media of money and power. In another place you have explained how your expression *norm-free sociality* has led to misunderstandings. Even after the modern uncoupling of system and lifeworld, system integration remains indirectly connected with the lifeworld through the legal institutionalization of the steering media. You claim only that the integration of the subsystems is not "in the final instance" dependent on the socially integrative accomplishments of communicative action. You write: "It is not the illocutionary binding effects [of speech acts] but steering media that hold the economic and administrative action systems together."[22] This answer makes your position more flexible, but you still maintain that the media of money and power demand that the agent adopt a strategic attitude. I have my doubts about this.

Your picture of the economic actor shares important traits with the model of neoclassical economic theory. Why do you neglect the arguments developed by institutionalist economic theory to demonstrate that the model of purely strategic and utilitarian action died out at the latest with Adam Smith's "invisible hand"? Amitai Etzioni's most recent book offers numerous arguments and copious evidence for the claim that "the most important bases of choices [also in the market] are affective and normative. That is, people often make non- or subrational choices, first because they build on their normative-affective foundations, and only secondly because they have weak and limited intellectual capabilities."[23]

JH: I think that this is a misunderstanding. I use "system" and "lifeworld" as concepts for social orders that differ in their mechanisms of societal integration, that is, in the intermeshing of interactions. In "socially integrated" spheres of action, this interlinking or sequential ordering is achieved either through the intentions of the agents themselves or through their intuitive background understanding of the lifeworld; in "systemically integrated" spheres of action, order is generated objectively, "over the heads of the participants" as it were, through the functional interlocking and reciprocal stabilization of consequences of action of which the agents need not be aware. The concept of the lifeworld must be introduced in the context of a theory of action. But only if the concept of system were introduced in a similar manner could one establish the clear, reversible relation between systemically integrated spheres of action and forms of purposive-rational action you attribute to me.

In fact, I introduce the concept of systemically differentiated, self-steering, recursively closed spheres of action in terms of mechanisms of functional integration, and specifically the steering media of money and power. The latter undoubtedly have correlates at the level of social action in the form of interactions steered by media. But this fact in no way compromises the rationality of the choices of participants in interaction. In each case, the medium specifies the standards by which conflicts are ultimately resolved. To this extent the structural limitations to which media-guided interactions are subject *occasion* more or less rational plans of action, but they neither necessitate that action be rationally orientated nor can they *obligate* actors to behave rationally. Hence, the empirical evidence you allude to is compatible with a media-theoretical description of economic and administrative behavior.

THN: You have taken over the concepts of the state as a system and power as a medium from Talcott Parsons, both of which entail the separation of politics and administration. Thomas McCarthy has criticized this separation as contrary to both empirical investigations and your own concept of democracy: "If self-determination, political equality, and the participation of citizens in decision-making processes are the hallmarks of true democracy, then a democratic government could not be a political *system* in Habermas's sense."[24] You have emphasized that the democratic state cannot be reduced to positive law. In the case of civil disobedience, legality must even be abrogated in favor of those who must ultimately safeguard the legitimacy of government—the citizens.[25] But how can civil disobedience be interpreted in this way without abandoning the separation of politics and administration underlying the concepts of the state as system and of power as a medium?

JH: I do not regard processes of legitimation per se as part of the administrative system regulated by power; they unfold in the political public sphere. Here, two opposed tendencies meet and intersect: communicatively generated power proceeding from democratic processes of opinion formation and will formation (Hannah Arendt) runs up against the production of legitimation by (and for) the ad-

ministrative system. How these two processes—more or less spontaneous opinion formation and will formation through public channels
of communication, on the one hand, and organized production of
mass loyalty, on the other—affect each other, and which gains dom-
inance over the other, are empirical matters. A similar form of interaction occurs in institutionalized forms of political will formation—
for instance, in parliamentary bodies. Only with the complete integration of political parties into the state apparatus would these institutionalized processes of will formation be *fully* absorbed into an
administrative system that was self-regulating (albeit within the limits
of existing laws).

But to return to your question: the boundaries between communicatively regulated political opinion formation and will formation,
on the one hand, and administration steered by power, on the other,
could be blurred under modern conditions of life only at the cost of
reversing differentiation within the system of public administration.
The production of power by communicative means obeys a different
logic from the assertion and exercise of administrative power.

By contrast, civil disobedience—in the sense of nonviolent
transgression of rules intended as a symbolic appeal to a differently
minded majority—is merely an extreme case that exhibits the interplay between noninstitutionalized public communication and constitutional processes of democratic will formation. The one can
influence the other because institutionalized will formation embodies
the idea just mentioned: in parliaments, opinion formation oriented
to truth should act as a kind of filter for majority decisions, thereby
lending them the presumption of reasonableness.

THN: How can power be compared with money, even if the former
is understood as a steering medium? In *The Theory of Communicative
Action* you enumerate (again following Parsons) differences in measurement, circulation, and storage that exist between the two media
but then maintain that both would equally make action coordination
independent of the resources of the lifeworld. Yet the mode of institutionalization of power in the lifeworld exhibits significant dissim-
ilarities from that of money. Thus, obedience is the appropriate
attitude toward administrative power, whereas the market calls for
an orientation to enlightened self-interest. The respective attitudes

must, for example, be correlated with different stages of moral consciousness. How can such differences be explained when both steering media occupy the same or a parallel place in the architectonic of your theory?

JH: The contradiction you have just set forth can be resolved as follows. The two media, money and power, function in a symmetrical fashion insofar as they serve to hold together differentiated, self-regulating action systems independent of any *intentional* effort, and thus of the coordinating *activity,* of actors. They behave asymmetrically in respect of their mode of dependency on the lifeworld, though both are legally institutionalized and hence anchored in the lifeworld. Whereas the capitalist economy also subsumes the production process, including labor power (as the substrate that generates exchange values), the democratic state apparatus remains dependent on the repeated provision of legitimation over which it can never gain *complete* control through the exercise of administrative power. Here communicatively produced power constitutes a substrate that can never be cut off from the roots of discursive—and to that extent, administratively nonregulable—processes of public opinion formation and will formation to the same extent that production steered by market forces can be severed from lifeworld contexts of active labor.

On the other hand, this asymmetry should not mislead us into thinking that the administrative system can be subsumed under lifeworld categories. It is indeed a necessary condition of the possibility of making demands on the administrative system in the name of imperatives originating in the lifeworld; and the latter, in contrast to consumer decisions, do not have to be formulated from the outset in the language of the steering medium in question, that is, in prices and institutional directions, in order to become "comprehensible" to the corresponding system. This can be seen from the different attitudes that politics and administration take toward law—respectively, a normative and a more instrumental one.[26] The administrative system treats law primarily in an instrumental fashion; what counts from the perspective of administrative power is not the practical reason employed in the justification or application of norms but rather efficiency in the implementation of a program in part laid down and in part developed by the administrative system itself. The normative reasons, which in the language of politics serve to justify positive norms, function in the language of administration as constraints and post hoc rationalizations for decisions occasioned by other considerations. At the same time, normative reasons remain the sole currency in which communicative power becomes operative. It can affect the administrative system by cultivating the pool of reasons on which administrative decisions, which are subject to the rule of law, must draw. Not everything *may* be done that could be done by the administrative system if the preceding political communication and will formation had discursively devalued the reasons required within a given legal framework.

THN: The last three questions can be drawn together in an argument to the effect that your analysis of the pathologies of modernity needs to be supplemented in ways that pull in opposing directions. You maintain that the system colonizes the lifeworld. But there also exist countervailing tendencies. Normative expectations and democratic processes of will formation can so influence the two subsystems that they can no longer be integrated exclusively through their systemic mechanisms. Thus, your analysis of processes of legal regulation, for example, could be supplemented by an analysis of social movements that have as their goal the democratization of the economy, user participation, and so forth. Why do you ignore this possibility? Would the results of such investigations undermine the architectonic of your theory?

JH: When I was writing *The Theory of Communicative Action* my main concern was to develop a theoretical apparatus with which the phenomena of "reification" (Lukács) could be addressed. But this approach to systemically induced disruptions in communicatively rationalized lifeworlds was one-sided; it failed to exhaust the analytic resources provided by the theory of communicative action. The question of which side imposes limitations on whose imperatives, and to what extent, must be treated as an empirical one that cannot be decided beforehand on the analytical level in favor of the systems. I have already emphasized in the preface to the third edition of the book, in response to similar objections by Johannes Berger, that the colonization of the lifeworld and democratic constraints on the dynamics of systems that remain unresponsive to the "externalities" they produce represent two equally legitimate analytic perspectives. A one-sided diagnosis of the contemporary scene is by no means implicit in the architectonic of the theory.

THN: In a series of articles that have appeared since the original publication of *Moral Consciousness and Communicative Action*, you have discussed the Hegelian concept of "ethical life" (*Sittlichkeit*) or, alternatively, of a "pragmatic ethics," in an effort to mediate between discourse ethics and social reality. You gauge the rationality of a form of life by the degree to which it enables and encourages its members to develop a moral consciousness guided by principles and to convert it into practice.[27] But can rationality be identified with morality? Ethical life or practical ethics would seem to be reducible to the existing norms of a given society. Then the question becomes whether the socially current norms are also valid or whether they at least promote such valid norms. You seem to want to preserve normative validity, or the pure "ought," exclusively within the framework of Kant's individual morality, while abandoning Hegel's project of uniting "is" and "ought" as untenable.

JH: The concept of communicative rationality comprises a number of different aspects of validity, not just the moral aspect of the normative validity of commands or actions. Hence the rationality of a form of life is not measured solely by the normative contexts or the potential sources of motivation that facilitate the translation of postconventional moral judgments into practice. Nevertheless, what seems to me to be essential to the degree of liberality of a society is the extent to which its patterns of socialization and its institutions, its political culture, and in general its identity-guaranteeing traditions and everyday practices, express a noncoercive, nonauthoritarian form of ethical life in which an autonomous morality can be embodied and take on concrete shape. Intuitively we recognize fairly quickly—like ethnologists who have been integrated into a foreign society—how emancipated, responsive, and egalitarian our surroundings really are, how minorities, marginal social groups, the handicapped, children, and the elderly are treated, the social significance of illness, loneliness, and death, how much tolerance there is toward eccentricity and deviant behavior, the innovative and the dangerous, and so on.

However, your question seems to confuse two issues. When I draw the distinction between morality and ethical life in the normative attitude of a moral theorist (or indeed of a participant in argumentation), I have something different in mind than when I compare, in the role of sociologist, the moral beliefs of individuals I observe, or the moral content of their legal principles, with the established practices and the concrete manifestations of ethical life in this society. But even from the sociological perspective, it is not as if the complete normative substance resides in the heads of those making moral judgments (or in the wording of their juridical texts) and thus would be exhausted by universalistic morality. The ethical practice actually obtaining in society also belongs to this normative substance, however much it may deviate from the socially accepted morality.

THN: In the Howison Lecture of 1988 you make a further attempt to mediate between discourse ethics and society. There you assert that "the *application* calls for argumentative clarification in its own right. . . . the impartiality of judgment cannot again be secured through a principle of universalization."[28] But how can a new form of relativism be avoided when a so-called principle of appropriateness serves as a substitute for the context-sensitive application of norms in all situations?

JH: The logic of discourses of application can be investigated from the normative point of view of the philosopher or the legal theorist. Ronald Dworkin provides examples of this and develops a corresponding theory, and Klaus Günther formulates this approach convincingly within a discourse-theoretical framework.[29] The latter shows that the principle of appropriateness, no less than the principle of universalization, brings impartiality to bear in judging practical questions and thereby makes rationally motivated agreement possible. In discourses of application, we also rely on reasons that are in principle valid for everyone, not just for you and me. One must be wary of making the fallacious inference that an analytic procedure that calls for sensitivity to context must itself be context dependent and lead to context-dependent results.

THN: In the Howison Lecture you emphasize that ethical questions—in contrast to moral questions—do not require a complete break with the egocentric perspective: . . . "in each instance they take their orientation from the telos of one's own life."[30] You also introduce maxims of action as a kind of bridge between morality and ethics "because they can be judged alternately from ethical and moral points of view."[31] How are maxims related to normative validity claims? Don't maxims somehow claim empirical and normative validity simultaneously?

JH: Yes, ethical questions, questions of self-interpretation, have as their goal your or my good life, or better, not unsuccessful life. We survey our life history or our traditions and ask ourselves, with the ambiguity that typifies strong preferences, who we are and who we would like to be. The answers must therefore refer to a particular perspective on life assumed to be valid for particular individuals or groups. Answers such as this cannot claim to privilege one form of life as exemplary and binding on all, as Aristotle privileged the polis. But relative to a given context, ethical questions can be answered rationally, that is, in such a way that they make sense to everybody and not just to those immediately affected, from whose perspective the question was posed.

You touched on another point: What are maxims? Following Kant, I understand by "maxims" rules of action or customs that constitute practices or even a whole way of life, in that they relieve agents of the burden of continually making decisions in daily life. Kant had in mind primarily the maxims of a professionally stratified, early capitalist society. In the lecture I said that maxims can be judged from either an *ethical* or a *moral* point of view. What may be good for me, given my view of myself and of how I would like to be seen, may not be equally good for all. But the fact that maxims can be judged from a twofold perspective does not confer on them a twofold nature.

Again, the normative discussion we have just been conducting must be distinguished from a sociological discussion. From the viewpoint of a sociological observer, maxims may recommend themselves as a class of phenomena with reference to which the concrete ethical life of a group can be productively studied. Maxims enjoy social currency; as such, they are normatively binding for the agents themselves, as least insofar as they are not mere conventions. Hence, we can change perspective and move from observation to judgment by considering whether the reasons for which *they* have chosen their maxims are also good reasons *for us.*

THN: You defend ethical cognitivism against skeptics but leave the consideration of moral feelings to one side. But these come into play once more, at the very latest, in the application of norms. What is the status of moral feelings? Don't feelings and "habits of the heart" have intrinsic worth? Or do they merely have a catalytic function in the development of moral consciousness and become superfluous once a certain level of moral competence has been reached?

JH: Moral feelings are both an important topic and a broad field in their own right, so I will limit myself to a few remarks.

First, moral feelings play an important role in the *constitution* of moral phenomena. We would not experience certain conflicts of action as morally relevant at all unless we *felt* that the integrity of a person is threatened or violated. Feelings form the basis of our *perception* of something as moral. Someone who is blind to moral phenomena is blind to feeling. He lacks a sense, as we say, for the suffering of a vulnerable creature who has a claim to have its integrity, both personal and bodily, protected. And this sense is manifestly closely related to sympathy or compassion.

Second, and more important, moral feelings, as you correctly observe, provide us with orientation in *judging morally relevant particular cases.* Feelings are the experiential basis of our initial intuitive judgments: feelings of guilt and shame are the basis of self-reproach, pain and resentment of reproaches against another person who offends us, anger and indignation of the condemnation of a third person who offends someone else. Moral feelings are reactions to disruptions of relations of intersubjective recognition or of interpersonal relations in which agents are involved in the role of first, second, or third persons. Hence, moral feelings are structured in such a way that they reflect the system of personal pronouns.

Third, moral feelings clearly play an important role not only in the application of moral norms but also in their *justification.* At the very least, empathy—the ability to project oneself across cultural distances into alien and at first sight incomprehensible conditions of life, behavioral predispositions, and interpretive perspectives—is an emotional prerequisite for ideal role taking, which requires everyone to take the perspective of all others. To view something from the moral point of view means that we do not elevate our own self-understanding and worldview to the standard by which we universalize a mode of action but instead test its generalizability also from the perspectives of all others. It is unlikely that one would be able to perform this demanding cognitive feat without the generalized compassion, sublimated into the capacity to empathize with others, that points beyond affective ties to immediate reference persons and opens our eyes to "difference," to the uniqueness and inalienable otherness of the other.

Of course, however indispensable the cognitive function of moral feelings, they do not have a monopoly on the truth. In the final analysis, moral judgment must bridge a gap that cannot be filled emotionally. Ultimately we must rely on moral *insights* if all of humankind is to have a claim to moral protection. The counterfactual idea that all human beings are brothers and sisters is already difficult enough to encompass, but the notion of a horizon including all human beings proves to be even more fragile if it is supposed to be held together by spontaneous feelings. So your question is not at all easy to answer. Certainly moral feelings initially sensitize us to moral phenomena, and in questions of the justification and application of norms, they have in addition an invaluable heuristic function. But they cannot be the *final* reference point for judging the phenomena they bring to light.

THN: You have often emphasized that a narrow concept of morality demands a correspondingly modest self-assessment of moral theory. On your conception, "the philosopher ought to explain the moral point of view, and—as far as possible—justify the claim to universality of this explanation. . . . Anything further than that is a matter for moral discourse between participants."[32] However, it seems to me that this modesty and separation of spheres is being superseded in your more recent writings by a new tripartite division in which a neo-Kantian moral theory (discourse ethics) is mediated with a curtailed form of Hegelian ethical life (a pragmatic ethics) through a broadened concept of practical reason or even a Kierkegaardian notion of "radical choice." How do you view this?

JH: I think that the task of philosophy is to clarify the conditions under which moral and ethical questions alike can be decided rationally by the participants themselves. The moral point of view enables us to grasp generalizable interests in common; an ethical decision to adopt a conscious plan of life first puts a person or group in the proper frame of mind to appropriate critically their own life history, or identity-constituting traditions, in the light of an authentic life project. But philosophy cannot arrogate to itself the task of finding answers to substantive questions of justice or of an authentic, unfailed life, for it properly belongs to the participants. It can help prevent confusions; for example, it can insist that moral and ethical questions not be confused with one another and thereby be addressed from an inappropriate perspective. But when it offers material contributions to the theory of justice—as Rawls does in some sections of his book— or if it becomes engaged in drawing up normative blueprints for an emancipated society—as do Ernst Bloch and Agnes Heller—then the philosophical author steps back into the role of an expert who makes proposals from the perspective of a citizen participating in the political process.

Anyone who goes beyond procedural questions of a discourse theory of morality and ethics and, in a normative attitude, *immediately* embarks on a theory of the well-ordered, or even emancipated, society will very quickly run up against the limits of his own historical situation and his failure to take into account the context in which his own development has taken place. Hence, I advocate an ascetic construal of moral theory and even of ethics—indeed, of philosophy in general—so as to make room for a critical social theory. Critical theory can contribute to the scientific mediation and objectivation of processes of self-interpretation in quite a different way; the latter should neither succumb to a hermeneutic idealism nor fall between the twin stools of philosophical normativism and sociological empiricism. This is more or less the architectonic I have in view—from the negative perspective of what is to be avoided.

Notes

Chapter 1

1. Ursula Wolf, *Das Problem des moralischen Sollens* (Berlin, 1984).

2. Hans Albert, *Treatise on Critical Reason*, trans. M. V. Rorty (Princeton, N.J., 1985).

3. Charles Taylor, "The Concept of a Person," in *Philosophical Papers* (New York, 1985) 1:97ff.

4. Hans-Georg Gadamer, "Hermeneutics as Practical Philosophy," in *Reason in the Age of Science*, trans. F. Lawrence (Cambridge, Mass., 1982), pp. 88ff.

5. Michael Sandel, *Liberalism and the Limits of Justice* (New York, 1982).

6. Hobbes, *De Cive*, III, 14.

7. Ernst Tugendhat, "Antike und moderne Ethik," in *Probleme der Ethik* (Stuttgart, 1984), pp. 33ff.

8. Kant, *Foundations of the Metaphysics of Morals*, trans. L. W. Beck (New York, 1959), p. 42 [425]. [Numbers in brackets in quotations from Kant refer throughout to the pagination of the Prussian Academy edition—*Trans.*]

9. Cf. Tullio Maranhao, *Therapeutic Discourse and Socratic Dialogue* (Madison, Wis., 1986).

10. Karl-Otto Apel, "The *a priori* of the Communication Community and the Foundations of Ethics," in *Towards a Transformation of Philosophy*, trans. G. Adey & D. Frisby (London, 1980), pp. 225ff.

11. Klaus Günther, *Der Sinn für Angemessenheit* (Frankfurt, 1988).

12. Ernst Tugendhat, *Probleme der Ethik* (Stuttgart, 1984), pp. 87ff.

13. Here I part company with Karl-Otto Apel and his "principle of complementarity" (cf. below, chapter 2, pp. 84ff.); see also Jürgen Habermas, "Volkssouveränität als Verfahren," in Forum für Philosophie (ed.), *Die Ideen von 1798 in der deutschen Rezeption* (Frankfurt, 1989), pp. 7–36.

14. This objection is raised by Martin Seel in *Die Kunst der Entzweiung* (Frankfurt, 1976).

Chapter 2

1. Kant, *Foundations of the Metaphysics of Morals*, trans. L. W. Beck (New York, 1959), p. 20 [403–404].

2. Bernard Williams, *Ethics and the Limits of Philosophy* (Cambridge, Mass., 1985).

3. Williams, *Ethics*, p. 163.

4. Williams, *Ethics*, p. 200.

5. See the remarks on the type of discussion pursued on the basis on mutual trust in Williams, *Ethics*, pp. 170f.

6. Williams, *Ethics*, p. 172.

7. Williams, *Ethics*, p. 152. For criticism of Williams's conception of science, cf. Hilary Putnam, *Realism with a Human Face* (Cambridge, Mass.,1990), pp. 163–178.

8. John Rawls, *A Theory of Justice* (Cambridge, Mass., 1971).

9. John Rawls, "Kantian Constructivism in Moral Theory," *Journal of Philosophy* (September 1980), p. 519.

10. John Rawls, "Justice as Fairness: Political Not Metaphysical," *Philosophy and Public Affairs* 14 (Summer 1985), p. 230.

11. "[I]t was an error in *Theory [of Justice]* and a very misleading one, to describe a theory of justice as part of the theory of rational choice, as on pp. 16 and 583. What I should have said is that the conception of justice as fairness uses an account of rational choice subject to reasonable conditions to characterize the deliberation of the parties as representatives of free and equal persons." Rawls, "Justice as Fairness," p. 237, n. 20.

12. Rawls, "Justice as Fairness," p. 223. With the shifting of normative premises from the procedure to the concept of the person already undertaken in the Dewey Lectures, Rawls presents an unprotected flank to the familiar neo-Aristotelian objections. Cf. Michael I. Perry, *Morality, Politics, and Law* (Oxford, 1988), pp. 57ff.

13. For a discourse-theoretical interpretation of Rawlsian constructivism, see Kenneth Baynes, *The Normative Grounds of Social Criticism: Kant, Rawls and Habermas* (New York, 1991), pp. 68–76.

14. Gadamer makes the connection between philosophical hermeneutics and a historically informed Aristotelian ethics: "Über die Möglichkeit einer philosophischen

Notes

Ethik," in *Kleine Schriften I* (Tübingen, 1967), pp. 179ff.; cf. Ernst Tugendhat, "Antike und Moderne Ethik," in *Probleme der Ethik* (Stuttgart, 1984), pp. 33ff.

15. Albrecht Wellmer, *The Persistence of Modernity*, trans. D. Midgley (Cambridge, Mass., 1991), p. 185.

16. For a critical discussion of important aspects of Wellmer's study, see Lutz Wingert, "Moral und Gemeinsinn" (Dissertation, Frankfurt, 1991).

17. In the original edition of *Moralbewußtsein und kommunikatives Handeln* (Frankfurt, 1983), pp. 102f., I employed an overly strong notion of normative justification. This error has been corrected in subsequent German editions and in the English edition: *Moral Consciousness and Communicative Action*, trans. C. Lenhardt and S. W. Nicholsen (Cambridge, Mass., 1990), pp. 92f.

18. A detailed proposal for carrying through this justification is outlined by William Rehg, "Discourse and the Moral Point of View: Deriving a Dialogical Principle of Universalization," *Inquiry* 34 (1991), pp. 27–48.

19. Wellmer, *Persistence*, p. 225. The same holds of the well-founded objection that Günther Patzig raises against the more comprehensive claims of K. O. Apel; cf. Patzig, "Principium diiudicationis und Principium executionis," in Gerold Prauss, *Handlungstheorie und Transzendentalphilosophie* (Frankfurt, 1986), pp. 204ff., especially pp. 214ff.

20. Wellmer, *Persistence*, p. 155.

21. Cf. Klaus Günther, *Der Sinn für Angemessenheit* (Frankfurt, 1988), pp. 23–100.

22. Günther, *Der Sinn*, p. 62.

23. Günther, *Der Sinn*, p. 50.

24. Günther, *Der Sinn*, p. 53.

25. Günther, *Der Sinn*, pp. 55ff.

26. Cf. also Günther, "Ein normativer Begriff der Kohärenz für eine Theorie der juristischen Argumentation," *Rechtstheorie* 20 (1989), pp. 163–190.

27. Günther, "Ein normativer Begriff," p. 182.

28. On Durkheim, cf. Jürgen Habermas, *Theory of Communicative Action*, trans. T. McCarthy (Boston, 1987), 2:43ff.

29. I have discussed Tugendhat's Gauss Lectures in another context (Habermas [1990], pp. 68ff.). Here I refer to the "Retractions" in Tugendhat, *Probleme der Ethik*, pp. 132–176, and to his contribution to the Fahrenbach Festschrift, "Zum Begriff und zur Begründung von Moral," in C. Bellut and Müller-Schöll (eds.), *Mensch und Moderne* (Würzburg, 1989), pp. 145–163. The transitional view between the earlier and later positions is represented by an interesting manuscript, "A New Conception of Moral Philosophy" (1987).

30. Tugendhat, "Zum Begriff und zur Begründung von Moral," p. 146.

Notes

31. Tugendhat, "Zum Begriff und zur Begründung von Moral," p. 147.

32. Tugendhat, "Zum Begriff und zur Begründung von Moral," p. 163.

33. Tugendhat, "Retractions," pp. 156ff.

34. Cf. the thoroughgoing critique developed by Wingert, "Moral und Gemeinseinn."

35. Cf. Tugendhat, "A New Conception of Moral Philosophy."

36. Tugendhat, "Zum Begriff und zur Begründung von Moral," pp. 158f.

37. Tugendhat, "Zum Begriff und zur Begründung von Moral," p. 157.

38. Tugendhat, "Zum Begriff und zur Begründung von Moral," p. 159.

39. The first-person plural perspective cannot be replaced, or even circumscribed, by an alternation between the first- and third-person perspectives. Thomas Nagel, whose thought is situated within the theoretical framework of the philosophy of the subject, confuses the standpoint of impartial judgment of moral questions with the "external standpoint" of an observer in *The View from Nowhere* (Oxford, 1986), pp. 138ff. This premise generates a dilemma between an objectivistic neutralization of the spheres of value—"If we push the claims of objective detachment to their logical conclusion, and survey the world from a standpoint completely detached from all interests, we discover that there is *nothing*—no values left of any kind: things can be said to matter at all only to individuals within the world" (p. 146)—and the subjectivistic dissolution of commands and values into preferences. Nagel believes that he can escape this dilemma through a procedure of expanding the subjective perspective by reflective integration of objective knowledge: "We simply aim to reorder our motives in a direction that will make them more acceptable from an external standpoint. Instead of bringing our thoughts into accord with an external reality, we try to bring an external view into the determination of our conduct" (p. 139). But preserving the connection to the first-person perspective prejudices the view in favor of ethical issues and closes off the dimension of moral judgment. Nagel cannot deal with the "obscure topic of deontological constraints" (p. 175), as can be seen from his counterintuitive treatment of the example on pp. 176ff.

40. See, for example, *Foundations of the Metaphysics of Morals,* p. 48, n. 14 [430].

41. Cf. Karl-Otto Apel, *Charles S. Peirce: From Pragmatism to Pragmaticism,* trans. J. M. Krois (Amherst, Mass., 1981), and "Sprachliche Bedeutung, Wahrheit und normative Gültigkeit," *Archivio di Filosofia* 55 (1987), pp. 51–88; also C. J. Misak, *Truth and the End of Inquiry* (Oxford, 1991).

42. Cf. Robert Alexy, "Probleme der Diskurstheorie," *Zeitschrift für Philosophische Forschung 43* (1989), pp. 81–93.

43. Stephen Lukes, "Of Gods and Demons," in John B. Thompson and David Held (eds.), *Habermas—Critical Debates* (Cambridge, Mass., 1982), p. 141.

44. Williams, *Ethics,* p. 197.

45. Cf. B. Peters, *Rationalität, Recht und Gesellschaft* (Frankfurt, 1991), pp. 227ff.

46. Cf. R. Alexy, "Nachwort" to the new edition of *Theorie der juristischen Argumentation* (Frankfurt, 1991), pp. 399ff. [In English: *A Theory of Legal Argumentation*, trans. P. Adler and N. McCormick (New York, 1989).]

47. On the communication-theoretical concept of the subject, cf. Jürgen Habermas, "Individuation Through Socialization," in Habermas, *Postmetaphysical Thinking* (Cambridge, Mass., 1992), pp. 149–204.

48. Cf. Marcus G. Singer, *Generalization in Ethics* (New York, 1971), p. 240; Wellmer, *Persistence*, pp. 123ff.

49. Wellmer, *Persistence*, p. 193.

50. See section 4.

51. Cf. Jürgen Habermas, "Labor and Interaction: Remarks on Hegel's Jena *Philosophy of Mind*," in *Theory and Practice*, trans. J. Viertel (Boston, 1983), pp. 142ff.

52. Bernard Gert, *The Moral Rules* (New York, 1970), p. 125; *Morality—A New Justification of the Moral Rules* (New York, 1988), p. 157.

53. Charles Fried, *Right and Wrong* (Cambridge, Mass., 1978), p. 29.

54. Cf. Henry Shue, "Mediating Duties," *Ethics* 98 (1988), pp. 687–704.

55. Fried, *Right and Wrong*, p. 118.

56. Cf. Charles Taylor, *Sources of the Self: The Making of the Modern Identity* (Cambridge, Mass., 1989). Page references to this book are noted parenthetically in the text.

57. The same claim is made by Dieter Henrich, *Fluchtlinien* (Frankfurt, 1982); see also the appendix to his *Ethik zum nuklearen Frieden* (Frankfurt, 1990), pp. 274ff.

58. Other neo-Aristotelians dispute the neutrality of the principle of justice regarding conceptions of the good life rooted in concrete forms of life and traditions but without taking into account, as does Taylor, the fact that the priority of the right over the good first emerges at a postmetaphysical or nonfoundationalist level of thought. Only in modern societies do cultural traditions become reflective in the sense that competing worldviews no longer simply assert themselves against one another in noncommunicative coexistence but are compelled to justify their claims to validity self-critically in the light of argumentative confrontations with the competing validity claims of all others. Modern conditions of life leave us without alternatives; we are not free to alter them at will, and hence they do not stand in need of retrospective normative justification. This fact was dramatically highlighted by the Rushdie affair: no culture that has, with the transition to modernity, integrated second-order concepts into its everyday practices and its collective identity can accord claims that are merely *asserted* in a fundamentalistic manner the same argumentative role as reflectively *justified* claims. Perry's critique (cf. Perry, *Morality*, pp. 57ff.) of the so-called liberal project of Ackermann, Dworkin, and Rawls fails to accord this fact sufficient weight. Perry's own concept is inconsistent in, on the one hand, subordinating the demands of an autonomous morality of justice to the claims of religiously or metaphysically grounded forms of life while, on the other, linking the coexistence of these life-forms to forms of communication in which it is not difficult to discern the existence of a moral principle, whose neutrality Perry nevertheless denies: "If one can participate in politics and law

Notes

. . . only as a partisan of particular moral (religious) convictions about the human, . . . then we who want to participate, whether as theorists or activists or both, must examine our convictions self-critically. We must be willing to let our convictions be tested in ecumenical dialogue with others who do not share them. . . . If necessary, we must revise our convictions until they are credible to ourselves, if not always or even often to our interlocutors" (p. 183). But how should the liberation theologians, with whom Perry sympathizes, deal with their pope, for instance, who does not even want to enter into ecumenical dialogue? How are they to defend the view that he should expose himself to such arguments when the appeal to authenticity has priority over deontological notions of impartiality, equal respect for all, autonomy, and so forth? "The relevant ontological category is not autonomy but authenticity. To have achieved some degree of (political) freedom is not necessarily to have achieved any degree of (human) authenticity" (p. 182).

59. Cf. Christoph Menke, *Die Souveränität der Kunst* (Frankfurt, 1988). [English translation forthcoming, MIT Press.]

60. Karl-Otto Apel, *Diskurs und Verantwortung* (Frankfurt, 1988), p. 348.

61. Apel, *Diskurs*, p. 347.

62. Apel, *Diskurs*, p. 352.

63. Jürgen Habermas, *Moral Consciousness and Communicative Action* (1990), pp. 86–98.

64. Apel, *Diskurs*, p. 350.

65. Apel, *Diskurs*, p. 352.

66. Apel, *Diskurs*, p. 69, and "Is the Ethics of an Ideal Communication Community a Utopia?" in S. Benhabib and F. Dallmayr (eds.), *The Communicative Ethics Controversy* (Cambridge, Mass., 1991), pp. 23ff.

67. Apel, *Diskurs*, p. 165.

68. Karl-Otto Apel, "Normatively Grounding 'Critical Theory' Through Recourse to the Lifeworld?" in A. Honneth, T. McCarthy, C. Offe, and A. Wellmer (eds.), *Philosophical Interventions in the Unfinished Project of Enlightenment* (Cambridge, Mass., 1992), pp. 125–170.

69. Karl-Otto Apel, *Transformation der Philosophie*, 2 vols. (Frankfurt, 1973) [English translation of selected essays: *Towards a Transformation of Philosophy*, trans. G. Adey and D. Frisby (London, 1980).]

70. Karl-Otto Apel, "Kann es in der Gegenwart ein postmetaphysisches Paradigma der Ersten Philosophie geben?" (ms., 1991).

71. See Martin Seel, "The Two Meanings of Communicative Rationality," in A. Honneth and H. Joas (eds.), *Communicative Action* (Cambridge, Mass., 1991), pp. 36–48, and my response, pp. 222–228.

72. Habermas, *Moral Consciousness*, pp. 1–20.

73. See Marcel Niquet, *Transzendentale Argumente: Kant, Strawson und die Sinnkritische Aporetik der Detranszendentalisierung* (Frankfurt, 1991).

Notes

74. Apel, "Normatively Grounding."

75. Apel, *Diskurs*, p. 467.

76. Cf. Wingert, "Moral und Gemeinsinn."

77. Cf. my remarks on the issue of civil disobedience in Habermas, *Die Neue Unüber-sichtlichkeit* (Frankfurt, 1985), pp. 79–120.

78. Thomas McCarthy, "Practical Discourse: On the Relation of Morality to Politics," in *Ideals and Illusions: On Reconstruction and Deconstruction in Contemporary Critical Theory* (Cambridge, Mass., 1991), p. 198.

79. McCarthy, "Practical Discourse On the Relation of Morality to Politics," p. 196.

80. McCarthy, "Practical Discourse On the Relation of Morality to Politics," pp. 191f.

81. Cf. Charles Taylor, "The Liberal-Communitarian Debate," in N. Rosenblum (ed.), *Liberalism and the Moral Life* (Cambridge, Mass., 1989).

82. Seyla Benhabib, "Autonomy, Modernity and Community," in A. Honneth, T. McCarthy, C. Offe, and A. Wellmer (eds.), *Cultural-Political Interventions in the Unfinished Project of Enlightenment* (Cambridge, Mass., 1992), pp. 39–59, and "In the Shadow of Aristotle and Hegel: Communicative Ethics and the Current Controversy in Practical Philosophy," *Philosophical Forum* 21 (1989/90), pp. 1–31; Kenneth Baynes, "The Liberal-Communitarian Controversy and Communicative Ethics," *Philosophy and Social Criticism* 14 (1988), pp. 293–315.

83. John Rawls, "Justice as Fairness: A Briefer Restatement" (ms., 1989) (page references in parentheses are to this text). Cf. also Rawls, "Justice as Fairness."

84. Alasdair MacIntyre, *Whose Justice? Which Rationality?* (Notre Dame, Ind., 1988). Page references to this book are noted parenthetically in the text.

85. Günther Patzig, *Ethik ohne Metaphysik*, 2d ed. (Göttingen, 1983), p. 132.

86. D. Birnbacher, "Sind wir für die Natur verantwortlich?" in *Ökologie und Ethik* (Stuttgart, 1980), p. 72.

87. Günther Patzig, "Ökologische Ethik—innerhalb der Grenzen bloßer Vernunft" in H. J. Elster (ed.), *Umweltschutz—Herausforderung unserer Generation* (Studienzentrum Weikersheim, 1984), 67. In *Ethik ohne Metaphysik* Patzig defends a Kantian approach in ethics that incorporates utilitarian arguments.

88. Jeremy Bentham, *An Introduction to the Principles of Morals and Government* (Oxford, 1789), chap. 17, I, sec. 4, footnote.

89. Patzig, "Ökologische Ethik," p. 74.

90. Patzig, "Ökologische Ethik," p. 73.

91. Patzig, "Ökologische Ethik." p. 7.

92. Günther Patzig, "Der wissenschaftliche Tierversuch unter ethischen Aspekten" in W. Hardegg and G. Preiser (eds.), *Tierversuch und medizinische Ethik* (Hildesheim, 1986), p. 77.

93. Cf. Joel Feinberg, "The Rights of Animals and Unborn Generations," in William T. Blackstone (ed.), *Philosophy and Environmental Crisis* (Athens, Ga., 1974), pp. 43–68.

Chapter 3

1. Jürgen Habermas, "Individuation Through Socialization," in Habermas, *Postmetaphysical Thinking* (Cambridge, Mass., 1992).

2. Lawrence Kohlberg, "The Current Formulation of the Theory," in Kohlberg, *The Psychology of Moral Development* (San Francisco, 1984), p. 286.

3. I have discussed how empirical assumptions and rational reconstruction are interrelated in Kohlberg's theory of moral development in "Reconstruction and Interpretation in the Social Sciences," in Habermas, *Moral Consciousness and Communicative Action*, trans. C. Lenhardt and S. W. Nicholsen (Cambridge, Mass., 1990), pp. 21ff.

4. Kohlberg, "Current Formulation," pp. 277ff.

5. Herbert Schnädelbach, "What is Neo-Aristotelianism?" *Praxis International* 7, pp. 225–237.

6. Bernard Williams, *Ethics and the Limits of Philosophy* (Cambridge, Mass., 1985), p. 69.

7. Albrecht Wellmer, *The Persistence of Modernity*, trans. D. Midgley (Cambridge, Mass., 1991), pp. 200ff.

8. Michael Sandel, *Liberalism and the Limits of Justice* (Cambridge, Mass., 1983), p. 173.

9. Alasdair MacIntyre, *After Virtue* (Notre Dame, Ind., 1984), pp. 51ff.

10. MacIntyre, *After Virtue*, pp. 218–219.

11. Richard J. Bernstein, "Nietzsche or Aristotle," in *Philosophical Profiles* (Philadelphia, 1986), p. 129.

12. Williams, *Ethics*, p. 200 (my emphasis).

13. Williams, *Ethics*, p. 155.

14. Richard Rorty, "Solidarity or Objectivity," in J. Rajman and C. West (eds.), *Post-Analytic Philosophy* (New York, 1985), p. 5.

15. Williams, *Ethics*, p. 172.

16. Karl-Otto Apel, "Der postkantische Universalismus im Lichte seiner aktuellen Mißverständnisse," in *Diskurs und Verantwortung* (Frankfurt, 1988), pp. 217ff.

17. William E. Connolly, *Politics and Ambiguity* (Madison, Wis., 1987).

18. Charles Taylor, "Die Motive einer Verfahrensethik," in Kuhlmann, *Moralität*, pp. 101ff.

19. Schnädelbach, "What is Neo-Aristotelianism?" pp. 234–235.

20. Kohlberg, "Current Formulation," pp. 230ff.

21. Kohlberg, "Current Formulation," pp. 232f.

22. David Wiggins, *Needs, Values, Truth* (Oxford, 1987), p. 82.

23. Klaus Günther, *Der Sinn für Angemessenheit* (Frankfurt, 1988), pp. 255ff.

24. Alan Gewirth, *Reason and Morality* (Chicago, 1978).

25. Robert Selman, *The Growth of Interpersonal Understanding* (New York, 1980); "Interpersonale Verhandlungen," in W. Edelstein and J. Habermas (eds.), *Soziale Interaktion und soziales Verstehen* (Frankfurt, 1984), pp. 113ff.

26. Fritz Oser, *Moralisches Urteil in Gruppen* (Frankfurt, 1981).

Chapter 4

1. Alfred Schmidt, *Die Wahrheit im Gewande der Lüge* (Munich, 1986); "Religion as Trug und als metaphysisches Bedürfnis," *Quatuor Coronati* (1988), pp. 87ff.; "Aufklärung und Mythos im Werk Max Horkheimers," in A. Schmidt and N. Altwicker (eds.), *Max Horkheimer heute* (Frankfurt, 1986), pp. 180ff.

2. Max Horkheimer, "Gespräch mit Helmut Gumnior," *Gesammelte Schriften* [henceforth cited as *GS*] (Frankfurt, 1985–1991), 7:387.

3. *GS*, 7:393.

4. Max Horkheimer and Theodor W. Adorno, *Dialectic of Enlightenment*, trans. J. Cumming (New York, 1972), p. 118.

5. Max Horkheimer, *Notizen 1950 bis 1969* (Frankfurt, 1974).

6. This holds above all for the philosophical articles that Alfred Schmidt already included in the appendix to the German edition of *The Critique of Instrumental Reason* (*Zur Kritik der instrumentellen Vernunft* [Frankfurt, 1967], pp. 177ff.).

7. Horkheimer, *Notizen*, p. 93.

8. Horkheimer, *Notizen*, p. 184.

9. Horkheimer, *Notizen*, p. 102.

10. Horkheimer and Adorno, *Dialectic*, p. 118.

11. Horkheimer, *Notizen*, p. 61.

12. *GS*, 7:178.

13. "Theismus-Atheismus," *GS*, 7:185ff.

14. *GS*, 7:184.

15. "Religion und Philosophie," *GS*, 7:193.

16. "Die Aktualität Schopenhauers," *GS*, 7:136.

17. Schmidt, *Die Wahrheit im Gewande der Lüge*, p. 121.

18. "Religion und Philosophie," *GS*, 7:191.

19. "Die Aktualität Schopenhauers," *GS*, 7:138f.

20. *GS*, 7:135f.

21. "Schopenhauers Denken," *GS*, 7:252.

22. "Pessimismus Heute," *GS*, 7:227f.

23. Horkheimer and Adorno, *Dialectic*, p. 101.

24. "Psalm 91," *GS*, 7:210.

25. Horkheimer, *Notizen*, p. 26.

26. Horkheimer, *Notizen*, p. 172.

27. "Die Aktualität Schopenhauers," *GS*, 7:138.

28. Horkheimer, *Notizen*, p. 26.

Chapter 5

1. English version: *The Theory of Communicative Action*, 2 vols. trans. T. McCarthy (Boston, 1984, 1987)

2. *Moral Consciousness and Communicative Action*, trans. C. Lenhardt and S. W. Nicholsen (Cambridge, Mass., 1990). Original version: *Moralbewußtsein und kommunikatives Handeln* (Frankfurt, 1983).

3. English version: *Legitimation Crisis*, trans. T. McCarthy (Boston, 1975).

4. Jürgen Habermas, *Vorstudien und Ergänzungen zur Theorie des kommunikativen Handelns* (Frankfurt, 1984), pp. 226–270.

5. "Vorlesungen zu einer sprachtheoretischen Grundlegung der Soziologie," in Habermas *Vorstudien*, pp. 11–126.

6. English version: Habermas, *The Philosophical Discourse of Modernity*, trans. F. Lawrence (Cambridge, Mass., 1987).

7. Cf. Habermas, "Theory of Communicative Action," 2:92 ff.

8. Michael Walzer, *Spheres of Justice* (New York, 1983), p. 6.

Notes

9. Cf. John Rawls, *A Theory of Justice* (Cambridge, Mass., 1971), pp. 446, 567ff.

10. Cf. Carol Gilligan, *In a Different Voice* (Cambridge, Mass., 1982).

11. Seyla Benhabib, "The Generalized and the Concrete Other," in Seyla Benhabib and Drucilla Cornell (eds.), *Feminism and Critique* (Minneapolis, 1987), pp. 77–96.

12. Cf. Benjamin Lee Whorf, *Language, Thought and Reality* (Cambridge, Mass., 1973).

13. Wolfgang Schluchter, *The Rise of Western Rationalism* (Berkeley, 1981), pp. 6ff.

14. Cf. Anne Colby and Lawrence Kohlberg, *The Measurement of Moral Judgment* (Cambridge, 1987), vol. 1.

15. Cf. Habermas, *Communication and the Evolution of Society,* trans. T. McCarthy (Boston, 1979), p. 120.

16. Cf. Habermas, *Autonomy and Solidarity: Interviews with Jürgen Habermas,* ed. Peter Dews (London, 1986), p. 160.

17. See Habermas, *Moral Consciousness,* p. 80.

18. Habermas, *Moral Consciousness,* p. 92.

19. Habermas, "Theory of Communicative Action," 2:149–150.

20. Cf. Wolfang Schluchter, *Religion und Lebensführung. Studien zu Max Webers Kultur und Werttheorie* (Frankfurt, 1988), 1:322–323.

21. Cf. Habermas), *Vorstudien,* p. 126 n. 94; also "A Reply to My Critics," in John B. Thompson and David Held (eds.), *Habermas—Critical Debates* (Cambridge, Mass., 1982), pp. 261f.

22. "A Reply," in Axel Honneth and Hans Joas (eds.), *Communicative Action* (Cambridge, Mass., 1991), p. 257.

23. Cf. Amitai Etzioni, *The Moral Dimension* (New York, 1988), p. 90.

24. Thomas McCarthy, "Complexity and Democracy, or the Seducements of Systems Theory," *New German Critique* (Spring, 1985), p. 44.

25. Cf. Habermas, "Civil Disobedience: Litmus Test for the Democratic Constitutional State," *Berkeley Journal of Sociology 30* (1985), p. 106.

26. Cf. Jürgen Habermas, "Volkssouveränität als Verfahren," in Forum für Philosophie (ed.), *Die Ideen von 1798* (Frankfurt, 1989), pp. 28f.

27. Cf. Habermas: "Über Moralität und Sittlichkeit," in H. Schnädelbach (ed.), *Rationalität* (Frankfurt, 1984), p. 228; also *Moral Consciousness,* pp. 207ff.

28. Habermas, "On the Concept of 'Practical Reason,'" Howison Lecture, ms. (University of California, Berkeley, 1988), p. 19. This lecture appears as the first chapter of this book (cf. above p. 13).

Notes

29. Cf. Klaus Günther, "Ein normativer Begriff der Kohärenz," *Rechtstheorie* 20 (1989): 163–190.

30. Cf. p. 6.

31. Cf. p. 7.

32. Habermas, *Autonomy and Solidarity*, p. 160.

Index

Postmetaphysical thought, 74, 94, 100,
123, 125, 128, 146
Postmetaphysical worldviews, 95
Postmodernism, 150
Poststructuralism, 140
Pound, Ezra, 74
Power, 16, 86, 169
communicative, 170
institutionalization of, 168
of labor, 169
political, 68, 89, 155
production of, 168
Practical deliberation, 21, 28
Practical reason, 2–3, 10, 20, 30, 42, 78,
80–81, 98, 118–120, 130, 135, 139,
154. *See also* Reason
and argumentation, 129
Aristotelian view of, 21
and contextualism, 96
exercise of, 4, 7
intersubjectivity of, 43
and justification, 9
Kantian concept of, 13–14, 28, 77
moral employment of, 15
normative content of, 28
and *phronesis*, 117, 123–124
unity of, 16–17
Pragmatic point of view, 5–6
Pragmatics, 3, 82, 149, 156, 158
Pragmatism, 17, 30, 113, 154
Praxis, 32, 150
Problematization, 22, 120
Prohibitions, 40, 63–64
Protestantism, 144
Public discourse, 49, 93
Public life, 26, 89
Public sphere, 60, 93
Purposiveness, 2, 43
Putnam, Hilary, 96

Rational choice, 3
Rational reconstruction, 25
Rationalism, 158
Rationality, 30, 81, 97, 100, 171. *See also*
Reason
communicative, 171
context-transcending, 95, 98
debate over, 96
forms of, 102
and nonagreement, 94
procedural, 125
purposive, 3
scientific, 124
standards of, 101, 104
suppositions of, 31–32

Rawls, John, 19, 29, 78, 97–98, 115–
116, 150, 176
constructivist account of justice, 27
on contextualism, 92
contract theory of, 25
and impartial judgment, 48
Kantianism of, 28
on the original position, 28, 57, 92–93,
105, 163
on overlapping consensus, 88, 93–95
Restatement, 92
on the right and the good, 153
social contract of, 27
Theory of Justice, 27–28
on truth, 26
Realism, 25
Reason, 2, 10–13, 34, 42, 134, 136, 139.
See also Practical reason, Rationality
architectonic of, 139
argumentative, 13
burdens of, 94
norm-testing, 15
passivity of, 27
poststructuralist critiques of, 149
procedural, 139, 141, 145
public, 27
pure, 120
reflective, 3
theoretical, 30, 117
Reciprocal perspective-taking, 64, 154
Reciprocal recognition, 60, 67, 68
Reciprocity, communicative structures
of, 67
Recognition, relations of, 131
Redemption, religious, 133, 143
Reflection, 21–22, 124
Reflectiveness, 22
Reflexivity, conditions of, 98
Relativism, 22, 76, 98, 100, 172
linguistic, 157
Religion, 47, 134, 136–137
Respect, 15, 40, 66–68, 80, 135
and admiration, 45
and esteem, 45
reciprocal, 44
symmetrical, 6
Responsibility, 66, 153
Right, 61, 119
Rightness, 29, 32
Rights, 40, 61–63, 65, 68, 87, 119
Rilke, Rainer Maria, 74
Rorty, Richard, 96, 98, 124
Rousseau, Jean-Jacques, 121, 153
Royce, Josiah, 113, 130
Rules, 3, 36

Index

Studies in Contemporary German Social Thought
Thomas McCarthy, General Editor